D0455904

SAME WAR
Different Battlefields

Inspiring stories from civilians impacted by WWII

Jean Goodwin Messinger

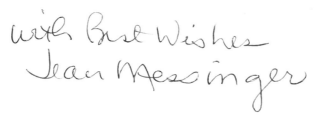

with Best Wishes
Jean Messinger

White Pelican Press
Loveland, Colorado

Other Works

A Closer Look at Beaver Dam

Faith in High Places (co-author)

Where Thy Glory Dwells (co-author)

White Pelican Press, Loveland, CO 80537

ISBN 978-1-60725-043-2

Dedication

To the Millions Who Didn't Survive to Tell Their Stories

● ● ●

Table of Contents

Acknowledgements

———————◆———————

This book relied heavily on the cooperation as well as contributions of the individuals recorded here. It was no small matter for them to open up to a stranger, describing in many cases details of their personal lives. I learned quickly not to take for granted a request for an interview would be accepted. In some cases it was not.

I hope they feel justice was done to their stories, and I believe there is good material here as basis for full-length biographies, novels, Hollywood films, and documentaries.

Many people came up with names to contact, and I was able to complete the text (regretfully) without exhausting that list, simply to keep the size of the volume within bounds. It remains for someone else to finish the task until there are no more stories and no more storytellers.

Thanks to Don Williams for his knowledge of the Arkansas Valley. Peggy Ford at the Greeley City Museum is a walking encyclopedia; a more helpful, diligent resource doesn't exist. Nancy Penfold, director of the Fort Lupton Museum, was particularly helpful, as she grew up in that area during wartime and knows personally many of the Japanese in the Platte Valley. Vic Bernhardt, "Mr. Windsor," now deceased, knew the resources of that part of Weld County. The staff at the Windsor Library can always be depended on to obtain difficult-to-find materials and be consistently patient and accommodating.

There were countless other friends and relatives of subjects who could drop names—like Eric Rosin, "You should talk to my dad," and Bill Marquardt, "You should talk to my neighbor." Several names came through Windsor churches like Faith United Church of Christ and Bethel Lutheran.

It's hard to imagine my first book was done on a typewriter. Bob Larson, popular Fort Collins genealogist and computer whiz, was quite simply the key to completing the manuscript via cyber tech skills I lack. He spent days preparing the text for layout, not a small task given the number of visuals and my general helplessness. (I hope we're still friends, Bob!)

Layout was done by Channing Meyer, graphic artist supreme and co-owner of Loveland's Full Circle Creative. Channing has served me admirably on previous projects and did another superb job putting it all together via the most creative conceptualization.

Rick Arneson, representing Citizen Printing of Fort Collins, is always a joy to work with and can be depended on to be patient, competent, diligent, and always accommodating.

Thank you to many friends and relatives whose calls have gone unanswered for weeks while I buried myself in this enterprise.

To dear husband Tom, who always finds the burden on himself while I indulge in these endeavors. Thank you, again; as we face more challenging times ahead, I promise to be more attentive in the future.

Preface

———— ● ————

Everyone should have the privilege of writing a book like this. For me, the unexpected bonus came from getting to know folks like those profiled on these pages. Actually, the getting acquainted part would be quite easy for anyone, anywhere, because such individuals exist within our families, among our neighbors and co-workers, at church, and throughout our communities. Now, as many reach their 80s and 90s, you are more likely to meet them at the senior center, or sometimes in a nursing home. They used to wait on us at the post office, teach at the middle school, and sell us insurance. Their distinction? They participated in World War II as civilians—anonymously.

The purpose for gathering and publishing these brief biographies and memoirs is to present facets of the conflict that have not received enough attention in the voluminous literature describing and analyzing the war. We have read veterans' accounts in such works as Tom Brokaw's *Greatest Generation*. Holocaust survivor stories reach audiences in print as well as at public forums such as the Holocaust Awareness Week symposia featured annually on many college and university campuses. All those accounts continue to horrify, instruct, and remind us, and make us proud of their narrators. We wish we could tell them how special they are and how much they inspire us.

It is important that these witnesses continue to be visible. But there is an additional category of "soldiers," who fought on different battlefields with different weapons— their courage, hope, and determination to survive. They suffered, were terrorized, and experienced severe losses. Not only were material possessions destroyed or left behind during a forced exodus, but members of their families were literally lost, as in "misplaced." Many of their communities were destroyed as well. Now, over sixty years past the ending of the war, reading about their lifetime experiences can inspire us by presenting examples of personal triumph over unimaginable adversity. Some will attribute their success to never wavering in their faith.

In collecting these stories, I have chosen to limit the subjects to mostly individuals presently living in Colorado, just to manage the abundance of material out there.

I didn't think there was a need to look to New Jersey or Oregon for such drama. As it turned out, readers will notice that the majority of subjects were recorded in north Front Range communities, in an area not far from the author's home base in Windsor. Laziness and the logistics of interviewing aside, that unintentional geographical bias makes a point worth noting—that a volume like this one is waiting to be written in other parts of Colorado and in every other state as well. Any large city could likely produce one of its own.

Some of the people you will encounter here are longtime friends of mine or at least acquaintances. A few others whose backgrounds I knew, wouldn't share—perhaps a privacy issue—but understandable for whatever reason. There are several explanations for this reticence. Ours is a generation taught not to pry and not to focus attention on oneself. Certainly not to complain. Secondly, some of these experiences were very traumatic, and victims have wisely chosen to get past them, moving on, although not forgetting. At any rate, they may feel it is unproductive as well as uncomfortable to dwell on the discomforts and injustices of the past, especially when reminiscing with people who haven't shared that experience. For those who did share, it was not always easy.

This volume is intended then to remind any generation willing to listen, how World War II impacted different people in different ways, and that the combat zone wasn't the only place to find fighters. I hope this endeavor will encourage the silent "others" to open up, so that these vital views into understanding our past will not be lost.

Introduction

———————●———————

There comes a time when a war is over. Combatants from both sides go home and become civilians again, even friends—dads and moms, sons and daughters, spouses, teachers, bricklayers, neighbors, and trading partners across the seas. But they aren't the same individuals they were before their wartime experiences, not in spirit, not in perspective, and sometimes not in body. A seventeen-year-old Marine who survived the ordeals of Iwo Jima grew to manhood pretty fast.

At the same time, it is important to remember that men and women wearing uniforms of the armed forces, facing the perils and disruption of war, are not the only ones impacted by it. Civilians supposedly are promised an immune status that sets them apart from the battlefield. It has rarely worked out that way. World War II rained destruction, terror, and disruption onto millions of ordinary citizens all over the globe. Even those who remained behind in a secure environment like the one the U.S. provided for its residents during the war often had life-changing experiences too.

As a result, the postwar era brought societal changes that created a new global order. In the U.S., age-old prejudices were tempered, paving the way for the Civil Rights movement two decades later. New roles for women brought freedoms and mobility undreamed of by their mothers and grandmothers. In the process, traditional family roles were challenged and modified. Immigration introduced new and different cultures to previously homogeneous neighborhoods and communities of earlier immigrants. Thanks to the GI Bill, the work force and college campuses welcomed new faces from previously unrepresented strata of society. For example, college students were often married with families, requiring separate housing from the customary dorm accommodations.

Citizens of Colorado witnessed and participated in all that. We were amazed at such progress (synonymous with "growth" in our state), and indeed the population increase after the end of the war has been stuck on explosion ever since. Many new Colorado residents were (and still are) vets who became acquainted with Colorado's glories during military training in the state.

At writing, more than sixty years since the end of the war, many veterans still are unable or unwilling to articulate their wartime experiences. It is not unusual for members of a family to be uninformed about Granddad's war record. It is equally regrettable that the personal stories of noncombatant witnesses to the events of the wartime era have not been given the attention they deserve. It took many years for Holocaust survivors to record and publish their memoirs, and longer still for those narratives to find their legitimate place in school curricula. So horrific were the details of those accounts, they were sometimes greeted with skepticism and even disbelief. Justifiably, some would-be chroniclers withdrew. They certainly didn't extend a hand, roll up a sleeve to reveal a tattooed, five-digit number and say, "How do you do? I'm Abraham and I survived Auschwitz. Let me tell you about it."

Thus, passage of time is robbing posterity of the educational value of intimate, personal histories which remain untold. Memories fade, and human resources vanish altogether as the Greatest Generation passes from this earth, which brings us to the rationale for this book. In my capacity as a facilitator for personal and family historians, I have discovered a remarkable array of silent heroes who haven't assessed their own civilian wartime experiences as being anything significant. That great numbers may have encountered similar circumstances seemed to dilute those events, thereby losing their distinction.

For example, millions of parents all over the world sent off their sons (as they have for centuries), and daughters, to be visibly accounted for in absentia in the U.S. by a blue star on a small flag hung conspicuously in a street-facing window in each home so honored. That it was a collective exodus didn't make it easier for any single family. Millions of wives, children, and parents grieved when gold stars replaced the blue. Their heartache and despair received little comfort from knowing that multitudes of other mourners were grieving across the planet—from Holocaust exterminations and living under Nazi tyranny, to enduring the London Blitz and fleeing Russian troops in East Europe. Victims of fire-bombings of cities on both sides of the conflict suffered equally.

All wartime stories were not tragic or even dramatic. Most families have some direct connection to the war; anyone alive during that era has a story to tell. And each one contributes to our better understanding of how life went on during those years. We can be inspired by learning about the personal impact of becoming Rosie the Riveter in a big city, away from home and a comfortable small-town environment, of being a USO entertainer on a remote Pacific island, of stepping unprepared into classrooms when male teachers were called suddenly into service. Life was different just not having the guys around, and unless you lived near a military base, there were few to date. For many others there was the anxiety of waiting and worrying. Young mothers quickly became more independent than they ever dreamed they could be, by being left alone to raise the children and also run the family business when Papa put on a military uniform and disappeared for months or years at a time, or forever. Being a farmer with crops to harvest and no one to do the harvesting happened on farms across the nation. Coming to the U.S. after the war as a young Japanese or German war bride was full of uncertainties, challenges, and disconnection from home. Arriving here as a displaced family from a devastated country, full of hope and an equal amount of anxiety, with literally no material possessions, was a different kind of immigration situation than our country had accommodated for three centuries before.

Readers will notice that the youthful memoirs recorded in the *European* section speak at different levels of the fear element as part of their experience and its lasting impact of those times. The point made here is that it is easy to overlook the anxiety of parents in these childhood accounts. It is regrettable we don't have their first-person recordings, because perspectives of different generations are as different as the age gap between them. The same situation would receive a different description. As readers, we naturally vicariously suffer for the children, thinking of our own. At the same time, as adults and parents it is hard to imagine ourselves fleeing a burning town to an unknown destination with the responsibility for several children and Grandma, feeding them whatever we could find along the side of the road, watching for planes that strafed the helpless refugees, then worrying about our daughters when enemy soldiers occupied the village—plus a host of other frightening conditions of war.

Resilient as the human spirit is, all these situations are recounted here as success stories, of rising to the challenge, and knowing we can do what we have to do. Didn't our mothers promise that? It is the American way, but not only in America. We see in many of the stories recorded here drama, heartbreak, and anxiety, as well as pride of survival and achievement, even good will, in all quarters here and abroad during the war years. All families have stories to tell from those times, memories to share, explanations to make, and feelings to deal with. These are not stories you will read in history books. But what follows are true stories, including many of courage and survival that will inspire us and reduce our own complaints to specks on the horizon.

Finally, keep in mind that this endeavor to record is not intended as an intellectual commentary about the causes and results of events described. Historians and academicians have filled bookshop and library shelves with comprehensive analyses. The stories presented here are told informally, generally in interviewees' own voices. It is intended that you will get to know them as individuals by learning about their lives before and after the war as well. They put a face on important wartime events and describe firsthand on a human level how World War II impacted the lives of ordinary people—the "innocents" who just happened to be in its path. Remember that every face behind barbed wire, or picking through the rubble after a bombing raid, or waving a flag to welcome American GIs liberating an Italian village has a story worth telling and remembering. Let the scholars make of it what they will; in the meantime, dear Reader, get a recorder or pen and paper and talk to Grandpa, Uncle David, and Cousin Bertha before it's too late.

Same War, Different Battlefields

Japanese Americans

Leila (Hinako), Mary (Takeko), and Grandmother (Obaasan)

Mary Shibao

"I wish there had been a different way."

—————————— ● ——————————

Mary Shibao's life story is as unique and dramatic as you will find among WWII memoirs. She is also strikingly modest, sincere, and open in relating her experiences. At eighty-two, Mary is a valued presence at the Brighton Senior Center, where she continues to work weekday mornings.

To put Mary's story into proper perspective and to fully appreciate its significance as part of describing the impact of the war on civilians, it is necessary to reach back a couple generations. Although there is a sizeable Japanese American population in certain areas of Colorado, their neighbors as well as other Caucasian citizens living outside these areas are not likely to be familiar with traditional Japanese ethnicity. In addition, cultural distinctions generally diminish the farther removed in time descendants of immigrants are from their immigrant heritage. This blurring happens to any group as they are assimilated into urban life styles, and/or separated geographically from the people and cultural entities that support the old ways: places of worship, markets, restaurants, neighborhoods, continuation of the native language, etc.

Mary's father, Yamamoto Shigeichi (first name is last), came to America from Hashirano, Japan, in 1905. He worked first as a wage earner helping to build a railroad in Wyoming, then moved to the beet fields of Colorado and changed his name to Harry. After nine years he was able to begin farming on his own, which meant he could bring a young woman from his home town to America to be his wife.

Times were hard for the growing family during the Great Depression of the 1930s. They moved frequently, farming in different locations around the state lines that separate Wyoming, Nebraska, and Colorado. Mary was born in 1926 at Hillrose, Colorado, a small farming community near Fort Morgan, third youngest of nine children and twin of Jack. In 1936, while the family was living in Gering, Nebraska, Mary's mother died in a domestic fire.

About the same time, Harry's father became ill in Japan. As eldest son, Harry was culturally required to assume the care of his aging mother, although he had siblings in Japan. Plans were initiated to return to Japan, but before the move was completed, Harry's father died. It was urgent then to pull up stakes in Nebraska and resettle the family permanently in Hashirano to care for his widowed mother. At the same time, Harry would return his wife's ashes to her homeland.

Not uncommon among the first generation (Issei), Harry had always expected to return to his homeland after he prospered in America. However, by 1937, after working hard for many years, his expectations had fallen short. Now he was forced to return to Japan with his nine motherless children.

It was soon apparent that Harry had been living in America too long, and he found he no longer fit into the Japanese society and lifestyle he had left thirty-three years before. He stayed just three months, until after he planted his mother's rice crop, and then took his three oldest children back to America. He left the other six to care for their seventy-six-year-old grandmother ("Obaasan" in Japanese). A year later, four more of his children were brought back to America, leaving behind Mary, age eleven,

Eleven-year-old Mary "Takeko" with her first grade class at Hashirano school. Standing far left, second row, she is easily identified by her American hairstyle and standing a head taller than her classmates.

and Leila, six (pronounced Lee-eye-la). Probably their return depended upon Obaasan's health as well as money to pay their passage. However, world events would later make this decision for them.

For a while, Mary and Leila were able to keep in touch with their American family, at the same time enjoying a comfortable and secure life as Japanese schoolgirls. They increased their proficiency in the Japanese language, helped with chores around Obaasan's small farm holdings, and learned what it meant to be Japanese. Nevertheless, it was a sad and uneasy time for homesick Mary and Leila as well as for Obaasan. Mary didn't have a clear picture of just how far away America was, and she expected that she and her sister would be able to return home at any time, especially after four siblings, including Mary's twin, Jack, left Japan.

The family of Harry and Moto Yamamoto. Photo taken in July of 1936, in Gering, Nebraska, four months before mother Moto passed away. Ten-year-old twins Jack and Mary flank their mother. Photo hanging on the rear wall is sister Coralee at twenty in a photo taken separately in Denver.

An initial adjustment involved changing their names, much as "Harry" had replaced "Shigeichi" for their father. Mary became "Takeko," which means "straight and strong like bamboo" and Leila adopted "Hinako." Because of Hinako's age, she hadn't yet started school in the U.S., and in Japan she entered elementary school with her age group. Takeko, on the other hand, lacked Japanese language skills to perform with her age group and was required to begin at first grade. This was a difficult and unfair sentence placed on this bright eleven-year-old girl, with so many other adjustments to make. A foreigner, she stood out for several reasons, including her size and maturity and American hairstyle; the other girls sported a traditional Japanese "bowl cut."

Takeko soon caught up with her age group, completing six grades in three years. Japanese schools were demanding of their students, giving them only one month off in the summer—"vacation" accompanied by demanding homework assignments. During the regular school year, students were required to attend classes five and a half days a week. Discipline was strict, and the obedience required didn't allow for the classroom interaction, individualizing, and creativity American students take for granted.

Nevertheless, both girls later appreciated the life-training lessons that resulted from such a tough regimen. Just attending Takeko's school required that she make an arduous, hilly, five-mile walk around intervening rice fields. She is still proud that she hardly missed a day. Carrying a lantern, she left home early in the morning, often in the dark, and returned in darkness at the end of the school day.

The attack on Pearl Harbor on December 8, 1941, (8th in Japan because of the international date line) changed Takeko and Hinako's world, as well as that of their family in America. In Hashirano as well as in other communities, the population celebrated. Takeko was given a small Japanese flag and against her choice had to march in a downtown parade with her classmates. There were subsequent Japanese military victories that also required her reluctant applause.

When Harry came back from Japan in 1937, he went to Los Angeles. At the outbreak of war, as Japanese Americans were removed from the coastal areas, Harry and the children still with him were able to avoid internment because he had friends back in Lyman, Nebraska. They resettled there for the duration. Coralee, the oldest, was in her twenties and already married. She and her husband were interned at Manzanar, the famous relocation camp in California. The Yamamotos in Japan were unaware of what happened to their family in the U.S., as letters "home" were being returned to Japan by late 1940 for no apparent reason.

Takeko, now sixteen, and Hinako continued their schooling under awkward and uncomfortable circumstances. They stood out as Americans, so their movements were kept under surveillance. Periodically military police would visit Obaasan's home to check on their activities to be sure they weren't engaging in subversive activities. Items like English language books and records were confiscated. This suspicion must have insulted as well as frightened loyal citizen Obaasan. It was ironic that the Yamamotos in America, equally innocent, were experiencing their own scrutinization and rejection.

Harry Yamamoto, Mary's father

Takeko attended a prestigious all-girl high school and generally got along cordially with her classmates. In fact, she was awarded "Outstanding Student of the Year" in her junior year and elected class president her senior year. But some students taunted her. The girls' older brother Kuni was in the American armed forces, and although he did not serve in the Pacific theater, Mary was accused of having family members intent on killing their family members.

Because money was short, during her senior year Takeko worked part-time in a factory that welded oxygen tanks. In some Japanese cities, because of the bombing and destruction, schools were closed and students were put to work at tasks that contributed to the war effort. Takeko worried that the tanks were being used some way in combat that would target American forces. All these feelings and apprehensions she and Hinako had to keep to themselves.

The war affected them in many ways. There were shortages of all kinds: no medical supplies, no fuel for wintertime heat, and currency was useless because there was little to buy. Merchants and black market dealers wanted to trade for merchandise rather than cash. The government even took from Obaasan's house all metal objects that could be reused and applied to the war effort.

Obaasan lived on a small farm, and Mary felt they were somewhat better off there than in town. They could grow some of their own food, but rice was in short supply and rationed. On occasion, dandelions, snakes, and grasshoppers were added to their diet, as well as vegetation not previously considered food. Fish was more accessible, and sea salt had several uses, such as for toothpaste.

American incendiary bombs easily destroyed the traditional Japanese wooden houses in the town, as well as its shops. One attack hit the Hashirano village school, killing eight children. Nearby bomb explosions twice damaged Obaasan's house, but she continued to live there with the girls by boarding up broken windows and patching holes in the structure.

During these difficult times the girls were maturing, and cultural differences created tensions. Obaasan had very conservative, traditional views about the behavior of her two teenage American granddaughters, as well as plans for their future. For example, she wouldn't permit the girls to have contact with the opposite sex, and she saw no need for Takeko to continue her education after completing high school. Obaasan could neither read nor write and had no understanding of or appreciation for modern technology. However, she carefully instructed the girls in traditional Japanese practices like the tea ceremony and the proper ways for a genteel lady to behave and to manage a household. She expected the girls would eventually marry and remain in Japan.

After Takeko graduated from high school, despite Obaasan's disapproval she enrolled at a local teachers college. Upon receiving her certificate, she secured a position teaching third grade in Misho, a village five miles from Hashirano and about eighteen miles from Hiroshima. She walked to school every day. One day a downpour of monsoon rains flooded both Misho and Hashirano and washed out roads so that Takeko was unable to return home. She stayed overnight with relatives, but the safety of Hinako and Obaasan was unknown. When she was able to make her way to Hashirano, she found they were safe, but the devastation to Obaasan's house was shocking. Their possessions were in shambles or lost; several feet of mud filled the house and covered the premises. With no manpower to help, cleanup was a physically demanding task for an elderly grandmother and two young girls. Coping with bombing was still another challenge to fear and to deal with its destruction.

Meanwhile, the Japanese population was assured that Japan was winning the war. The public was told that Japanese living in America were having their noses and ears chopped off. Takeko and Hinako couldn't believe such stories, nor could they publicly refute them. It was a regular challenge to the girls to conceal their true feelings, their loyalty to their homeland, and anxiety about their family in the U.S. Both groups knew nothing of the whereabouts of the other, as communications had been discontinued five years previously.

Then one day in early August of 1945, the children at Takeko's school in Misho were assembled in the gymnasium for a special program. The principal was speaking when there was suddenly a bright flash of light, like lightening. The day was clear and there was no sign of oncoming rain. Then there was an enormous boom, the earth began to rumble, and sirens screamed. The school building itself shook, shattering windows. Thinking it was an earthquake, staff quickly evacuated the building. Takeko hurried her class into an assigned school dugout shelter. When they emerged after the sirens stopped, they saw the infamous mushroom cloud over Hiroshima, caused by the atomic bomb explosion. Mary remembers clearly the fright and bewilderment over what she was witnessing. It was definitely bombing like no other that anyone had ever experienced.

The true nature of that nuclear explosion was not disclosed initially, perhaps not realized, nor was the extent of its devastation. Three days later, volunteers were requested to help relief efforts in the city, and Takeko joined a group of her colleagues. Apparently no one at this point recognized the danger from radiation poisoning. They were able to take a train part way to Hiroshima, but as they walked closer, they saw nothing but black skeletons of the former city. No sign of life.

Blackened corpses littered the ground. Mary describes the shock of seeing the river literally flowing with corpses. Fortunately, the destruction of the bridge over that river kept Mary's group from continuing into the city. Wisely conceding that there was nothing to be done at the site, they returned to Hashirano, overcome by what they had seen.

Hinako experienced the bomb in a different way. Her school had been converted to a factory, and young as she was, she worked at various tasks associated with the war effort. She, too, heard and saw what was happening in the skies over Hiroshima. She jumped into an irrigation ditch and watched the mushroom cloud forming over the city, terrified that the world was coming to an end. Mary speculates that the hills and small mountains between Hiroshima and Hashirano may have protected her village somewhat from the possible spread of radiation.

Vivid images and the stench of fire and death remain with Mary to this day. She is fortunate that potentially dangerous radiation exposure affected her no more than a blister on one leg, which has left a small circular scar. When I asked her, as probably others have, how she felt about America dropping the Bomb, she hesitated, looked away, and answered softly, "I wish there had been a different way."

Three days after the August 6th bombing of Hiroshima, a second nuclear bomb targeted Nagasaki. The Japanese began to sue for peace, and on August 15th the Emperor addressed his people on the radio. He announced that Japan had capitulated in order to save the rest of the country from total destruction. The war was over.

This was the first time the people of Japan had heard the Emperor's voice. Obaasan did not believe it was the Emperor who spoke. He was never to be seen or heard by ordinary people, as he was considered a god.* Obaasan felt she could never face her ancestors after such disgrace. There were elements of the population that felt betrayed by the military—betrayal by being led into what turned out to be such a destructive war, and betrayal by disgrace from the defeat that followed.

*This speech had actually been pre-recorded the day before, a strategy intended to maintain the mystical distance between the Imperial One and his subjects. To prevent the Emperor's public announcement of surrender, there was a last-minute attempted coup by certain fanatic, high-ranking military officers who intended to use every resource remaining in order to reject what they considered a humiliating peace treaty. The Emperor urged compliance, but to the military, surrender would bring unacceptable dishonor to the nation and its citizens. And so, they intended to resist Allied occupation no matter what the cost to both sides.

The recording of the Emperor's speech was carefully hidden and never found. What caused the coup to fail was a last bombing mission by the Americans. The target of the mission was not Tokyo, but bombers passed Tokyo close enough to set off the city's radar warnings. This triggered a citywide blackout, which included the imperial palace. Although the palace was ransacked by rebel forces using flashlights, because of the blackout, the recording was not found, and the coup failed. Consequences of its success are unfathomable. For a hair-raising, detailed account of this event, read *The Last Mission: The Secret History of World War II's Final Battle*, by Jim Smith and Malcolm McConnell, Broadway Books, New York: 2002. This story has also been featured on The History Channel.

PEACE RETURNS

Now, new challenges and a new era would begin for the Japanese people as well as for Takeko and Hinako Yamamoto.

The end of the war did not immediately or automatically return Takeko and Hinako to America. For one thing, Obaasan's health was failing and she needed the girls, but there were other issues. For the time being, Takeko transferred to Hashirano Elementary School, which she had attended as a young student. Now she would teach fifth grade there.

As Takeko had reached marriageable age, Aunt Akimoto and Obaasan decided to match her with a suitable husband. Takeko wasn't consulted about this and had other plans for her future—plans that were predicated on her return to America. A worthy young gentleman was chosen for the union, a young man she already knew from a youth organization they both belonged to. Arrangements were made between each family, without Takeko's knowledge. Her fiancé had gone off to fight in the war, and when he returned, she refused to go through with the wedding.

This conflict of culture and the accompanying unforgiveable "disobedience" exhibited by Takeko resulted in much heartbreak and tears by all the female parties involved. Particularly hurtful to Obaasan was the girls' determination to be reunited with their family in America. One thinks of the Japanese parents whose daughters married American servicemen and entered America under quite different circumstances. How would their beloved daughters be accepted? Would they ever see them again, or ever know their grandchildren? Mary notes how Japanese parents were no more enthusiastic about their daughters marrying Americans than Americans probably were when their sons brought home Japanese brides.

Obaasan's resistance was not the only obstacle Takeko and Hinako faced. They learned that without proof of citizenship, they could not get passports or permission to go to the U.S. When Harry Yamamoto emigrated from America, he intended to remain in Japan permanently. Consequently, he brought all important personal papers with him. Such documents that had been left with Obaasan perished in the flood and bombing of her house. The girls had no way of proving their legal American status.

Meanwhile, the Red Cross succeeded in locating Harry Yamamoto in Nebraska and were able to forward one of Takeko's letters to him. She still has the postcard that came in response, the first communication since before the war, which let her know all was well with the family back in America.

In 1947, Takeko found employment as an interpreter with the British occupation forces in Iwakuni. Personnel there took an interest in her predicament and suggested that if she knew where her birth records were filed in Colorado, they would verify her American citizenship. Naturally a good bit of bureaucratic red tape was required before this was successfully accomplished. In February, 1948, the girls found themselves on an Army troop ship leaving Yokohama, bound for America and HOME. Takeko realized then just how much distance separated her from America.

Leaving Obaasan and the extended family that had taken such loving care of them for eleven years was heartbreaking for them all. Takeko and Hinako had grown to young womanhood under their care and guidance. They had suffered through the difficult challenges of the war together, and now they all could look forward to peace and prosperity again. Strong bonds had formed during their time together, bonds now threatened to be severed perhaps forever. Takeko and Hinako were torn apart by this situation, but their choice to return to America seemed inevitable and appropriate to them. Harry's younger brother Tai, who had been an important father figure for the girls, took over the role of caretaker for Obaasan.

After a difficult fifteen-day ocean crossing accompanied by much sea-sickness, the girls were greeted by the welcome skyline of San Francisco. Papa Harry was there to meet them, although the parties didn't recognize each other at first; it took a loudspeaker announcement to bring them together. It was a happy and emotional day for them all. They had been separated, involuntarily, for nearly twelve years. Many changes had occurred within the family during that time.

Lyman, Nebraska, where Harry had resettled during the war, was no longer home to Mary and Leila. Now the girls faced some of the same adjustments Harry faced in 1937 when he returned "home" to Japan. The girls' formative years had been spent in a totally different environment, and they now struggled again to fit in, even with the English language. Mary was twenty-one years old and needed to establish herself vocationally as well as socially. She went to Denver and attended Opportunity School to sharpen her secretarial skills as well as to re-learn English, and most of all, to establish her independence. Leila soon joined her there. Leila later went to college, married, and settled in California, where she still resides.

In 1950, Mary married Harry Sakata and settled in Brighton, Colorado. The Sakata family is well known as farmers and community leaders in the area north of Denver. Two boys were born from this union, but Mary's bliss and security were soon shattered when husband Harry died five years later.

If there was one thing Mary's wartime experiences taught her, it was how to survive. The resulting resilience and confidence that she could face the future assured Mary she could once again create a new life for herself. This time she had the added responsibility for two young sons. Papa Harry came to live with them, giving the boys a much-needed father figure. He died in 1959, a year before Mary remarried in 1960.

Mary's new husband was Tom Shibao. Tom enthusiastically assumed the role of father to Mary's sons, whom he adopted. He was devoted to the boys, and then a baby daughter, Pam, joined the happy family. But tragedy struck Mary again when her older son, Howard, died in 1985, and Tom passed away in 2001.

Mary has revisited Japan on three occasions; one visit included Hiroshima. She was amazed at the recovery of the city, literally rebuilt from ashes. Obaasan died at age 83 in 1952 and Mary never saw her again; Mary's first return to Japan was in 1955, when she, Harry, and the two boys made the trip. Harry became ill on that trip and died before the end of the year. She has since had meaningful reunions with former students and relatives, and in 2006 she took eight members of her family to Japan to see where she taught, where she lived, where she attended school, etc.

A very touching and personal incident reveals the sensitivity of our Japanese American neighbors' traditional culture. Papa Harry didn't return again to his homeland, but he requested that if and when Mary made such a trip, she secure part of her mother's ashes and bring them back to Colorado, to join him in a final resting place. The ashes were placed inside Harry's casket.

Today Mary keeps very busy with family, her job at the senior center, community volunteering, crocheting and knitting, and savoring what life still offers her.

" I have no regrets about what has happened to me. I am what I am because of all that. I'm stronger; I have more compassion, and I appreciate what I do have. I believe there is a reason and a purpose for what comes our way, and we can learn from it."

And we can learn much from this gentle, gracious lady—her words and her inspiring example.

**Mary and friend,
Brighton, Colorado**

POSTSCRIPT

On September 2, 1945, the treaty to end World War II was signed on the battle-ship *U.S.S. Missouri* by a delegation of Japanese military and civilian officials and representatives of the Allied governments. As the proceedings ended, formations of American planes flew overhead as a dramatic and symbolic closing to the ceremony. One airman looking down on the history-making spectacle below, was Lt. Stan Morrison, presently enjoying retirement in Windsor, Colorado. Lieutenant Morrison, (Lt. Col. Ret.) was a navigator on one of the participating B-29 bombers.

The lieutenant has his own story to tell about Hiroshima. His bomb wing was stationed on Tinian Island, the base from which the bombing of Hiroshima took place.

"On the night of August 5-6, we went on a bombing mission to a city on Kyushu. On the return, we ran low on fuel and stopped on Iwo Jima for refueling. This took some time, and it was past noon before we headed south (to Tinian). Our radio man tuned in to Armed Forces radio on Saipan, and we heard about the atomic bombing of Hiroshima that morning. After landing and debriefing, we had been up some 36 hours so we went to bed. Meanwhile the Hiroshima bomber (the *Enola Gay*) landed back on Tinian. Later I learned the plane was met by generals and the news media. So I missed being present at an historic moment taking place a short distance away."

Railroad tracks ran across the hill behind Hashirano School, shown. The tracks were a target for Allied bombers, and errant bombs hit the school.

The Japanese American Creed

I am proud that I am an American of Japanese ancestry, for my very background makes me appreciate more fully the wonderful advantages of this nation.. I believe in her institutions; ideals, and traditions; I glory in her heritage; I boast of her history; I trust in her future; She has granted me liberties and opportunities such as no individual enjoys in this world today. She has given me an education befitting kings; She has entrusted me with the responsibilities of the franchise.. She has permitted me to build a home, to earn a livelihood, to worship, think, speak, and act as I please - as a free man equal to every other man..

Although some individuals may discriminate against me, I shall never become bitter or lose faith, for I know that such persons are not representative of the majority of the American people. True, I shall do all in my power to discourage such practices but I shall do it in the American way; above board; in the open, through courts of law, by education, by proving myself to be worthy of equal treatment and consideration.. I am firm in my belief that American sportsmanship and attitude of fair play will judge citizenship and patriotism on the basis of action and achievement, and not on the basis of physical characteristics..

Because I believe in America, and I trust she believes in me, and because I have received innumerable benefits from her, I pledge myself to do honor to her at all times and in all places; to support her Constitution; to obey her laws; to respect her Flag; to defend her against all enemies, foreign or domestic, to actively assume my duties and obligations as a citizen cheerfully and without any reservations whatsoever, in the hope that I may become a better American in a greater America..

As read before the United States Senate and printed in the Congressional Record May 9, 1941.

Mike Masaoka

Mike Masaoka is the founder of the JACL (Japanese American Citizens League). This poignant and ironic testimonial was read before the United States Senate and printed in the Congressional Record May 9, 1941.

Internment

———●———

Federal executive order 9066 was issued in February of 1942, which decreed that enemy aliens (not specifically naming them as Japanese) were to be evacuated from the security-sensitive coastal areas of the U.S. It would take several months to provide housing for 110,000 prospective evacuees in ten camps scattered throughout the western states and Arkansas (an additional 10,000 voluntarily found placement in the interior). In the meantime, they were temporarily "accommodated" in fairgrounds and race tracks in California.

The internment after Pearl Harbor of Americans of Japanese descent was regarded at the time with mixed feelings, depending on certain factors. For example, at least some non-Japanese West Coast residents knew the Niseii (second generation immigrants) and their Issei elders (first generation immigrants) as good neighbors, industrious workers, prosperous farmers and owners of businesses, professionals, and gentle folk devoted to their families. These non-Asians must have been disturbed and confused about their own feelings—caught between patriotism, compassion, and wartime fear. At the same time, there was also a long tradition of anti-Asian prejudice as the immigrants and their progeny became more successful and therefore more competitive. For their rivals, separation meant "good riddance." Americans in other parts of the country who weren't acquainted with Japanese Americans first-hand were either indifferent or applauded the move for national security. Likely not many acknowledged or cared that re-location was also promoted as a means to protect the Japanese from the hostility of their fellow citizens. Nor was there much if any public outcry from sympathetic individuals. It would have been considered un-patriotic to question the appropriateness of the strategy, given circumstances of the time.

After the war, with a different perspective, issues of civil rights and humaneness came to the fore. The national consciousness began to equate the Internment right up there with the Civil Rights movement, slavery, and the treatment of Native Americans. Each of these had its contemporary rationale, of course. For the Internment, war hysteria serves as justification, or at least explanation, for something that seems impossible to contemplate doing today. It too was blatantly incompatible with the very founding principles of this nation and its democratic society.

Historians have amply examined and chronicled the Internment—the process, its statistics, conditions, and ramifications. The subject requires and deserves more description than can be provided here. Readers are urged to refer to those more comprehensive resources.* Although author's sentiments are obvious, it is not my intent or skill to make a political analysis of the situation. Our purpose here is simply to present in their own words the experiences of individuals who lived the Internment, to "put a face on it." We shouldn't forget how ordinary law-abiding, productive citizens' lives were disrupted, their futures put on hold. They were needlessly humiliated, confused, frightened, and impoverished by what they must have considered betrayal by the very institutions they trusted. Meanwhile, German friends and relatives in countless communities of Wisconsin where I was growing up, carried on life as usual. They, too, were loyal citizens.

*Excellent descriptions of Colorado's involvement are found in Sandra Dallas's *Tallgrass,* St. Martin's Griffin, Publisher, 2007. This novel is an accurate and powerful narrative about the impact Camp Amache had on its Caucasian neighbors around Lamar and Granada.

Another is Robert Harvey's *Amache: The Story of Japanese Internment in Colorado During World War II,* Taylor Trade Publishing, 2003.

Bill Hosakawa, former Denver Post editor was held as an internee at the Heart Mountain Camp in Cody, Wyoming. He was an outspoken writer about the prejudice Japanese Americans faced, as well as other victims of injustice. His book *Nisei: The Quiet Americans,* University Press of Colorado, 2002, is strongly recommended as a first-person account of conditions about which most Americans were unaware. Mr. Hosakawa passed away at 92 in November of 2007.

INTERNMENT CAMPS

Location of the ten American "Relocations Centers"

Onishi family portrait, Oki standing at far right

Okiko Onisi Matsushima

"Tokuhei felt the atom bomb was properly used by the U.S., and he was happy to have the war end."

———————●———————

Oki is a neighbor of John and Daisy Kiyota, and she works in the Kiyota green-houses during the springtime rush. Her story is typical of internees, but for the anguish, humiliation, or anger over the situation, one must look elsewhere. More thorough descriptions and analyses are found in other, often Caucasian, sources like Robert Harvey's Amache *(recommended reading). Of the Japanese American interviews I conducted, every subject was humble and modest, without a trace of bitterness, self-pity, or resentment over the betrayal by their government and some of their fellow citizens.*

You will notice in reading these camp memoirs how summarily the situations are described, and without complaint. Yet each one is loaded with implications of hardship, deprivation, and unfairness—conditions to which most ordinary Americans have never been exposed. Comforts and conveniences we take for granted were lacking for three years of confinement for many internees. Many of them were people of means, professionals, business owners, and skilled craftsmen, whose pre-war standard of living was considerably higher than the minimal, makeshift facilities provided in the barracks. Even shelter was inadequate from cold, heat, wind, blowing sand, and creepy critters working their way into hurriedly-built, spartan, living spaces. Waiting in line was expected and privacy unknown. Nighttime illumination came from a single bulb hanging down from the center of the ceiling. Despite all that, in hindsight it seems that daily life in the camps was not totally grim for everyone, especially for the young. Oki's perspective is that of a teenager For kids, camp life often had an acceptable complexion.

I was born in 1925 in California at Los Gatos, a suburb of San Jose. I had eight living brothers and sisters, and I was the middle child. While I was growing up, my father farmed on rented parcels around Los Gatos. We did truck farming, raising strawberries and vegetables. The family first lived in Monterrey and on several other farms, but I grew up at Los Gatos.

My father was a bachelor here for a number of years; I don't know exactly when he came to the U.S., but it was before the San Francisco earthquake of 1906, because he talked about it. Actually, he had gone to Hawaii first. He was around five feet tall and couldn't do heavy work; his small stature kept him from doing many jobs. He couldn't work in the sugar cane fields, so he was given the job of water boy.

His marriage was arranged in Japan, and my mother arrived in 1916. She worked first as a domestic, and my dad was a gardener.

My parents didn't speak English. My older siblings spoke only Japanese when they started school. They learned English there, then taught English to the younger siblings. As we got older, we spoke less and less Japanese, and we didn't communicate well with our parents because of the language barrier So, much of this wartime situation I really don't know how it affected my dad emotionally. We weren't able to discuss it.

From the Onishi family history comes a description of the post-Pearl Harbor response in California and its effect on the family. Oki's father, Tokuhei Onishi, had an active leadership role in the Japanese American community, specifically in developing a Japanese school, and he was also Issei. These combined factors made him suspect in those initial days of war hysteria and its accompanying blatant racism.

A friend warned him that he would be picked up and possibly separated from the family if we didn't move immediately. We were living in the most strategic-sensitive area near the coast, Zone #1. We had to sell personal belongings quickly and at great loss. Then those family members still living at home moved inland to Orange Grove near Fresno, which was in Zone #2. They found employment as migrant workers. Housing was scarce, and some families were forced to live in converted pig pens, chicken coops, and tents. I remember living in a chicken house.

We talked about the vitriolic, hateful, fear-filled invective directed toward the Japanese, coming out of California, some of it in Colorado. Weren't you afraid?

I suppose my father was; we didn't talk about it. I was young, and I don't remember a lot. It didn't seem that terrible to me at the time. We went to school. We weren't there long because the order came in a few weeks to move to the camp at Poston, Arizona.

The account of the train trip to camp is consistent with other evacuee memoirs; they all describe a long, uncomfortable trip across the desert to an unknown destination. Shades were kept down to keep the passengers from seeing where they were. Ironically, some military personnel were also being transported in other cars on these same evacuation trains.

It was so hot and dry; the wind was blowing, and the sand. They gave us salt pills as soon as we got there. We didn't have much to take to camp, because we had already moved and gotten rid of whatever we could. We didn't have to worry about what to take and what not to take; we had already done that. There wasn't much room for anything anyway. Evacuees were instructed to take only what they could carry.

My sister Toshi lived in San Francisco with her husband and two small children. They spent time at one of the racetrack assembly centers in California before being transferred to Topaz, the camp in Utah. We never had to go to an assembly center because we had moved inland before the evacuation order was issued. But we had friends, besides my sister, who were sent to one of those places. They all said the odor in the horse stalls was awful. Of course they had cleaned them up, but that's a tough odor to get rid of.

All this was harder on the parents. Older people saw the injustice and disruption and everything, but the kids probably thought there would be certain aspects about it that would be fun. They would make new friends, didn't have chores to do, didn't have quite so many rules. My mother did a lot of knitting and crocheting. I'm sure she didn't have time for that before.

Much has been written about the psychological effect on male heads-of-household losing control of the family and not being able to provide for them.

I wasn't aware of that. I probably didn't question my father about it, either.

Camp life was not bad for us kids. We were away from the intimidation in California. I had never been around so many Japanese kids, and I made many friends. We didn't have to work after school, so we were able to do more extra-curricular things than we would have been able to do at home. We learned Japanese dancing, and I really enjoyed that. I had never done that before.

School was in the barracks. Each barrack was divided into four rooms. Classes weren't very large. Some teachers were Japanese, but not all. We girls didn't do sports, but probably the boys did. We had Sunday School there too, and church. Mostly we had the types of groups associated with Sunday School. We were Buddhist. I go to the Buddhist church in Ft. Lupton.

Oki's treasured diploma from Los Gatos High School

Mostly we had a lot of free time. I never got into trouble, but my brother did. He got arrested with some other boys when they climbed up the water tower. There were sentries, and when the sirens went off, the boys got picked up. I think he got let off because one of the policemen was dating my sister.

I graduated from high school at Poston. However, at the time I didn't think the camp diploma would be worth much, so later I wrote to the principal at Los Gatos, and he gave me a diploma. Recently, they told all those people who missed out getting their diplomas during evacuation that they were going to present it to them, all these years later.

We got transferred to Topaz (*Utah*) in May of 1943, because my parents wanted to be with my sister and her family. I really cried when we left Arizona, because I had had a good time there and had made good friends in the camp. We had been together a year or two. I kept in touch with some for a while, but now so many years have passed.

Was one camp better than the other? What were their differences?

At Topaz the barracks were built better, and we had bathtubs. In Arizona there were cracks in the floorboards. We could just sweep and sweep the dirt through the cracks in the floor. Critters would come up through the cracks. Of course it never got cold. We had these big towers of water and took our baths with the water straight from there; the air was so warm, and the water was warm. Bathhouses were one room; there was no privacy for bathing.

Our family lived in one room. Some people had a little camp stove. We went to the mess hall to eat. There wasn't even privacy within the family, just curtains. The mattresses in Arizona were just filled with straw, but when we got to Topaz, we slept on regular mattresses on cots. I don't remember bunks. With seven children, there wouldn't have been room for anything else. But by the time we went, my brother was working in Montana, and two sisters were married, so there were only five of us in that room. If you stayed there long enough, you improvised.

When all this trouble started, my oldest brother, Mas, was determined to avoid internment. He found a job on a farm in Malta, Montana. He sent for us, and the whole family was able to leave the camp and go there in April, 1944. Mas helped us get work. We all went to work—my mother, father, all of us. If you could show that you had a job on the outside or that someone was willing to hire you, you were able to go away from the camp. Sometimes companies would contact the camps looking for labor. We stayed in Montana almost a year. Later in 1944, Mas was drafted and sent to a post in Utah. Since there wasn't any reason for us to remain in Montana, we moved back to Utah, this time to farm. We didn't have to go back to the camp. It was toward the end of the war.

After the war I went to junior college in Utah to study business. You didn't have as many choices as there are now. My sister worked as a domestic, and she helped me out financially. I finished two years and got my diploma. My family was in Murray, Utah; they were farming—truck gardening and renting. They couldn't go back to California yet. I'm not sure when they were allowed to go back, but as soon as they could, my dad wanted to go back. The minute they opened it up, they had to go back. They went to the Los Gatos area again. They had old friends, Caucasians, that helped them out, and they found a place. That was the way they got their first place, and then they share-cropped. They did that until they got enough money and were able to buy their place.

Did your dad have a bad experience when they returned to California? We read of such terrible things about the way they were treated when they went back home.

Not that I know of. Maybe in the cities it was worse. But my parents were out in

WAR RELOCATION AUTHORITY

CITIZEN'S INDEFINITE LEAVE

This is to certify that OKIKO ONISHI, a United
States citizen residing in Block No. 28 - 7 - A, B
within CENTRAL UTAH Relocation Area is allowed to
leave such area on April 17, 1944, and subject to
the terms of the regulations of the War Relocation
Authority relating to issuance of leave for depar-
ture from a relocation area and subject to any special conditions or restrictions set forth on the reverse side hereof, to enjoy leave of indefinite duration. The holder's first destination is Malta, Montana.

Roscoe E. Bell
Acting Project Director

I understand and accept the
conditions of this leave.

Okiko Onishi
Signature of Leaver

FOR VICTORY
BUY
UNITED
STATES
WAR
BONDS
AND
STAMPS

WRA authorization which allows Oki to leave the camp at Topaz to join brother Mas in Montana

the country, in small towns, among people they knew.

Was everybody pretty healthy in the camp?

Yes, they came through the camp OK. My parents both lived into their nineties; my father was ninety-seven. They continued to live in California—never went to live with one of their kids.

According to the written Onishi family history, Oki's father, Tokuhei, "felt the atom bomb was properly used by the U.S., and he was happy to have the war end."

I went back to Los Gatos and worked at what was a tuberculosis sanitorium at that time. I worked in the office, then moved to Los Angeles, where I had a friend. She was rooming with several other girls, and I moved in with them. I worked for some Japanese people who had an appliance store.

My husband had always lived here in Colorado, and he went on a vacation out there; that's how we met. We called him "Tick" but his name was Takashi. We got married in December of 1950.

We moved here to Platteville. Farming was altogether different and so was the climate. He said it was a ranch, so I assumed he had animals. I had lived on a farm before the war, but we raised strawberries, did small-scale truck gardening, and things like that. I had never driven, but you have to drive here if you want to go anywhere!

When I first got married, my husband said that when we retire, we can go back to California. But after living here for more than fifty years and watching my kids grow into responsible adults, I doubt that I'll ever go back. Even with severe winter weather and the hardship of life in the country, this is still home.

THE WHITE HOUSE

WASHINGTON

A monetary sum and words alone cannot restore lost years or erase painful memories; neither can they fully convey our Nation's resolve to rectify injustice and to uphold the rights of individuals. We can never fully right the wrongs of the past. But we can take a clear stand for justice and recognize that serious injustices were done to Japanese Americans during World War II.

In enacting a law calling for restitution and offering a sincere apology, your fellow Americans have, in a very real sense, renewed their traditional commitment to the ideals of freedom, equality, and justice. You and your family have our best wishes for the future.

Sincerely,

G. Bush

Overdue but welcome official apology signed by president George Bush, 1990

A memorial portrait bust of Ralph Carr at Sakura Square, downtown Denver
Photo courtesy of Betty Buchanan

Ralph Carr

"Carr stressed their rights as granted by the Constitution."

When Executive Order No. 9066 was issued in February, 1942, to evacuate 120,000 residents of Japanese ancestry from the west coast, where to relocate them safely and conveniently became a major concern. And when Adam Schwager's book *The Principled Politician: The Ralph Carr Story* was published in 2008, few Coloradoans knew anything about its subject, Governor Ralph Carr, and how he figured into the relocation controversy in Colorado. The content of this essay relies substantially on Schwager's study.

Ralph Carr, a smalltown lawyer from Antonito, Colorado, served two terms as Colorado's Republican governor from 1938 to 1942. As governor, Carr was a pivotal figure when Japanese relocation to our state became a divisive and significant issue. It is generally considered that his position on internment cost him his political career.

After the bombing of Pearl Harbor on December 7, 1941, and America's entry into the war, there was early talk of forcibly removing those individuals from the coast to less security-sensitive areas inland. They were also urged by the federal government to relocate voluntarily. So, 10,000 of the 120,000 decided to leave their homes and businesses under their own terms and to destinations of choice before they were required to resettle. Colorado became a target refuge for many West Coast Americans of Japanese descent. Colorado had an existing population of Japanese farmers in the Platte River valley around Ft. Lupton, Brighton, and Platteville, as well as in communities along the Arkansas River in the southeastern part of the state. Many local families took in relatives and sometimes strangers, who sought to avoid internment.

Sentiment arose early throughout Western states to keep those "potential saboteurs" out of their territories. The ugliest, most despicable racial epithets found their way to the front pages of newspapers in states (including some in Colorado) that might be affected by such an evacuation. Vitriolic, even threatening, public rhetoric came easily from named civic leaders, farmers and ranchers, ordinary citizens, and particularly from governors of those states affected. Except from Ralph Carr. Humaneness aside, Carr defined and justified his position as civic duty—patriotic responsibility to the nation in time of war. If the federal government wanted them resettled in Colorado, they would be accepted, if not welcomed. After all, if removal from the sensitive strategic coastal areas was mandated, and other states were determined to keep them out, where could they go? (Objectors unanimously responded, "Back to Japan!!")

Carr was also concerned about the civil rights of these Americans. He recognized that the animosity accompanying their assumed "enemy alien" status was compounded by their being easily identified ethnically. Issei were restricted from citizenship by law. But second generation Nisei were native-born and automatically American citizens. Most of the people in question were citizens. Carr stressed their rights as granted by the Constitution, emphasizing that depriving any group of their legitimate rights could pave the way for similar attacks on other groups of Americans.

The governor's stand was bold, and unpopular to say the least. Yet, he did not have the authority to issue a directive from the governor's desk one way or the other. The federal government decided, without his knowledge or approval, to establish Camp Amache near Granada. The governor responded by promising the feds that the Colorado National Guard would NOT be used to guard American citizen "inmates." In the meantime, Carr was personally threatened to the point where he was accompanied by a bodyguard when making personal appearances around the state. There was also justifiable concern for the safety of the new arrivals. Hunting licenses were advertised, to be used to "hunt Japs."

Later in 1942, Carr lost a close senate election campaign to incumbent "Big Ed" Johnson and retired from public life. He was of course vindicated by the end of the war decade, and in 1950, Republicans nominated him again for the governor's office. He reluctantly accepted but died shortly before the election, at the age of sixty-two. Republican Dan Thornton became the next Colorado governor.

For a comprehensive description and analysis of the Ralph Carr story and how it affected Colorado, read Adam Schwager's thoroughly-researched, fascinating work, appropriately titled *The Principled Politician: The Ralph Carr Story* published by Fulcrum Publishing, Golden, Colorado, 2008.

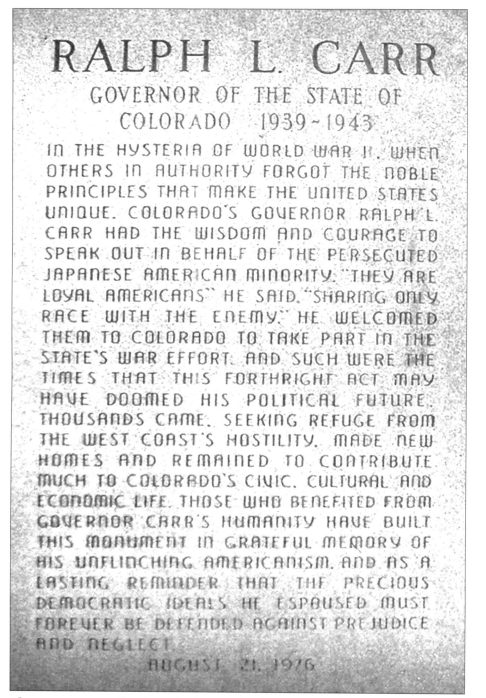

The commemorative inscription on the Carr memorial
Photo courtesy of Betty Buchanan

An annual memorial service is conducted at Camp Amache, attended by Caucasians and Japanese   *Photo courtesy of Eiichai Imada, 2004*

Camp Amache

In August of 1942, Camp Amache opened as a "relocation center," less than a mile from the small town of Granada in southeast Colorado and about eighteen miles east of Lamar. It would serve as home to nearly 10,000 internees before it closed in 1945. Amache was a Cheyenne princess married to John Prowers, nineteenth-century cattle baron who operated in the area. Prowers gave his own name to the county in which the camp was located.* It is ironic that the name of an innocent Native American personage was chosen to designate yet another ethnic injustice.

When trains unloaded their human cargo after three or four days' uncomfortable journey from California with shades down to obscure the destination, the bewildered passengers were surprised by the scene laid before them. Each recorded impression expresses the initial dismay about the inhospitable landscape that greeted them. The bleak, barren, windblown landscape must have heaped more despair onto an already stressful situation. These were people uprooted from a mild California climate with favorable growing conditions. Colorado's more popular image projects beautiful, dramatic scenery of snow-covered mountains, brilliant blue skies, and rushing trout-filled streams. The camp's facilities weren't even finished when the first inmates arrived.

Considering the numbers affected, we haven't heard much from the survivors. Many of us in Colorado have friends and acquaintances who were interned, but have you ever heard them talk about it? Whatever is in their hearts and memories, bitterness is not displayed. There were only smiles as Harry and Kimi Shironaka reminisced, never a complaint about the gross unfairness of it all, no "poor me," only an occasional chuckle over some inadequacy or restriction that horrified their interviewer. For example, when I lamented over living for all that time without handy hot water, Harry remarked, "Well, it was better than no water at all." Not a lot of specifics, and an interviewer has to sense how hard to press, how comfortably personal details can be shared with a world of strangers eager to learn about their experiences and feelings.

In view of that brevity, readers are advised to pause and reflect on the ramifications of each sentence recorded here.

* Amache's father, Chief Lone Bear, was among those murdered by the Colorado Militia in the Sand Creek Massacre in 1864.

Harry and Kimi Shironaka

"There was nothing we could do about it but accept it and make the best of it."

───────── ● ─────────

It is easy to see that some boys never outgrow their love for our national pastime. Until his ninety-fifth year, Harry and his wife Kimi spent winters in Florida at St. Petersburg, where Harry played softball on a Kids and Kubs team. This is a remarkable assemblage of seniors— an understatement, as participants only become eligible at age seventy-five. Membership runs over fifty players on four teams, many of whom are well beyond the entry age. There is even an "over-eighty" division. (Now ninety-six, Harry claims his last good year was when he was ninety-two.) There was a spot for Kimi as well; she served as bat girl for sixteen years.

The Kids and Kubs season runs from early November until April 1, which has given the team time to compete in tournaments around the U.S. Harry is proud to report the successes of his team; they came home with national championships in 1998 and 2002. Harry was eighty-six when his team won the national title for the over-eighty division in Chicago in 1998. For sixteen years, Harry was captain of the Kids division.

He used to play infield for a semi-pro team in Stockton, California, playing spring exhibition games in California and Scottsdale in the Pacific Coast League. All this adds up to a lifetime dedication to his favorite sport. It is appropriate that for his participation in baseball during the war (while at Camp Amache), Harry was honored with four other Japanese Americans by having their pictures and memorabilia displayed at the Baseball Hall of Fame in Cooperstown, New York.

Otherwise, the atypical Shironakas' story is very similar to other evacuee sagas. Harry and Kimi were born in California; their parents were first generation—Issei.

Their respective families farmed in California.

Growing up there, Harry recalls that Filipinos and Orientals went to one school, Caucasians to another. There were no African Americans in his town, Walnut Grove. It was a small town and there was only one high school, and it was not segregated.

Before WWII, distinctions were made in California between Chinese and Japanese. Fearful of the competition and of being "overrun," Californians didn't allow Japanese to own property, and Issei were not allowed citizenship or its accompanying rights. However, Harry admits that after Pearl Harbor, friends and neighbors treated them pretty much the same. Walnut Grove was small, and everybody knew everybody.

Harry and Kimi were newly-married, living in Walnut Grove. Harry was raising tomatoes on fifty irrigated acres of a rented farm.

We didn't have much time to get ready to leave— a month or two. Some people had less than that. At first, newspapers and notices warned us that we weren't allowed to leave the area. Notices were posted all over; you didn't get an individual notice, and the word spread pretty fast. You were allowed to go out of state if you had friends or relatives to sponsor you, but we didn't have anyone to take us in. I had never been out of California.

Since we were young and recently started, our equipment and household possessions were new. You were allowed to take one suitcase each, just what you could carry. Everything else had to be left behind—stored, sold, or given away. We stored some things at a church; neighbors kept some for us, but we never were able to recover our stored things after the war. I had a new car, for which I paid $900, but I could only get $200 for it. We rented out our house to Caucasians. We didn't own the farm, because Japanese couldn't own land at that time. Fortunately, we hadn't started the tomato planting yet.

In May we were ordered to report to the assembly center at Merced, because Amache wasn't ready yet. We were taken on buses, and everybody was pretty anxious about the situation. Merced was a former racetrack, about fifty miles from Walnut Grove, near Stockton. We were housed in former stables.

Harry does not describe in detail the living conditions at the Merced racetrack, but from all other accounts, they were appalling. The uncertainty of being assigned for an indefinite period of time was one more of the difficulties that interfered with adjustment to these primitive facilities. Simple issues like only occasional hot water, not much furniture, lack of privacy, and minimal, inconvenient toilet and laundry facilities were more aggravating than those encountered on a camping trip, and of course quarters were crowded.

All food was provided; we ate in a mess hall. You could hear your neighbors over the partition.

Partitions between stalls did not go to the ceiling; there was no need for the former, equine occupants. For all inmates, the humiliation and unfairness of being housed in stinking stables, although whitewashed, having no control over meals and child discipline, plus lack of mobility, added despair to the unreasonableness of the situation. But Harry doesn't dwell on these things.

There was nothing we could do about it but accept it and make the best of it. And we did survive.

In September we were put on a train to Granada. Our Walnut Grove neighbors, everyone at Merced, was sent to Amache. The camp opened in August, but it wasn't nearly finished when we got there. We were among the first to arrive. You couldn't see the camp from the station; Granada is about a mile away. There were military guards in watchtowers with guns. The area was fenced in. No one wanted to venture out; they didn't know the area, and it was nothing but cactus. There was no transportation into Granada, but we could walk, and later we would occasionally go into town. We weren't afraid while we were there, just of rattlesnakes.

We had one room. Kimi's mother was with us, as her father had died. They gave one room to a couple or three people, two rooms for four or five, and larger rooms in the middle of the barracks were for bigger families. There was no bath or toilet, no running water, no kitchen. Light came from a bulb hanging down from the center of the ceiling. Laundry was in a common room. There were six blocks on each side of the camp; twelve barracks in a block; the bathroom was shared by everyone in the block. Showers were in the same building.

The lack of privacy in the toilets and showers was particularly intimidating and offensive to the elderly ladies in the camp. Each recorded camp memoir describes this specific complaint.

We had a pot-bellied stove that burned coal; there was no wood except scraps left from construction. Some people built furniture and shelves from those scraps. We made a table with borrowed tools, from boards and nails we found. We also had a chair and beds. There wasn't room for much anyway.

Harry's parents were interned at Rohwer in Arkansas. Harry and Kimi were given permission to visit them at the camp. Enroute, they had to change in Kansas City, Kansas, and before making the connection into Arkansas, they had to spend the night in Kansas City. Turned away from motels and hotels because of their ethnicity, they returned to the station and spent the night there.

Into this situation at Amache came the new baby, Keith, born at the camp hospital, delivered by a resident Japanese doctor. Kimi was kept busy caring for her baby, with minimal conveniences, and crammed into a small space that didn't insulate the neighbors from a crying infant.

Besides the MPs and other Caucasian administrative staff, much of the work force came from camp inmates. Employment helped pass the dreary days that turned into months and years. However, the minimal compensation seemed more equivalent to volunteering.

Physicians at the hospital were Japanese, paid $19/month. Assistants got $16; others, like mess hall workers, got $12.

Harry volunteered as recreation director and organized boys and girls baseball and softball teams. The school offered athletics as well, but Harry says he was not involved in that. The camp had a recreation hall where Japanese games were played, and basketball was popular at the Amache High School gym.

In 1943 and 1944, enlistment into the armed forces was encouraged; later the draft was applied. Harry at thirty was given a physical but deferred because of his age.

They were looking for younger men—eighteen and nineteen-year-olds.

We were there only a year. I left first because my brother-in-law had a Caucasian friend in Crowley who knew about a place in Ordway I could buy to farm. Things were reasonable then. The government wanted those Amache internees to find other places to work and live. They helped them to get out, even helped financially. They knew that what they had done to us was wrong, and there was no danger in letting us out. Kimi stayed behind for a while until I got settled. My brother-in-law came to work with me.

38

I had thirty acres and raised corn, turkeys, and alfalfa. I soon learned that Colorado isn't a reliable place to raise tomatoes. Thirty acres isn't much, so I farmed other places as well.

Until recently, Harry and Kimi continued to spend half the year in St. Petersburg. They now live with son Kevin in Eaton, Colorado, and at a lively ninety-six, Harry no doubt keeps pretty close watch over the baseball scene on television.

Alma Sekiya as a mischievious two or three-year-old

Norma Sekiya and Alma Sekiya Shironaka

Nobuko's family quickly learned how different life in rural Colorado was from farming in California.

———————— ● ————————

Alma Shironaka is Harry and Kimi's daughter-in-law, married to their son Kevin. Alma and Kevin are presently sharing their home in Eaton with Kevin's parents, who are retired from farming in Ordway and baseball in Florida.

Like many children of the war generation, Alma was not directly affected by the war because she was born during the war. But she and her two siblings were impacted by what their parents experienced. Consequently they have perspectives of their own, filtered through the passage of time and changing public attitudes.

Alma's mother recorded her memoirs and the family history carefully, as a novel. The resulting, amazing chronicle is a personal and intimate record disguised as fiction— which reveals something about her mother's intent and willingness to record but wishing to do so anonymously. However, this two hundred and twenty-five pages of vivid documentation was rejected by the literary agency to which she submitted it, because it appeared to be "too autobiographical." Therein lies its value! Ironically, the rejection letter applauded her skillful writing. Be that as it may, the manuscript is a treasury of insights into what a particular Japanese American family experienced before and during the war. Perhaps it would have been accepted if the author had written the narrative in first person, but with typical Japanese modesty (more so because she was a woman?) she apparently couldn't bring herself to present this material using the "I" word. Instead, she identifies the lead character as Nobuko, her own given name. In private life, she added "Norma" to Nobuko, because it sounded more American, and during her lifetime she was known as Norma Nobuko Sekiya.

Some of the account is common to the immigration pattern of the Japanese in the early 1900s. Nobuko's story describes how her father left Japan for Hawaii as a lone teenager. This separation broke his mother's heart, as it must have done in many families sending their sons off half a world away, wondering if they would ever meet again. In Nobuko's father's case, the family never saw each other again. From Hawaii, he moved on soon to America and found employment as an agricultural worker in California, later taking a bride from Japan. He returned to Japan to see his mother, but she died before he arrived. As for his bride, she was the sister of an acquaintance who played matchmaker for the pair on that trip "home." Grandfather was thirty years old; his new wife may have been sixteen or eighteen.

Alma's grandmother

Prewar life on a California farm was hard for this young, hardworking family. One particularly poignant incident Nobuko describes involves a landlord/farmer who leased land to Nobuko's father (because at that time, Issei were not allowed to own land in California). There were cordial relations between the parties, until Nobuko discovered herself that the landlord was a sexual predator. When she threatened to reveal the situation to her father, the man made it clear that her family would be thrown out if she made trouble for him. Nobuko understood, even at her young age, that the racially tinged circumstances of her family were critical, and she never told anyone of the situation until many years later. In the meantime, she became skillful in avoiding contact with this individual. Such betrayal by a person of trust was to have a lifelong effect on Nobuko. She was paranoid about her own security and that of her two daughters. Alma reflects with amusement that a "babysitter" was nearby even when her sister Brenda was eighteen years old.

The saga proceeds smoothly until the bombing of Pearl Harbor brings war between the two nations and jeopardizes the status and security of thousands of West Coast Japanese Americans. Nobuko describes without rancor the animosity and unfairness of wartime prejudice as her California family suddenly becomes the object of suspicion and rejection. She had learned a lesson about prejudice as a little girl, when a Caucasian neighbor snatched her young son away from a play group because Nobuko was Japanese. But reeling from the attack on Pearl Harbor, there were more serious irrational responses. For example, a local grocery store immediately replaced all its Japanese employees. Checking accounts were frozen, and banks as well as other businesses made excuses to avoid service to Japanese customers.

Alerted to the possibility of being forcibly assigned to a concentration camp inland, Nobuko's father made a desperate attempt to re-locate, not easily done, as he was operating a farm. None of the family had ever been out of California. An acquaintance set machinery in motion which allowed the family to relocate in Colorado, leasing land in Rye, near Pueblo. They left California abruptly in March of 1942, leaving crops in the field ready to harvest. They also left family pets and valuable livestock behind. That original arrangement in Rye didn't work out, but

assisted by sympathetic Caucasians needing agricultural workers and ranch hands, they all found ready employment.

Nobuko's family learned quickly how different life in rural

Alma's mother Norma "Nobuko" and in maturity

Colorado was from farming in California. Exposure to extremes in the weather of the High Plains was a challenge. There was hail, grasshopper infestation, wind, and a sense of being disconnected. They were not prepared for the isolation. A few evacuees were living in Pueblo, and a Japanese community existed in Denver. Eventually the family re-settled in Denver.

They were snubbed by some businesses and served cordially by others. There were incidents of being taken advantage of and being cheated in real estate and other business transactions. Nobuko doesn't editorialize, but the implication is that because they were Japanese, they were vulnerable; they lacked both resources and "clout" to have recourse for any such kind of injustice.

Nobuko relates another reminder of how deep were the feelings toward the Japanese and how close to the surface. (There are still people out there who won't drive a Toyota, although it might be made in Kentucky.) When Alma's brother Floyd, now a Denver dentist, was born in a California hospital shortly after the bombing of Pearl Harbor, one of the attending nurses, an older woman, was noticeably abrupt and unaccommodating.

She clearly had a chip on her shoulder, and Nobuko was uneasy in her presence. She later learned the woman had lost a brother at Pearl Harbor. It may have given her some satisfaction to transfer her grief and anger to a helpless young Japanese mother experiencing the joy of bringing a son into the world. Later, the nurse regretted her attitude and before Nobuko left the hospital was gracious or repentant enough to wish Nobuko and baby Floyd the very best in the future.

Grandfather remained a conservative, old-world patriarch, devoted to and proud of his family. His only disappointment was in the female progeny his wife and daughter Nobuko brought into the world, because he regretted the loss of the Hatauye family name. Alma has compensated by giving that name as a middle name to her two sons.

Alma cherishes her heritage and is grateful her mother left in writing the stories Alma and her siblings heard while growing up. The general public, however, will unfortunately remain ignorant of the lessons contained in this important saga and its verification of how the war affected yet another innocent, law-abiding, American family and thousands of others like it.

Floyd Sekiya, Alma's brother, defending his country as a Lt. Commander in the U.S. Navy. Dr. Floyd is currently practicing dentistry in Denver.

This delightful candid shot of Alma and her siblings is of special interest because of the "coiffed" curly hair on Alma and her sister. It was an attempt to duplicate the current "Shirley Temple look" popular at the time, particularly appealing to the traditional, naturally straight bob of Japanese girls.

The Funikoshi family of six children minus one son who would be born later. Daisy is the little girl in the middle front row. We looked at photo albums consisting of studio portraits of the growing family—young boys dressed in suits, shirts and ties, little girls in their Sunday best. No candid shots like those in many other American albums. Daisy explained, "We took a lot of pictures and would send them to Japan. It was our only connection."

John & Daisy Kiyota

"Japanese farmers around here raised large families to help with work on the farm."

───────────● ●───────────

The earliest Japanese immigrants settled in the area in the first decade or two of the 1900s. Typically they came as single men to work building the railroad, then gravitated farther east and south into Colorado to farm—first as hired hands and eventually they owned their own land. Or, if a family was already established here, a relative might come directly and begin the process from that point. Before long, a bride would arrive and then a large family of children to add to the work force on the farm.

From John and Daisy came a fountain of information that attests to how Japanese traditions have for decades blended and melded into rural Weld County communities. The contrast between the two cultures is as strong as between rural Colorado and almost anywhere else, and both can claim people and life at their best. The harmonious coexistence of these two groups during wartime is a real tribute to their values, their different faiths, and the individuals who practiced them under extremely trying times. It is one of the most positive narratives of this collection, and for that it is reassuring. Plus, it well represents what we like to think is the real Colorado, after the disturbing and disgraceful behavior recorded in the preceding Ralph Carr narrative.

The reason for including all this background is to show how assimilated these Colorado Issei and Nisei were long before Pearl Harbor. They were living essentially the American life style, similar to other immigrant families from Europe working American farms. They brought their high standards of responsibility, diligence, dedication to family, and good citizenship. Yet, as we shall see, they maintained a number of traditions from the old country.

John and Daisy are both Nisei. John's father went to Hawaii from Japan by himself when he was thirteen. He worked there for a while, then came to Wyoming and worked on the railroad and eventually settled in the Platte River valley in Colorado. He married a picture bride in 1916. (A picture bride is exactly what the term implies; marriages were arranged overseas by presenting portraits of the lady under consideration and the gentleman seeking a bride. This procedure could be somewhat problematic, as succeeding narratives will describe.)

Daisy comes from a large family of Funakoshis, who were an early Ft. Lupton family established by three bachelor relatives who came from Japan.

My father had so many in his family; I think there were nine. Families in Japan are large. He figured there was no way he could progress there, so he came to Ft. Lupton. My mother's uncle was already in Ft. Lupton.

My parents were married in 1915. They were only eighteen or nineteen years old. It probably wasn't an arranged marriage, because they were first cousins. But all parents look into backgrounds carefully to make sure everything is OK. When he came here a year later, in 1916, he came by himself. He worked for two years farming. In the wintertime he went to Denver and worked as a houseboy to learn English. After three years, he called my mother out. Then they started a family.

My mother was the oldest of five or six girls, and my father took her name. It is common for a man to take his wife's family name if her family is all girls. We have a number of relatives in Japan that took the wife's name; it preserves the family name.

I was born in 1926 on a farm five miles east of Ft. Lupton, one of seven siblings, all of them living. My oldest sister is eighty-eight, and my youngest brother is seventy-four. Japanese people are often pretty long-lived. They live a healthy life style; they walk a lot, and obesity isn't as common as it is in the U.S. I have two aunts in Japan; one is 105, one is 101. I talked to one at New Year's time; she's always glad to hear from me.

When I was five years old, my father bought a farm west of town. It became the family farm. There was no house on the property, so we lived in the garage while my dad built a house. He was a carpenter in Japan. He never worked on the railroad like John's father did; he started farming right away. He just hired one Caucasian fellow and they built the house together. We don't own it any more; it is owned by my youngest brother Sam and his wife.

My siblings and I went to Ft. Lupton schools and all graduated from high school there. We had only four or five Japanese classmates when the war began, but as families moved in from California, fourteen graduated in my class with me in 1944. Because of wartime shortages, we didn't have a senior banquet. There was rationing of several things, like sugar, coffee, gas, butter, etc. They gave us a gift instead.

When I asked for photos of high school activities . . . Japanese kids didn't participate in after school extracurricular activities because we went home after school to work on the farm.

There was a small schoolhouse in town that was used as a summer school to teach the Japanese language to those interested in learning, including Caucasians. Japanese students had to work attendance around their responsibilities at home.

The three Funakoshi bachelors were Methodists. There was no church building at the time, so they met in each other's homes. I met John much later through the Youth Fellowship group. We married in 1946 right after the war; I was nineteen.

Our parents used to take us to the Japanese Methodist

Daisy's parents went back to Japan for a family wedding in 1939 or '40. The bride's family could not afford a wedding kimono so Daisy's dad bought one for her. It was passed on to Daisy. (The photo was taken after Daisy was married.) Daisy's daughter has it now, and it will be passed on to Daisy's granddaughter. Traditionally, the wedding kimono is passed on from generation to generation.

church in Denver. The pastor and his wife took good care of us, taught us songs, etc. Once we had children of our own, one of the ministers said, "We have a good Methodist church in Platteville; why don't you go there?" It was more of a social thing to go into Denver. There is a Japanese Methodist church in Arvada, but more and more Caucasians are going there now. They have a Caucasian minister. Worship, ritual, hymns are the same. Around here it's probably about half the Japanese that are Protestant, the others are Buddhist. My family never was Buddhist. At the present

Fort Lupton High School class of 1944. Daisy Funakoshi at right end of front row. Notice the number of Japanese American faces. Today there are none, as Daisy explains in her narrative.

time, John and I are the oldest members of the United Methodist Church of Platteville.

Among the Japanese traditions Daisy described is the "picture bride."

The mother of my brother in-law was a picture bride. She said that in reality they would send a picture of a real handsome person to a prospect and tell her they would meet in Seattle or San Francisco. When the girl arrived, he was bald and not what she was expecting! And what do you do about it when you come? You don't have any money to go back, so you just have to accept it and go through with it. Divorce is not common among the Japanese.

No doubt the same strategy was employed on occasion by the opposite sex. At any rate, there was room for misunderstanding along with misrepresentation. A story is told about a group of Filipino workers employed on the railroad with Japanese immigrants. The Filipinos thought the picture bride was a good idea, so they secured a Sears catalogue. One picked out a pretty face, sent off an order for his selection, then was surprised when a box arrived containing a lady's sweater!

Our family ate traditional Japanese food, and we still do. You can buy it at markets in Denver and in Boulder.

My parents' farm had a Japanese bath outside. We invited neighbors to use it on Saturday night, because everyone didn't have a bath house. We made it a social affair. Kids played hide and seek, adults visited, there were table games, and everyone had a lot of fun.

Japanese farmers around here raised large families to help with the work on the farm. Kids were obedient and we expected to contribute. My father didn't hire anyone in; we kids did the work.

Nevertheless, education is important, and today these farmers send their children to college to be doctors, lawyers, engineers, etc. Then those graduates don't come back to the area afterward. Consequently, the Japanese population here is dwindling. There aren't any graduating now from Ft. Lupton High School, and no one is a candidate for the annual scholarship JACL *(Japanese American Citizens League)* grants. There are ten students in the entire area that will apply this year for that scholarship.

In line with the tradition of family responsibility and the importance of education, John, as eldest son, and Daisy helped put their siblings through school.

The grandparents were old and without means, and they didn't know the English language. It was a handicap to come here being illiterate, not knowing the language, plus a totally strange cultural setting. Most of our oldest siblings didn't know any English when they started school, but they all graduated. No one babied the Japanese kids in school. There was no English as a Second Language program; they just had to manage the best they could until they learned the language.

But you know, by the time the war broke out, my father spoke English quite well. He traded at Safeway all the time. One time soon after Pearl Harbor, after he bought his groceries they said, "We can't take your check." So he had to leave all the groceries there. He probably knew people who worked there. There was another grocery store in Ft. Lupton, an IGA store, so he went over there to see if he could buy groceries. A lady ran that business because her husband farmed, and they were good people. She said, "You can charge it. Come in any time," and we started doing our business there all the time. The Japanese were also cut off at the bank and couldn't write checks or anything for quite a while.

When John and I were first married, we had no money, but in Platteville there

Willie K. Kiyota Cited for Heroism

...shing Officer ...m Colorado Returns

w York Ciy—A blushing nisei, won a field commission last tmas Day, returned home Sept. a patient on the Army hospital Ernest Hinds.

Willie Kiyota, 22, of Platteville, Colo., winner of the Bronze Star, the Purple Heart, Presidential unit citation and four battle stars, led the nisei unit, the only one to get through the German line at Vosges Mt. His unit also led the allied drive along the Po Valley in Italy last April and cracked the German line.

He is suffering from stomach ulcer and was transferred to Halloran Hospital.

John's brother Willy on the right, a decorated hero with the celebrated all-Japanese American 442nd Combat Team — while the Shironakas and Oki's family were interned as potentially "dangerous aliens."

were some good people. The gas man, Stub Bruce, let us charge for all our gas until crops were in. We had a great local grocery family, and they also let us charge for all groceries until harvest time. Imagine!

What is more commendable is the likely size of these smalltown businesses. Probably independent, "mom-and-pop" operations, they wouldn't have the financial back-up resources that today's Safeway, for example, has. They may have had to ask for credit themselves when cash was slow coming in because of their generosity toward their customers.

John and Daisy had five children— three boys and two girls, and now seven grandchildren. The eldest son died from leukemia when he was three years old.

Somehow we managed to send all four of our kids to college. Karen and Susan went to UNC and became teachers; Howard to CSU, Roger also to CSU, is part owner of the greenhouse.

John at ninety-two has retired from farming and from the family-owned greenhouse nursery business on the property. John and Daisy are part owners, sharing with a brother, nephew, son, and daughter.

Daisy's recollections of wartime are fortunately not as horrific as stories from expatriate survivors from Europe. Given the animosity initially shown when the prospect arose of bringing Japanese to Colorado, it is a credit to both sides that those years passed ami-

MERRY CHRISTMAS
442ND
COMBAT TEAM

Colorado Nisei Hero Lauded By Comrades in New York

Nisei Lieutenant Blushes and Won't Explain Decorations

NEW YORK, — A blushing Japanese American Army lieutenant who won a field commission last Christmas Day returned home last week as a patient on the Army hospital ship Ernest Hinds.

Lieut. Willie Kiyota, 22 years old, of Platteville, Colo., was too modest to explain his promotion or his decorations and ribbons, which include the Bronze Star with cluster, the Purple Heart, with two clusters, a Presidential unit citation and four battle stars. But other Army officers who returned with him sang his praises.

A lieutenant said Lieutenant Kiyota got the promotion for "unadulterated leadership," and a captain said: "You know why? Your Jap unit was the only one to get through the German lines to the lost battalion in the Vosges Mountains last November."

The lieutenant and captain added that Lieutenant Kiyota's unit had spearheaded the Allied drive along the Po Valley last April and cracked the German line.

Others joined in tribute to Japanese American troops in Europe, saying the only cases of AWOL among them were men who escaped from hospitals to get back to the front.

Lieutenant Kiyota stood quietly waiting for transfer to Halloran Hospital, and when a reporter asked him how he happened to be on the hospital ship he squirmed for a minute and then answered: "It was stomach ulcers. Cognac, not the Jerries, did it."

cably and good relationships emerged intact.

The Japanese people were well-known in the area; they had been farmers and business people for many years. There was no trouble, even going to school. I was a sophomore or junior when the war broke out. Nobody picked on us. We knew all our classmates. When evacuation came, because of Governor Carr more came from the

John and Daisy at the nursery

West Coast. We had relatives that came to our place in Ft. Lupton when the war broke out. Some we had never met before, because they had always lived in California. *(John and Daisy went to Japan one time, in the 1980s, an opportunity to meet many other relatives for the first time.)* They lived with us for quite some time. How did we find room? With seven children of our own, they had to double or triple up or sleep on the floor.

At least one Japanese family in the Platte River valley had unknown California residents contact them because they shared the same name. The Californians asked if they could come and stay with the Colorado family in order to avoid evacuation. The Colorado hosts accepted them, gave them a place to live on their farm, and hired them for the duration.

We knew a man from California who was at Amache with his family and worked on a farm off the camp premises. At the end of the war, when they were released, he went back to California and found everything had been taken by the neighbors, and they didn't have anything left. So he came back to Colorado and lived in Alamosa.

There was another man here whose parents divorced, and the father had to raise all the kids. His mother moved to California. When the war broke out, he heard that his mother came to Amache, and he got permission to go to see her.

The large Kiyota Nursery near Platteville is still a thriving, family operation. It supplies garden centers throughout the area with the very highest quality nursery stock.

As representatives of the Japanese community in Colorado, John and Daisy Kiyota continue to uphold the highest principles of that community and of their American homeland as well.

Chicako's graduating class of the all-girls high school she attended

Chikako Murata

"When I saw the sun going down in the western sky, I became very sad and wanted to go home to Japan."

────────── ● ──────────

This modest and refined lady is an artist among other things, and her home near Greeley is filled with lovely watercolor paintings from her travels and especially of flowers. They are reminiscent of the exquisite renderings one associates with traditional Japanese floral painting.

Chikako's memoir describes her coming to America as the bride of an American GI, who was also of Japanese heritage. Her adjustments were somewhat easier than some Japanese brides, but nevertheless there were many challenges.

Chikako was born in 1926 and grew up in Fukuoka. Her father manufactured texiles and silk sashes for kimonos. She attended an all-girls high school, then graduated from a women's college with a major in Japanese classical literature.

We graduated six months earlier than usual because of the war. It affected us directly because my father's looms were all destroyed. Anyway, that business wasn't needed for the war. His factory became a house. He didn't restart the business after the war because he wasn't in good health. He died in 1949.

Chikako had studied English in Japan, enough to assist a photographer who took pictures of American GIs and developed their personal films, and he needed an interpreter's services. One of the servicemen who came into the studio was Takeshi "Tak" Murata from Kuner, Colorado.

Chikako and Tak were married in 1947, and the next year they traveled on a military ship to Seattle, where Tak was discharged.

The trip took ten days in the month of May, when it was calm, so I didn't get seasick. But I couldn't eat on the ship because it wasn't familiar food. I only ate things like oranges. When I saw a grocery store in Seattle, we bought bananas and ice cream. I tell my children the story of how I ate a whole quart of ice cream. We looked for a

Japanese restaurant and couldn't find one.

The next leg of their journey took them by train to Denver and on to the family farm near Kuner, a small rural community east of Greeley near Highway 34.

Tak's parents came to get us in their car. On the way back to Kuner, they had a little incident. They didn't stop at a stop sign, because their car wasn't in good condition. A patrolman came and talked to us (and I'm sure gave them a ticket). After that the car wouldn't start up again, and they had to be pushed. I was so embarrassed!

Farm life in America was not like anything Chikako could have imagined. In fact, she didn't have any idea she would be a farmer's wife or what that entailed. Her upbringing was urban; she was college-educated.

Even in Japan I didn't know farmers or what they did. So I just came and I watched and experienced. I did it bit by bit. I was young and I guess naïve, and I wasn't too much afraid. After twenty-five years when I went back to see my classmates, they said, "You had such guts to go to a strange country."

Tak's mother and father came from Japan. His grandparents came to America a long time ago. Then his grandfather called Tak's father to come. When he got to marriageable age, he went to Japan to get a bride. Some people saw only a picture of the bride before meeting her to get married. So what I did was not as scary as that.

Lots of Japanese people raised onions, cabbage, and other vegetables. Compared to today, their acreage wasn't big. Mostly they didn't hire people but instead they helped each other. They worked hard all day. We had hardships farming in Kuner. Almost every year hail destroyed the crops.

I had to cook lunch and supper, but I wasn't cooking-experienced. I had taken cooking class at college, but when I went home, my mother cooked and washed dishes. When I got married and came to America, I had to wash dishes day and night! I became the cook for my husband, his parents, and his brother. My husband teases me about the first time I cooked shrimp for tempura. I forgot to peel the shell. Tak's parents had a little garden beside the house. I picked all their regular green peas thinking they were Chinese edible pod peas. We ate them with the tempura.

In 1949 my daughter was born, so I didn't help farm until four or five years later. Even when I started going to the fields, I didn't know how to do it. I didn't have experience. It was a sad time for me because, oh, I came this far, and I was doing this kind of things, and I cried.

I was lonely, too. I wept on my pillow so many times. When I saw the sun going down in the west sky, I said, "I want to go home so bad." But then my daughter was

The scrapbook Chikako made of her Christmas greeting cards
Photo credit Georgia Wier

born, and my son five years later, and I got used to it. When I went to Japan for the first time, twenty-five years later, I said, "I have to go home, and my place is in America." Even the second and third times I went, I liked to see my friends and family; I wanted to visit but not to live there.

To learn English, while in Japan Chikako took night classes, meeting once a week. She admits to not knowing much at first.

I had been to college, so I knew more than the others. When I write in English first, it doesn't come out well. Writing a letter in English is hard. Writing a short one I can write, but a long letter I can never write it. I regret I didn't study harder. Speaking is not good, but I get by.

In Japan we don't celebrate Christmas so much, but we exchange end-of-the-year cards. They are sort of the same as Christmas cards. My classmates send them to me. I collected them until about three years ago when I took a drawing class at the senior center. We had an opportunity to make something, and I decided this was the time to do something with my Christmas cards. My children don't read Japanese, but they will be able to see the book after I'm gone.

The scrapbook contains beautiful Japanese script captions. To non-Japanese , that script seems undecipherable, not to mention the difficulty learning to form the exquisite characters. Incidentally, Chikako's English handwriting is to be envied. It is clear, fluid, and would be a penmanship teacher's pride.

I had two boys and two girls, and I thought that was perfect. Then Brian came, and he helped me a lot. I felt so guilty when he told somebody that he wasn't sup- posed to be born.

Chikako proudly points out her hand-painted renditions
Photo credit Georgia Wier

The Murata children are called by their English names but all have Japanese names as well: Gladys (Miya), Wes (Hiroshi), Diane (Elko), Gene (Shuji), and Brian (Akio).

Chikako and Tak sent all five of their children to college, to Colorado state universities.

Japanese people think that it's our duty to at least send our children to college. My husband and I always think as long as you give your children education, they can do anything they want after that.

Chikako and Tak lived with Tak's parents for a time, helping on the farm. When their second daughter was born they got their own house. Chikako's in-laws never owned a farm; Chikako explains that they were at "survival stage."

As part of the first generation, they were satisfied with that. Second and third generation make it bigger and bigger. But farming is getting hard now.

At present, Tak and Chikako rent their own farm; Tak at seventy-seven still helps in the fields.

We go to the Buddhist temple and did from the time we arrived. My husband's parents did a reception for us at the church. In those days, they made all the Japanese feasts with friends helping. They served all kinds of things—fish, sushi, and all that stuff. Every time someone dies, Buddhists have a seven-day service. People come and church members made lunch. Nowadays people go to restaurants. When the first generation pioneers were still alive, we made everything from scratch. But they are almost all gone now, and the second generation is getting to be that age—seventy to eighty-five.

The third generation has mixed marriages now; mostly the boys go to the wife's side and are Christian. So membership in our church is getting small.

Lastly, for the record, Chikako would like to say:

I think America is the richest, nicest place in the world. Prejudices never go away, but I think this is the Number One country in the world. I've been to Japan four times, and I'd like to go one more time, but I don't think I can make the trip myself anymore.

Examples of Chikakos floral designs
Photo credit Georgia Wier

Georgia Wier, Greeley folklorist, recorded an interview with Chikako in March, 2002. This narrative is based largely on excerpts from that interview, plus my own meeting with Chikako. Georgia's original tape is in the archives at the Greeley Museum.

Reiko and Mary Jane

Mary Jane Rust

"I loved living in Japan because I could see over everybody's head."

———————⬤———————

Yes, it is evident that Mary Jane's stay in Japan as part of the occupation forces' families has indeed left a very positive impression of that experience. Beautiful porcelain plates and other decorative tableware adorn high shelves constructed for that purpose throughout the living areas of her home. Three-dimensional pieces occupy flat, display surfaces, while exquisite fabrics are displayed on walls. Japanese furniture is easy to pick out among an otherwise contemporary setting.

Mary Jane would have been a good American ambassador for her native culture in that precarious occupation situation after the war ended in August of 1945. She viewed this assignment as a privilege, a learning experience. She recalls that she particularly appreciated that the opportunity was presented to her as a young woman— an opportunity to learn first hand the commonalities shared by the human race.

The occupation of Japan by American military forces and their dependents presented an historic and unique challenge in 1945. The issue of intermixing diverse populations didn't exist in the occupation of postwar Germany, because America historically contained a large population of German immigrants. Japanese culture, on the other hand, was quite unknown to Americans, and few Americans had traveled to Japan. During her assignment there, Mary Jane concluded that people are people, with many of the same problems, goals, fears, feelings, no matter their language, dress, or faith, no matter what continent they call home.

Mary Jane and I have been best friends for twenty-five years, have traveled overseas together on several occasions, and have co-authored two books. She has proven to be the most open-minded, culturally-literate, talented, and classiest dame one could be privileged to know. Her legion of friends and admirers in Colorado Springs will be delighted to learn this additional dimension to a popular community personality, who served the city for many years as its Supervisor of Cultural Affairs.

It was 1949, just four years after the end of the U.S. war with Japan and the world's only nuclear bombing. I was twenty-two and on my way to join my Army husband, a lieutenant serving in the occupation forces in Japan. One of many military dependents on the Army ship, I wondered what life would be like in the country of such a foreign people, who so recently were our country's enemies. Also of concern was the fact that my first baby would be born in Japan in just a few months. Never had I been out of the U.S. in my life, but I was thrilled and excited about what lay ahead.

After my husband met me at the ship, we found ourselves in the middle of the Gion Festival in Tokyo, a huge celebration with balloons so tall that power wires were temporarily removed. It was to be my first experience among the many surprises ahead as we began to settle in for the years to come.

My husband was assigned to the 24th Infantry Regiment of the 25th Army Division. It was to become the last segregated regiment in the U.S. Army. All the soldiers were African American. Half the officers were African American and half were Caucasian. We were settled in Otsu, near Kyoto. Kyoto was the ancient capital and cultural and art center of Japan.

Soon a Japanese housemaid joined the household. Reiko became a close friend as well as a helpmate. She knew not one word of English, nor had she ever held a fork in her hand. I wanted to learn Japanese. So began a long, interesting mixture of languages and customs. We were the same age, and we learned to laugh together as we struggled to communicate. When my first baby boy was born in the nearest Army hospital, Reiko was as thrilled as we were and just as proud. For a year, with Reiko's help I was able to sign up for lessons in the Japanese language and flower design. But soon our lives were to change drastically.

In July of 1950, North Korea attacked South Korea and another war began. The nearest American troops were in Japan and were the first to be sent to Korea. On the Fourth of July, Reiko, baby Carl and I stood in a railroad station and watched the train leave carrying American soldiers, including my husband. Suddenly the world was a different place. Most of the American dependents left for home in the U.S. at the request of the Army. I chose to stay in the military compound where I not only felt safe but also closer to Korea, where my husband was.

Due to the proximity of Korea, it could eventually be a threat to Japan if the war moved to the south where American troops were still assigned. So, it was understandable that air raid warnings had to be practiced. That meant that when the siren sounded, all the women and children had to run up a hill into a bamboo forest and wait until the all-clear sounded. You never knew how often this would happen or whether it would one day be real. Meanwhile, the war lingered on.

The compound was small, but big enough to become a tiny community for the Army wives and their children, all waiting for husbands to return. The worst worry occurred when the chaplain's jeep drove into the compound. The chaplain was a young Marine priest who had the terrible responsibility to inform a woman that her husband was either wounded or killed in combat. We dreaded the arrival of the chaplain's jeep, and when it stopped at someone's quarters we all gathered together in that special relationship so natural for military women. Soon someone would be leaving for the States.

Mary Jane performing in a USO program in Tokyo, 1950. On one occasion she appeared in a show with Bob Hope when he came to entertain the troops.

Meanwhile, I enjoyed attending the nearby Japanese Catholic Church, where I was able to take part in the Latin Liturgy. The priest was a German who had spent the WWII years in prison in Japan. He had learned what he could of English from American GIs, but he retained a heavy German accent. So there we were—all three different languaged people brought together by the Latin of our religion.

Phone calls were few and far between, but one night a very familiar voice called, and I didn't know whether to laugh or cry. My husband was saying, "... Don't worry, I was shot by a sniper, but nothing important was hit," (comedian as always). He had

Reiko and baby Carl

been shipped to Osaka by the medical ship *Hope* and would be home in Otsu in a couple of days to recuperate.

Those few days went swiftly by, and before long he was assigned back to the front in Korea. Now I was more worried than before, because I knew how likely it was that he could be hurt or killed. And, incidentally, I discovered that I was pregnant again. This one would be known as a "Purple Heart Baby" in the annals of military language. As he had said, "Nothing important was hit."

My husband was awarded the Purple Heart and two Bronze Stars, one with a "V" for valor. Because he had been wounded and had twice spent time in Korea, we were one of the first American families allowed to return to the U.S. That meant temporary duty at Fort Dix, New Jersey, followed by Fort Bragg, North Carolina. Next came three years in Austria and Germany. A final assignment to Fort Carson, Colorado, led to our love of the Rockies. And so we have stayed since 1957 with our family, which soon consisted of seven children.

For many years Reiko and I kept in touch. One picture she sent showed her husband, herself, and six children. It must have been catching!

Life in Wartime Europe

● ● ●

St. Louis **survivors in Ottawa, 2000. Dr. Jacobson and Clark Blatteis in back row left. Jacobson on far left.**

Dr. Rudolph Jacobson

The Story of the *S.S St. Louis*

———————————— ● ————————————

My name is now Dr. Rudolph "Rudy" Jacobson, born Rudolf Cohen in Insterburg, East Prussia, Germany, in 1933, just five months after Hitler came to power. My mother divorced my biological father, Erwin Cohen, in late 1933 and then married Erich Jacobsohn a year later. Erwin Cohen emigrated to Israel with his mother and sister about 1935. For some unexplained reason he returned to Germany in the late 1930s and was subsequently murdered in Auschwitz during WWII. I was adopted by Eric Jacobson here in the U.S.A. in 1947. Once in the United States, my parents Americanized our names. In Germany my mother was known as Margarete Jacobsohn, my step-father as Erich Jacobson, and I as Rudolf Cohen. Eventually, the spelling was changed to Eric, Greta, and Rudolph Jacobson.

I have several recollections of my early childhood, going back to before I was four years old, and these have been verified by my late mother. (I lost her in 2000 at the age of 92.) I have heard that professionals say ones childhood memories usually don't go back beyond five and a half or six, but I have to disagree. In my case, my earliest memories are of a traumatic nature, and I firmly believe that life-threatening memories go back much earlier. My earliest memory is that of a young Hitler Youth girl getting hurt playing soccer in a park and being taken away in an ambulance. To this day, every time I see such an old Packard ambulance with a single back door that swings open, like in a WWII movie, or an old hearse, that scene flashes to me.

My survivor story is that I was a passenger on the ship *S.S. St. Louis*. If you're not familiar with the story, look up the book *Voyage of the Damned* (1974 by Thomas & Witts). My mother was interviewed by the authors during their research and is listed as a resource.

I grew up in Nazi Germany from May 11, 1933, until we left May 13, 1939, just two days after my sixth birthday. I am an eye witness to what happened on *Kristallnacht* ("night of broken glass") on November 9, 1938, when I saw the Brown Shirts set fire to our Synagogue in Bamberg. Dad and I were standing diagonally across the street in the shadows behind a house, where we couldn't be seen. In March of 2002, I was back in Bamberg and retraced those same steps my dad and I ran that fateful night in November of 1938. We even stood behind that same house on the exact spot Dad and I had stood on Kristallnacht.

I also recall the events of the following day when the Gestapo came to our house to arrest my dad, as they did all Jewish males between sixteen and sixty-five—most of the breadwinners. They were arrested and sent to one of three concentration camps— Dachau, Buchenwald, or Sachenhausen, depending on which one you lived closest to. It was three weeks before we received a post card from my dad telling us that he was OK and had been taken to Dachau (since we lived in Bamberg, Bavaria. Dachau was near Munich). I still have two of those cards. So when these revisionists say it didn't happen, I say differently because I have proof it did.

My dad was released when my mother showed the authorities proof the family was ready to leave Germany. This meant having a visa or landing permit for another country and that she had booked passage to get to that country, namely Cuba in our case. Prisoners were released with the understanding that they were going to leave Germany within sixty days, never to return. My mother showed the Gestapo the necessary documents to leave.

All assets had to be sold and proceeds turned over to the state. That included stocks, bonds, real estate holdings, businesses, art, antiques, cash value on insurance policies, jewelry, furs, silver service, cameras, etc. Each adult was allowed to take only ten marks (approximately $4.30) in cash out of the country for shipboard expenses. They even made the *St. Louis* passengers buy one half a return ticket in order to get more money out of them. By the time these people left, they were practically penniless. Most of the men had been beaten into a submissive state by the time of their release.

We had landing permits for Cuba, but when we arrived, the authorities there told us the landing permits were invalid, and that unless we had a Cuban visa we could not get off the ship. The American government wouldn't let us in either, even though most of the Jewish refugees on the ship had U.S. quota numbers and would have been eligible to immigrate within six to nine months. If the U.S. had accepted the *St. Louis* passengers, all would have been saved, since none would have been returned to Europe, where two-thirds were caught again by the Nazis and deported to the East. They could have been interned in the U.S., and when their quota numbers came up and they received their visas, their sponsors could have come and picked them up. However, President Roosevelt was advised by his political bosses that if he let these

"About 7 P.M. on *Kristallnacht*, Dad and I hid behind No. 10 Amalien and saw the S.A. breaking the stained glass windows as the flames were shooting out our Synagogue."

907 Jews into the country, he would lose the 1940 election, because four organizations had enough political clout to defeat him: the KKK, Rev. Coughlin and his radio audience, the labor unions, and the German American Bund.

We would be interned because we didn't have visas and could not enter the country legally. We had to be kept somewhere so we wouldn't infiltrate into the country and take jobs from legal citizens who were out of work, since there was still a lot of unemployment due to the Depression. The FBI was also afraid of a German Fifth Column and spies infiltrating—a legitimate concern, but in actuality a smoke screen for the U.S. State Department's blatant anti-Semitism.

As it turned out, the ship was forced to go back to Europe, and these Jews ended up in France, Belgium, Holland, and England. We left the *St. Louis* in Antwerp, Belgium.

Of course, all those who stayed in England were saved, but less than half of those that returned to the European continent survived. Our family was in the group of 181 the Dutch government allowed in because the Queen wanted to save those families with infants; my brother was just a year old.

We were interned in Holland for many of the same reasons we would have been a problem in the U.S. We were not regular citizens anymore. Germany had revoked the citizenship of the Jews after the Nuremberg Laws. We were stateless refugees and without resources, since all the adults were allowed to take on board was ten marks. Maybe we had some skills, but Holland had plenty of unemployed workers with skills looking for work, which they weren't going to give to illegal, foreign Jews. We had to be kept somewhere so we wouldn't infiltrate into the country and take jobs from legal citizens who were out of work.

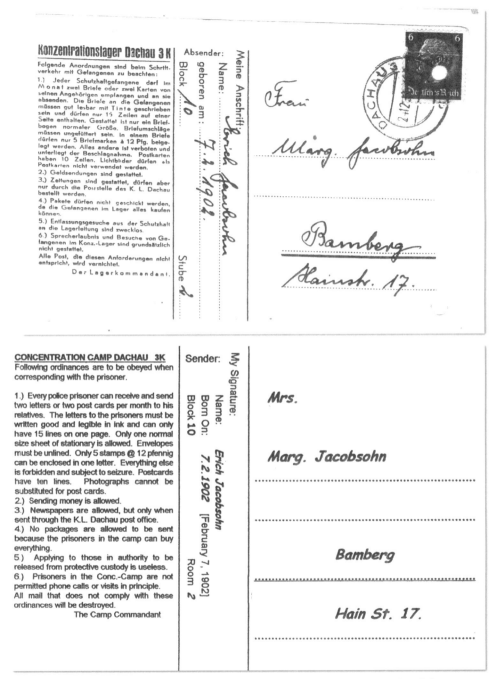

Konzentrationslager Dachau 3 K

Folgende Anordnungen sind beim Schriftverkehr mit Gefangenen zu beachten:

1.) Jeder Schutzhaftgefangene darf im Monat zwei Briefe oder zwei Karten von seinen Angehörigen empfangen und an sie absenden. Die Briefe an die Gefangenen müssen gut lesbar mit Tinte geschrieben sein und dürfen nur 15 Zeilen auf einer Seite enthalten. Gestattet ist nur ein Briefbogen normaler Größe. Briefumschläge müssen ungefüttert sein. In einem Briefe dürfen nur 5 Briefmarken à 12 Pfg. beigelegt werden. Alles andere ist verboten und unterliegt der Beschlagnahme. Postkarten haben 10 Zeilen. Lichtbilder dürfen als Postkarten nicht verwendet werden.
2.) Geldsendungen sind gestattet.
3.) Zeitungen sind gestattet, dürfen aber nur durch die Poststelle des K. L. Dachau bestellt werden.
4.) Pakete dürfen nicht geschickt werden, da die Gefangenen im Lager alles kaufen können.
5.) Entlassungsgesuche aus der Schutzhaft an die Lagerleitung sind zwecklos.
6.) Sprecherlaubnis und Besuche von Gefangenen im Konz.-Lager sind grundsätzlich nicht gestattet.
Alle Post, die diesen Anforderungen nicht entspricht, wird vernichtet.

Der Lagerkommandant.

CONCENTRATION CAMP DACHAU 3K
Following ordinances are to be obeyed when corresponding with the prisoner.

1.) Every police prisoner can receive and send two letters or two post cards per month to his relatives. The letters to the prisoners must be written good and legible in ink and can only have 15 lines on one page. Only one normal size sheet of stationary is allowed. Envelopes must be unlined. Only 5 stamps @ 12 pfennig can be enclosed in one letter. Everything else is forbidden and subject to seizure. Postcards have ten lines. Photographs cannot be substituted for post cards.
2.) Sending money is allowed.
3.) Newspapers are allowed, but only when sent through the K.L. Dachau post office.
4.) No packages are allowed to be sent because the prisoners in the camp can buy everything.
5.) Applying to those in authority to be released from protective custody is useless.
6.) Prisoners in the Conc.-Camp are not permitted phone calls or visits in principle.
All mail that does not comply with these ordinances will be destroyed.

The Camp Commandant

Sender:
My Signature:
Name: Erich Jacobsohn
Born On: 7.2.1902 [February 7, 1902]
Block 10
Room 2

Mrs.

Marg. Jacobsohn

Bamberg

Hain St. 17.

Front of KZ-Dachau postcard (the bottom is translation) received from Erich Jacobsohn. Erich was arrested on November 10, 1938, the day after "Krystallnacht," and for the three intervening weeks his family did not know where he was or if he were alive.

We were interned in a camp called Heijplatt. It was nothing like the German concentration camps you've read about—more of a transient camp. I have many memories of that camp; some are even funny, despite our desperate situation. Two of my fondest are these:

The camp was surrounded by a chain link fence; I can't remember if there was barbed wire along the top. There were only a few openings, guarded by Dutch police and German Shepard dogs. Adults could only leave the camp with a written permit, but we children made friends with one of the guards and his dog at one of the gates that was not very far from a railroad siding. One day three of us young boys wandered over to this track and watched the workers unload bananas from a box car. They had a metal platform connecting the railroad car to a canvas-covered truck. As they carried the stalks of green, unripe bananas on their shoulders, sometimes one would drop off the truck, bounce on the platform and onto the ground, where one of us would grab it.

I knew what these green things were, but I don't think the other two ever saw a banana before. The workmen saw us picking up the fallen bananas, and feeling sorry for us, gave us each a burlap sack to put them in. They must have known we were from the camp and hadn't seen any fresh fruit in a long time. Once we had the gunny sacks, they made sure many more bananas than before suddenly fell to the ground due to those wonderful, careless workers.

When all our sacks were full, we took them back to the camp and gave them to the elders in charge. They were divided among the families in our barracks. Since these bananas were green, everyone put them under the blankets on their bed hoping that would help ripen them quicker. After a few days, the people became impatient and even though they were still somewhat green, they were eaten by these people who hadn't seen any fresh fruit in quite some time. That was a big mistake, because most of us ended up with a case of the "scoots" from these unripe bananas, and then the plumbing got a real workout.

The other memory has to do with my distaste of milk as long as I can remember. The Queen wanted us children to have a healthy afternoon snack, and so every afternoon all of us children were herded into the dining room. There on the table were white coffee mugs filled with milk and some chocolate shavings floating on top. Who knows how long this milk had been sitting out, and I wasn't about to find out. I couldn't stand milk from the day I was born. My parents had to add a few teaspoons of coffee to change the color and taste so I would drink it. It had to be ice cold or I couldn't get it past my nose. To this day I can't stand the smell or taste of tepid milk.

So, I would take my mug of tepid milk and slip to the back of the dining room unnoticed, where there was a huge buffet consisting of a lower chest of drawers at least six feet wide, with an equally large hutch sitting on top, but which wasn't as deep as the chest of drawers it sat on. Since both pieces were placed so they were flush across the front, the back of the hutch didn't touch the wall, and that left a narrow shelf in the back which was actually the uncovered top of the chest. That is where I would slide these cups of room temperature milk day after day for at least ten days until it ended abruptly during a cleaning session when one of the ladies noticed this smell while dusting the buffet. My crime was discovered when they found all these mugs filled with sour, smelly milk. Who could have done this?—the elders wondered. My mother knew immediately who the culprit was. I was severely paddled and barred from any further afternoon treats, which really broke my heart!

As all the adults were only allowed to take ten marks each out of Germany, for shipboard expenses, they did not have any money to buy passage to come to the U.S. Luckily, Eric Jacobson had a second cousin in Milwaukee, Wisconsin, who was willing to send us the money for passage to the United States, and he agreed to be our sponsor. Our quota number came up on December 7, 1939, while we were interned in Holland. We arrived in the U.S. on February 5, 1940, landing in Hoboken, New Jersey, via the Holland American Line's *S.S. Veendam.* Ellis Island was already closed for the duration, since the war in Europe had already started in September, 1939.

Trying to assimilate into our new American life and culture is a whole other story in itself. My childhood didn't really start for me until I arrived in Milwaukee and started to attend the first grade. In prewar Germany, children were to be seen but not heard. By the time my dad came home from work, I had already eaten. He would put me to bed, kiss me good night, and then have dinner with Mother. I did have a nanny for a companion. I remember the boy from upstairs; we lived downstairs in a duplex, and I used to play in my sandbox in the back of the house. Sometimes my cousins would visit from out of town, and all of us would play in the sandbox. At such a young age, one really doesn't make many friends, and certainly my parents would not have left me alone to play with them. Besides, there weren't any day cares in those days for young kids to meet each other.

On Sunday mornings my dad would put me on his bicycle (he had gotten a special saddle for me that was bolted to the bar), and the two of us would ride out into the country for a second breakfast. That was my special time with my dad. Some Sunday afternoons the three of us would go to a local restaurant called "Die Weise Taube" (The White Dove), which had a beer garden where we would sit. This was one of the few places Jews could go to socialize, since gentile establishments were off limits to Jews after the Nuremberg Laws were passed in 1935. This restaurant was owned by

Jews. I always ordered my favorite, *Butter Brote*—bread with butter. It was good German dark rye bread, open face, with butter spread on it, and the butter was scored with a knife so it made a diamond pattern. Boy, that really impressed me! I'm not sure if it was the diamond pattern on the Butter Brote or the taste.

Once in the U.S., I was put back into the first grade because I could only speak

Mother Greta, Rudy, Dad Eric and Grandmother Eva Simon, 1935

two words of English, "yes" and "no." This got me into a lot of trouble. One day the teacher motioned for me to come to the blackboard. On my way to the blackboard, I accidentally stepped on my teacher's foot. She grabbed me by the arm and said, "You just stepped on my toe. You're supposed to say you're sorry. Would you like me to step on your toe?"

I didn't understand a word, and I was so frightened. I knew if the teacher asked a question, it's better to say "Yes" than "No," so I said, "Yes." Whereupon she promptly stepped on my toe, and I started to cry, not knowing why she did that. Mother was told this by a refugee girl from Germany who escorted me to school.

When all the first graders were moved to the second grade, I was kept in the first grade, and my parents were told I was going to remain there until I learned English so I could keep up.

That first summer of 1940, my parents sent me to Camp Sidney Cohen, a Jewish summer camp on Lake Nemabin, for six weeks. Mom said that by the time I came home, I spoke English pretty decently, and I was able to keep up during the rest of the school year. By the time I completed third grade, they let me skip fourth grade so I could be put back where I belonged, and I was able to graduate from high school at eighteen.

Emotionally, not only was I robbed of my childhood, as were all the children of the *Shoah*, but I was also deprived of the love and nurturing that children back then received from their parents, because my parents had no time for such display of affection. They were in a new country, no family, no friends, and couldn't speak the language. They had to learn English and earn a living. My dad went to work in a warehouse for his cousin who had sponsored us. He rode the streetcar for an hour to go to work, worked his shift of eight to nine hours and then rode the streetcar home again. This went on five days a week and from 8:00 to 1:00 on Saturday. By the time he came home, he was exhausted.

My mother started a business during the war called Kiddie Fashions. So she was busy with doling out home work to the ladies who worked for her. She would give them the cut materials, and they would sew them together at home. They made children's fashions and accessories. My first job was working for Mom punching holes for drawstrings in velvet bags, for which I got a penny a hole. She traveled a lot to get orders from the likes of Marshall Field, Macy's, and Sachs, not to mention some of the children's specialty shops in Milwaukee. My brother and I were kind of left to fend for ourselves, now called "latch-key kids."

Sunday was my dad's day of rest. After all, the man had put in close to fifty hours during the week and all for a lousy $35. The one luxury he would allow himself was to take me to the baseball game on Sunday afternoons. We went to see the old Milwaukee Brewers, when they were still AAA (*and Casey Stengl was coach*). Usually it was a double-header, which meant we would get to the ball park around 12:30 and stay until 6:00. He just loved to sit out in the bleachers—25 cents for adults and 10 for kids—under the hot sun. I would get a coke and a hot dog during those five-plus hours of broiling in the sun. He really loved the game of baseball.

Too bad he died of a heart attack in November of 1952, just months before major league baseball arrived in Milwaukee. He was only fifty years old but a severe diabetic, and the time he spent in Dachau before we left Germany aged him severely.

At the age of twelve I started selling newspapers. At fourteen I got a job in a flower shop for 50 cents an hour, and I've been working ever since. Once I turned sixteen I sold men's furnishings at J.C. Penney Co. where Dad worked, once he learned English. (There's a story about J.C. Penney letting my dad go because he was Jewish.) At eighteen I was working construction during summers. While going to dental school, I worked in the various Milwaukee breweries and drove cab on weekends. Still I had to borrow almost $4,000 from the physician dad of my best friend. Those are stories for another time.

One of the fondest memories of my trans-Atlantic crossings on the *S.S. St. Louis* was on the return trip to Antwerp, Belgium. Here is the amazing ending to this story sixty-one years later.

My wife and I were invited to Ottawa in October of 2000, for a gathering of *St. Louis* survivors, so that the members of this Pentecostal Christian group called "Watchmen for the Nations" could personally ask us survivors for forgiveness for the sins of their ancestors for not allowing Canada to offer a safe haven to these nine hundred Jewish refugees. Upon our arrival, we were whisked through customs, my wife was given a bouquet of white roses, and we were chauffeured to the Marriot Hotel's revolving dining room. An informal dinner was on the agenda so we could meet some of the attending Watchmen members, who had come from all over Canada as well as from the rest of the world. Introductions were made all around, and when it was our turn and I mentioned that I was one of the invited survivors, they were beside themselves that they had the honor to be sitting with a *St. Louis* survivor. The other couples at our table made me promise to tell my story, and during dessert I did. Whenever I speak of my Shoah experience, I always include this story:

I found myself a playmate on the ship, and during our return voyage to Europe this young friend and I were playing a game of hide-and-seek as seven-year-old lads often did. We found the canvas cover of a lifeboat loose, so we pulled it back and crawled underneath to do some exploring, not realizing the time. When the passengers sat down for dinner, we were discovered missing. The worst was feared, and a search for us began immediately. An observant crew member saw that the lifeboat cover was ajar, looked inside, and found us. If I remember right, neither of us could sit down for dinner after our parents finished paddling us.

For years I have wondered whatever happened to this playmate? Where did he end up? Did he survive or was he murdered? He was not in the group that went to Holland, because I never saw him in the camp we were in. So, for sixty years he has been on my mind. Whatever happened to him? I could not begin to find out since I didn't even remember his name. Mother said to forget him; he's probably been killed.

On the second day in Ottawa, we were all signed up for a city tour. The first stop was to see the Houses of Parliament. In the center of the complex of three buildings was what they called their "peace fountain," with a flame of freedom in the center. This memorial was surrounded by a seat wall about twenty inches tall. Our hosts wanted the group, both survivors and spouses, to stand near the flame for pictures. Then they wanted a picture of just the survivors. So, my wife stepped down, and in so doing she bumped into another lady and excused herself. The two of them started a conversation and she asked my wife if her husband, meaning me, was a survivor of the ship. She was told yes. Then the woman proceeded to tell my wife that one of the reasons her husband decided to attend this meeting was to see if he could find the little boy he got into so much trouble with when they played in one of the lifeboats sixty-one years ago. I overheard that conversation, turned around and yelled, "That was me!!" You could have knocked me over with a feather, because my knees just turned to butter. It was like finding a long lost soul mate. After that, the four of us became inseparable.

My playmate on the *St. Louis'* return trip to Europe was a young boy a year older by the name of Klaus Blatteis. I didn't remember his name until I found him again at our reunion in Ottawa. By that time he had become an American citizen and changed his name to Clark Blatteis. He and his family were among the group of 224 that were selected to go to France. When the Germans invaded France, they fled to the southern part of the country, which was controlled by the Vichy government. Once the U.S. entered the war after Pearl Harbor, the Germans occupied all of France, and they fled across the Pyrenees Mountains to Spain, made their way south to Gibalter, and eventually crossed over into Morocco. They spent the war years in Casablanca. After the war, they emigrated to the U.S. Clark got a Ph.D. in physiology, teaches at the University of Tennessee Medical School in Memphis, and that's where they live now.

Following are some of the questions students have asked Dr. Jacobson. They show surprisingly mature sensitivity and understanding of the implications of his Shoah experience.

Did the Holocaust seriously weaken your religious faith? At first it did, and that is because my religious feelings reflected that of my parents. My mother was raised in an Orthodox household and so was my biological father, Erwin Cohen. After our arrival in this country, and upon hearing of the murder of her parents by the Nazis, my mother lost some of her faith and didn't want to have much to do with traditional Judaism. She would not attend a service in an Orthodox synagogue. She would go with my brother and his family to their Reform temple until she died at ninety-two. She did insist that when I was thirteen, I would be a *Bar-mitzvah*. I think that was done in memory of her parents. Basically, I was raised as a Reform Jew. It was not until I had a near-death experience (I was hit in the head with an airplane propeller), that I made a pact with G_d, that if he let me live, I would become a better Jew. My faith was restored, but Mother's was definitely diminished.

Since the Holocaust, have you ever been mistreated for being a Jew? Yes and no. While going to grade school, I must have been nine or ten years old, the neighbor boy from across the street and I had a fight on the way home from school. I don't remember what the fight was about. I do remember us rolling around on the ground, and he purposely smashed my sunglasses with the heel of his shoe. Then I really got mad and beat the H out of him. When I finally let him up off the ground, he called me a "Damn Nazi." You would think he would have called me a dirty Jew or a Kike, but certainly not a Nazi from whom we had fled.

Are there any sights, sounds, smells, etc. that trigger your Holocaust memories?

Smells—yes. I love the smell of a banana, and every time I peel one I think about the time we brought back those sacks of green bananas while interned in Holland.

Sights—yes. Whenever I watch a movie and suddenly I see pictures of concentration camps being liberated or jack-booted Nazis marching, I get very upset, to the point of having trouble sleeping. I try to avoid movies such as *"Schindler's List."* However, I couldn't avoid that one because my wife and some friends wanted to see it. I got very upset watching it and had to walk out into the lobby. Sounds—oh yes! If I hear the whistle of an old steam engine in the movies or in the Colorado mountains where they run them for tourists, I immediately associate a steam engine with the one that was taking my grandparents to a concentration camp in 1943. Only they never got there. On the way, the train stopped and all were herded out to relieve themselves, only to run into a hail of machine gun bullets. A sixty-five-year-old couple who never harmed anyone, only that they were Jewish.

As you look back on your life, please share a lesson life has taught you. A deep one, indeed. One lesson is that there is a G_d for those who want to believe. During my lifetime I have been spared from death many times, beginning with our escape from Nazi Germany and then again from Holland. We were some of the lucky ones. Remember that two-thirds of the *St. Louis* refugees that returned to the European Continent were again captured by the Nazis and killed. Since then, I have been spared death several more times. The last incident made me a born-again Jew. I was driving down the Interstate at 55/mph pulling a fifth-wheel trailer and passed out from loss of blood due to a ruptured small intestine. I flew off the road into a swamp—without a scratch.

Secondly, I have learned the hard way that HATE is a bad trait. I have had two divorces and am now happily married to my third wife. I believe both previous marriages went sour because, as I was told, I had this chip on my shoulder. I have trouble getting along with my fellow Jews. When I sit in a synagogue and see all these clean, well-dressed, ostentatious, pious Jews, I think to myself what were they and their parents doing from 1941-45 to help their fellow Jews who were being murdered by the Nazis. I'll tell you what—making money! Now they are living in luxurious houses, riding around in their expensive cars, and over six million of their blood brothers are dead. What really galls me is when I see a Mercedes Benz parked in a synagogue parking lot. I have tried to seek professional help, and I feel I'm getting better, but under the right circumstances, the hate seeps back in. I really wish I could lose it, and maybe in time I will. They say "time heals all wounds" but maybe sixty years is not enough time.

You might ask, "Why should he hate? He was one of the fortunate ones. Now he's a retired dentist and has a nice life. He was never in a concentration camp, starving, facing death and disease." I'll tell you why. I was lucky enough to have been born into a well-to-do family. My mother's dad owned a small department store and several farms. My dad was the buyer for the ladies ready-to-wear department in a large department store in Bamberg called Herman Tietz, now known as Herte. All this was taken away from me.

I was deprived of my childhood and my parents' love during my childhood years. My dad was doing hard labor in Dachau while my mother was trying to make all the arrangements to get us out of the country and him out of Dachau. Once out, he was never the same and died an early death at the age of fifty from his Dachau incarceration.

When we got to this country I was set back a year because I couldn't speak any English. My parents both worked like heck to make ends meet. No one had time to spend with us kids. Had Hitler and the Nazis never existed, I would have had the finest education and possibly gone into business with my grandfather in his store, or maybe become a dentist over there. But we'll never know. You could say that all this adversity made me a better person; I doubt it. It was not by choice but rather a matter of necessity.

One thing I have learned from going to some of these *St. Louis* conferences and reunions like in Ottawa, Ft. Lauderdale, and the most recent in Hamburg, Germany, and Israel, is that by learning to forgive, the hate starts to dissolve, if one wants it to. It also makes it easier once you learn that you can forgive, but that doesn't mean you have to forget. The Ottawa gathering taught me that you can't blame the children for the sins of their fathers any more than you can blame this third generation of Germans for what their grandparents did seventy years ago to mine. But, it took me a long time to learn that. So, my message to students I speak to is "Don't hate, because you are only hurting yourselves." That is the big lesson life has taught me—the hard way!

I always finish my lectures by playing "You've Got to be Carefully Taught" from the musical *South Pacific*. It is OK to listen to the words of this song, but then forget them and remember the lyrics to a better song.

"You've Gott'a Accent-u-ate the Positive and Eliminate the Negative"

The Historical Holocaust Significance of the *St. Louis* Voyage

Ten days after arriving in Havana and sailing up and down the southeastern U.S. coast, entry had been denied to the *St. Louis* refugees by the United States, Canada, Mexico, and finally Cuba. Then Hitler ordered the Hamburg Amerika Line to tell Captain Schroeder to bring the *St. Louis* home, and they did under the pretext that they had to prepare it for the upcoming cruise season. Once the ship was on its way back to Germany, Joseph Goebbels announced to the world, "We *(Germany)* admit to the world we don't want the Jews. We are willing to let them go and even made one of our finest ships available for them. But the Western Democracies don't want them either; only they won't admit it. They are nothing but a bunch of Hypocrites." Then he sits down with the rest of his Nazi henchmen at one of their meetings, and announces: "Gentlemen, if the rest of the world doesn't care about these 900 Jews on the *St. Louis*, do you think they will care what we do with the rest of Europe's Jews?"

This gave the Nazis the Green Light for the Final Solution.

Unfortunately, the St. Louis episode is not well-known by Americans. It is a shameful chapter in our history. Many thanks to Dr. Jacobson for sharing his memories and his very personal thoughts about this issue, how it affected him, and how strongly he still feels about it. He is a popular and sought-after speaker at Holocaust Awareness events.

**The borrowed wedding dress made for a more attractive and
romantic wedding party than the required military uniform.**

Skip Johnson

"At five o'clock on the morning of June 6ᵗʰ, the camp was awakened by deafening rumbling that shook the ground."

Sadie "Skip" Johnson was a nurse in the U.S. Army. Yes, the requirements for inclusion in this collection of WWII first-person narratives specified being a civilian at the time of the experience. Technically Skip doesn't qualify, but readers will be glad her story is included for reasons that will become clear as it unfolds. And after all, she was a noncombatant while in the military.

Skip and I were hiking and quilting buddies in Fort Collins for several years before I learned she is Jewish. (At ninety-one, she still does both.) That revelation came only in the course of these interviews. Nor did I know the story recounted here, which reinforces my contention that we often are ignorant about details in the lives of our friends and even relatives, things we would like to know about them. For example, Skip's mother was Austrian-born and came to America at seventeen as an indentured servant. Skip's father was born in Poland, left home at thirteen—not uncommon in families who had too many mouths to feed—and worked his way across Europe until at eighteen he could get passage to the U.S. He worked in the dry-cleaning business in New York City and later farmed. The farm was lost during the Great Depression and the family was forced to move back to the city in order to find employment.

What I did know about Skip Johnson had long ago earned my admiration and that of her legion of friends. To name a few additional assets: her wit and ready smile, eyes that are stuck on "twinkle," a back straight as a board from years of dance training, and get this, post-menopausal ladies—she can still wear her shirts tucked in.

In discussing her wartime experiences of more than sixty years ago, Skip reminisces with enthusiasm, clarity, and modesty.

I'm proud of my service and glad I served, but not impressed by it.

That's Skip.

It is not surprising that Skip chose nursing as her career; she was introduced early to the workings of health care operations.

When I was six, I experienced severe swelling in the glands of my neck—"bull neck" they called it. My mother wouldn't accept that I was ill and sought no treatment. At age eight I was diagnosed with tuberculosis and confined to a sanitarium until I was twelve years old. My illness was attributed to drinking contaminated milk from the family's own herd of dairy cows. Milk consumed by the family was not pasteurized. We lived on a farm near Albany, New York, because my dad didn't want to raise his family in the city. The sanitarium was about ten miles from Albany.

Skip's life-threatening condition and long confinement were naturally stressful to her mother, who would weep and become depressed when she visited her young daughter. The danger of other family members becoming ill was also a continuing concern. Skip showed remarkable maturity for her age when she adopted a posture of cheerfulness during her mother's visits, in order to mollify her mother's behavior and make their time together more agreeable. Skip was able to control her own emotions to avoid crying—a strategy she maintains to this day.

She received her nursing training in Brooklyn. After initial assignment to the delivery room of the obstetrics ward at the same hospital where she trained, Skip wanted to see what was going on in current TB treatment. She subsequently went to work in a newly-opened sanitarium in Queens.

After the bombing of Pearl Harbor and America's entry into the conflict, Skip realized she could assist in the war effort, and should.

I was twenty-five years old, unmarried, and had no responsibilities at home. Serving would advance my education and experience. I thought of it as good experience, with nary a thought of its dangers or the possibility of not returning home safely after the war. I volunteered immediately for overseas duty, then told my parents of my decision.

Although Skip was the youngest of her siblings, she was the first to go, in July of 1942. In fact, medical careers ran in the family. Her two brothers—David, a urologist, and Abraham, an internist—also served in the Army. Sister Nettie entered the military as a nurse, but sister Gertrude, also a nurse, had a child and remained at home.

Fort Monmouth, New Jersey, was the first step toward Skip's journey overseas. The nurses there were not informed where their next assignment would take

Assignment in Iceland. The same quonset-type structures served as barracks and hospital—bleak surroundings during any season.

them, but they were given a clue when they were issued cold weather gear. In August, Skip and a few other nurses were shipped out on a British ship, H.M.S. Ormandy, enroute to Iceland. The media of the time did not reveal to the public much about this isolated station, and it remains a less-discussed wartime site. But for Skip and her colleagues, the trip across the north Atlantic put them into a dangerous combat zone and exposed them for the first time to the realities of war. German submarines were active in the area, targeting supply ships to Europe, and were particularly devastating to oil tankers. On several occasions, the Ormandy engaged in evasive tactics to vary their course in order to avoid torpedoes. As a result, the trip from Boston to Iceland took eleven days.

Skip's contingent was assigned for the next fifteen months to the 327th Station Hospital near Reykjavik, a post hospital that served 1200 soldiers and medical personnel.

The area was protected by American troops guarding the airport and bases for U.S. fighter squadrons. Germans had initially occupied the territory in order to control the airport, which they used as a refueling station. Before the Americans chased out the Germans, swastikas hung in local windows, and Hitler's speeches were broadcast on the radio. German reconnaissance planes were not uncommon, but bombers that invaded the air space were not successful in targeting the airport nearby. Nevertheless, we girls were instructed when hanging our laundry outside to cover white undergarments with army khaki as camouflage to avoid attracting attention from the air. Another minor challenge the nurses faced was getting our patients to bed down during summer months of long daylight.

The next transfer, which brings us to the meat of Skip's story, was to Blockley, a small town near Cheltenham, in Gloucestershire in southcentral England. The hospital was an American-run facility for American personnel in the area. The campus consisted of a cluster of huts erected on the grounds of a large estate owned by Winston Churchill's nephew. England's historic country mansions were often turned over to the war effort for rehabilitation facilities and/or hospitals.

At Blockley the property included a private mansion and outbuildings some distance down the road and away from the hospital. Military personnel were instructed to stay away from the private part of the estate; nevertheless, at night hospital personnel would occasionally sneak a dip in the family's swimming pool.

Nurses were billeted in huts, six or seven nurses to a hut. Six other huts were designated for male personnel, and there was also an officers' club and mess hall. The hospital functioned as an Army camp, maintained by 200 enlisted personnel, fifty officers, and fifty nurses. My future husband, First Lieutenant Don Johnson from

Columbus, Nebraska, was Detachment Commander in charge of enlisted personnel. Non-medical personnel were assigned to detail in maintenance, food service, equipment management, and supply. The camp and hospital were well-equipped.

The hospital came into existence eight months before D-Day, and not one of us suspected it was intended to receive combat casualties from France. In the interim, local American service personnel were treated there. The hospital operated at full capacity at that time.

There were several airbases in the area around Cheltenham. This part of south-central England seems a bit far from the coast to be the staging area for the Normandy invasion, but apparently there wasn't room available farther to the south. Also, security was an issue, reflecting the need to avoid German reconnaissance picking up on the volume of preparation traffic and activity.

Nevertheless, off-duty time was sometimes spent on excursions to London, where Skip and her friends could find themselves caught in sporadic bombing raids.

On June 5th, the day before D-Day, orders came to evacuate the hospital and get supplies and facilities in order. Patients able to make the trip back to the States were sent home. A handful who were too ill or had had recent surgery were retained.

At five o'clock on the morning of June 6th, the camp was awakened by deafening rumbling that shook the ground. Words can't describe the noise. Nurses hurried outside in their nightwear, to see squadrons of bombers pulling gliders. At this point, there still was no suspicion that the invasion of Europe had begun. No one was allowed to discuss such a security-sensitive subject, and anyone's speculations had been kept private for the preceding months. However, as the skies remained filled for several hours, it became apparent this was the BIG ONE.

Skip remembers being more baffled than frightened, then fascinated by the scale of what they were witnessing.

Our life at the hospital was rather secluded, and we weren't aware of the amount of military installations in the area capable of carrying out an operation of such magnitude and significance. The gliders and bombers went over so low, spectators on the ground could see the faces of those on board, and troops waved as they went by.

Nearing their destination in France, a horrible and tragic ending awaited many of those young soldiers.

Some of those gliders went in too low, detached too early, unloading their cargo prematurely and dropping the troops into the Channel, too distant from the beach.

Hundreds, maybe thousands were drowned.

Soon trainloads of German prisoners were arriving at the Blockley hospital. They were generally older men and young boys; some in critical condition, some ambulatory. Casualties of other nationalities were included; they had been detained by the Germans to work in forced labor camps in Normandy. These noncombatants were in poor health; they had been physically mistreated and poorly fed. They likely arrived fear-filled from the ordeal that brought them to Blockley, relief over being liberated, yet apprehensive about their future.

Triage was complicated by the language problem. "Triage" is a term applied to the immediate survey of a critical situation. In a hospital setting it involves preliminary examination to determine whose needs are most urgent in order to prioritize care. Fortunately I knew some German from my Austrian-born mother. An American Jewish doctor and I were the only German-speaking personnel on the premises. Later, military interpreters who spoke several languages were assigned to interrogate the patients.

As Skip was already an experienced surgical nurse, she was assigned to the surgery and anesthesia units. I immediately reacted to the irony of these two American, Jewish professionals assigned to perform lifesaving procedures on the Nazi enemy— more enemy than to their non-Jewish colleagues. Sixty-four years later at this time of writing, perspectives are obviously and thankfully changed, and a non-animus response seems natural. But at the time, it would take a mature and enlightened individual to be able to proceed without hesitation according to their Hippocratic oath, an oath taken at a time when no one would anticipate being placed into such a situation.

At the same time, it was during this emergency that Skip heard a particularly offensive remark, not directed at her personally nor by a colleague in the hospital, but inappropriate and hurtful nevertheless. "We wouldn't be in this mess if it weren't for the Goddam Jews." Skip was also offended by the segregation of African-Americans in the military, which gave open sanction to yet another kind of bigotry.

Skip responded predictably to my observation of the irony of the situation.

The human beings before us were viewed by all medical personnel as patients, not enemies. It did not occur to us to treat them any differently from anyone else who needed our healing and caring skills. Really, the commitment and dedication of my outfit to their work was inspiring to us all. We took care of them the best we could. Politics had nothing to do with what we were doing at that moment. For the most part, both German and Italian prisoners were glad to be taken care of so well, and they treated the staff with respect.

On other the hand, some prisoners had the reverse mentality. One sixteen-year-old German had been machine-gunned diagonally across his torso. As critical as his condition was, he was scared to death of his situation there in an American, enemy hospital.

One cannot avoid wondering about the fate of that young man as well as his comrades, returning to occupied Germany after the war, their lives saved by the very people they had been taught to hate and fear most. Despite that, a few prisoners committed suicide while in the hospital.

We suspected that at least two soldiers were killed by others in their squadron to prevent them from talking to U.S. military intelligence who came to interrogate the prisoners. Staff found one soldier hanging in a bathroom, and it never was established if it was suicide or murder. Two Germans (*who must have been in pretty good condition*) escaped to the nearby airstrip, stole an American plane and took off, presumably over the Channel. They were brought down without incident by U.S. planes.

Military wounds are obviously different from civilian wounds. For example, drive-by shootings result in one or a few wounds in the upper body. Machine gun damage, on the other hand, can traumatize a large area, riddling the target. Inner city violence often involves knifings. Swords have disappeared, fortunately, but they have been replaced by more devastating weapons like bombs, grenades, and shrapnel, which inflict damage indiscriminately, sometimes resulting in loss of limbs. One patient's injuries in the back and one leg resulted in paralysis. He suffered terribly from bed sores, and I literally washed the bones of his lower spine.

For the following ten days and nights, emergency care was addressed 24-7, with staff getting very little rest. We worked for six hours, then took a break for a snack, and were supposed to nap for an hour. Despite the constant stress and fatigue, nurses rarely took their full allotted break time, rushing back to the wards and ER. None of them broke under those stressful conditions.*

After those first hectic days of D-Day, order returned to the hospital. Ambulatory patients helped take care of their own buddies. Despite the non-threatening, almost cordial environment in the wards, at night when nurses were at the unit office charting and doing clerical work, an un-armed, uniformed ward boy stood guard at the

A young Jewish physician from my home town was assigned similar stressful duty in the South Pacific. He suffered a heart attack and died at age thirty-five.

door. Like medical personnel, ward boys were considered noncombatants and not allowed to carry arms on duty. An aggressive prisoner could disarm one and create some real trouble. Some German patients remained apprehensive about their situation as POWs and couldn't be completely trusted. SS prisoners arrived with an 'SS' tattooed on their inner upper arm, and you can believe they were attentively monitored.

Female nurses, called "schwester" (or "sister" in English), were included in some POW groups. They weren't injured, just captured, and occasionally we were confronted by one that was pregnant. They often had items in their possession to do needlework and knitting, an otherwise productive and therapeutic activity. But we had to confiscate their scissors, crochet hooks, knitting needles, etc.—anything that could be used as a weapon against our personnel. That really upset them. Don was in charge and he hated to do it, but it was a prudent policy.

Blockley was maintained as a combat hospital for eight more months, at which time the premises were converted to a POW camp. Concertina barbed wire was added as well as watch towers. A cadre of medical personnel was left to take care of most of their medical needs. They were supplemented by interned German doctors and medics, but our staff had to first show the Germans how to run the hospital.

In November of 1944, Skip and her unit shipped to France. By this time she and Don were engaged, but he was transferred to another unit. Arriving at LeHavre, Skip described the landscape that greeted them as

. . . nothing but rubble and destruction as far as you could see. The group was first deployed to Neufchatel in northeast France. It was not a hospital; it was a staging area. A pool of nurses was stationed there temporarily as a source of supply for other hospitals. The nurses quarters there consisted of a large old barn heated by potbellied stoves. We weren't accustomed to luxury, but it took some getting used to bathing in cold water. And have you ever taken a sponge bath out of a helmet?!

The time spent at Neufchatel was generally not as crisis-filled or hectic as the situation at Blockley. When things weren't too busy we marched, hiked, and did group physical activities to stay in shape. We sometimes had leisure time that we could visit nearby towns. There were occasional air raids, and at one point during that winter of 1944 when the U.S. received so many setbacks, I felt I might not return home. I even wrote to my mother and told her to get rid of my clothes and other possessions because I had no further need for them. I made up excuses about gaining weight and changing fashions, but I had it in my mind that I wouldn't return to the U.S. alive.

At this point, Skip had a memorable meeting with her brother David. They hadn't seen each other in four years. Although he was stationed in England while she was at Blockley, an attempt to get together there didn't work out. He called her one day to say he would come over to see her the next day. Skip knew her unit was on "red alert," meaning they were due to be shipped out at any time to an unknown destination. Because of security, she was unable to disclose this to him—that she might not be there when he came to see her. Anticipating that possibility, she did tell David that when he came, he should first contact a particular officer who would be able to advise David of her redeployment. During the night, Skip's unit was shipped out.

Eventually, when David was stationed near Neufchatel at one of the camps named after cigarettes (like "Camel," "Lucky Strike," "Chesterfield," etc.), he surprised her by showing up. She was excused from duty so they could spend a leisurely day together by the river, reminiscing over a bottle and a loaf of bread.

We still talk about that day as being very special and how much it meant to both of us to be together at that time at that place.

Don and David also had a chance meeting while both were in the Neufchatel area. Don approached David, who was working with a patient in a field hospital. David looked up and said, "What can I do for you, soldier?" Without an introduction, Don stuck out his hand and responded, "I'm going to be your brother-in-law."

Considering the possible world-wide deployments all three could have been assigned, these connections were truly serendipitous.

Skip was reassigned a couple more times within France, including a much-appreciated stint near Paris. On the continent, American GIs were their patients. As the war drew to a close and Americans took over more and more of German-occupied territory, German-operated hospitals revealed some sad conditions.

Supplies were depleted, dressings not changed, and crepe paper, not fabric, was used for bandages. The insect infestation was particularly bothersome as well as unhygienic.

In August of 1945, Skip and Don were married at the camp at Etampes, with hospital and military personnel serving as attendants and well-wishers. The camp commander, through a required application to General Eisenhower's headquarters, had to give Skip permission to be married in a traditional white wedding dress instead of her military uniform. This was no small matter. Weddings had been prohibited during the war, but even in August, after the war had ended, red tape intervened. The wedding gown itself was borrowed, arranged by a French civilian *employee at the hospital.*

Subsequently Skip was sent back to the States, honorably discharged in October, 1946, and pregnant. Her term of duty had ended over a year earlier, but anticipating Don's reassignment to the invasion of Japan, she volunteered again, opting to spend their last months together in France. A few months later, she returned home to Albany, and Don to his home in Nebraska.

The GI Bill took Don and Skip to the University of Wyoming, where Don graduated with a degree in botany. He subsequently worked for the U.S. Department of Agriculture as a soil conservationist in Gillette, Sheridan, and Wheatland, Wyoming. Skip also attended the University on the GI Bill as a pre-med student. But when the babies came along, she became a stay-at-home mom. The family grew to two children, four grandchildren, and three great-grands. Don passed away in 2005 at age eighty-five.

**Skip—a role
model for all ages**

Ursula's sister Irmgard, age five and Ursula age eight

Ursula Stack

"On this last meeting, he explained he was a hunted man because of his political affiliations as a Nazi; then he disappeared and was never seen or heard from again."

———————————⬤———————————

Ursula's story presents distinctive insights to which we haven't previously been privileged—a description of growing up in wartime Berlin within a Nazi household, where fear of the government was not a concern like some other contributors have reported. However, being "connected" didn't spare the family from the ravages of bombing, food shortages, and the terror of Russian occupation of postwar Berlin.

When Hitler took over in 1933, Ursula's family enthusiastically embraced his message. He promised the German people bread and jobs. He responded positively to the despair Germany experienced as a result of the terms of the Treaty of Versailles which ended World War I. Most importantly, he gave back hope and assurance that things would get better, that Germany would be a great nation once again.

With such promises, it isn't surprising that Ursula's father became a Nazi, joined the S.A. (the dreaded Brown Shirts), and then a member of the Gestapo. Exactly what he did during the war years wasn't known to the family, although it is known that he spent time in Poland. He turned mean and rough, and when he became abusive toward Ursula's mother, they divorced.

I had a wonderful childhood, the oldest of six kids about two years apart. I was born in 1927, and we lived in Berlin. My dad was an electrician until he started off with Hitler. I remember when I was little, a few times they brought my dad home and he was unconscious. They were fighting the Communists out in the street, and he had gotten hurt.

We had one room that was always locked; it belonged to a friend of my father. There was a two-story-long flag with a swastika on it hanging from the window of that room. I remember from my mom talking about it, but I do remember myself holding

on to my mom's apron when the police came to the door to take down the flag. My mom told them, "Sorry, but I can't get in there; it is rented out, and they should take down the communist flag at the bar across the street if they want this flag down." The flag at our apartment stayed up. All this was before Hitler took control of the government.

My dad later became Gestapo (undercover state police.). He wore a Rohm dagger with his uniform. Rohm was a man who got shot. I remember

A tender photo of four-year-old Ursula with her beloved father Karl Wesner in better times

my dad taking me to work with him at his office across the Reichs Kanzlei from Hitler's house, up a beautiful stairway. Halfway up the stairs was a plaque; that was where Rohm was killed.

I was in the Jung Made or BNM (Bund Deutscher Madchen). It was for German girls, like the American Girl Scouts. There was a group from age seven to fourteen, then a senior group until age sixteen, then to a women's group. I stopped at fourteen, because after eight years of schooling you go to work. You learn a trade for three years or go to high school and university. In BDM we had lots of fun. Like here in the U.S. we respected the flag, and we were very proud of it. We had meetings about things that we were going to do, like service projects, learning handiwork, raising money, being courteous and helpful, and so forth.

We went to parades and took part in rallies. We went on streetcars (no autos), and we did lots of walking. And if any high officials came to Berlin, we went out and waited for hours to see them. The police always let us stand in front because we all looked so nice in our uniforms—dark blue wool skirts, white blouses, and a triangular, black scarf rolled up and held by a braided leather knot. We had gold-colored jackets like corduroy, very fitted, with little pockets to hold money. We had always to look neat. I remember seeing Churchill, Chamberlain, and Mussolini. Mussolini was supposed to come at two in the afternoon and didn't get in until midnight. It was raining cats and dogs, and we stood under the Brandenburg Gate to stay dry. How fanatic you get when you are young!

One time I was at a parade when Hitler's car came. Everyone was so excited and kept pushing. The police had a line holding hands to hold the people back, and they let me stand in front of them because of the crowd. And then the people started pushing, and the line broke, and I got pushed forward and fell in front of Hitler's car. They stopped, and the police picked me up. I wasn't hurt, but the funny thing is, I remembered it when I came to Colorado Springs. We went to the Old Town Museum, and here was one of Hitler's cars parked! It made me laugh. It was an older car; he had lots of them. Another time I presented a bouquet of flowers to the Fuhrer.

I also remember being at the opening for the 1936 Olympics in Berlin. We had to wear our jackets and sit in seats that were marked, so that when we were told to take off our jackets, it spelled out "*Gross Deutschland*" (which means Great Germany) on our white blouses.

In the summer we had trips to the country, taking about two hours to a farmhouse where the farmer would let us stay in the barn, and we would sleep on the hay, washing in the morning with cold water from the outside pump and cooking on a little oil stove. We carried a backpack just like the soldiers did, with a blanket rolled up around it. It was very heavy, so some of the bigger girls carried mine for me, and all I had to carry was my guitar. We would walk around in the woods, sing folk songs, and play the guitar.

In winter we were busy with building toys for needy children. With a jigsaw and blocks of wood and light weight wood, we would make trains, cars, dollhouses, building blocks. We painted and decorated the dollhouses. Every year for three months before Christmas, we did things like that.

During the war years I was working for a salon as a tailor's apprentice. We did just designer originals, but with so much bombing going on, we had to go into ready wear. There was a little basement built out into a bunker, so every night we had to carry all the finished clothes and all the material down into the basement. Every morning we had to carry it all upstairs again to work on it.

I was fourteen when I started to work. You are treated as an adult, and "you will act as an adult." So you grow up fast, but that's not so bad. No time for BDM anymore but still going to the theater and opera and movies. I was an autograph hunter, and some of our customers were movie star wives. My boss used to send me to deliver sometimes. She would say, "No, Ursula, no autographs." When I came back, she would stand there laughing and say, "OK, what did he write down for you?"

My boss was a very elegant lady; I looked up to her. She trained me a lot faster than some of the other apprentices; she had three of them. She taught me more than she had to. She made me learn some office work and paid me more money than the others. It wasn't much, but I tried to do my best.

We had duty twice a month to stay overnight. Each company needed one person each night in case of fire from bombing. We had cubicles in a downstairs room with a cot and blanket and pillow. I was on duty with a men's tailor and a furrier. Instead of sitting and playing cards, they went upstairs to work. I went along, so I also learned from them men's tailoring and to work with fur. I made myself a jacket out of scraps of white rabbit fur, all by hand.

On Saturday we did not work; we had trade school. They taught us all the little tricky things that they thought our bosses didn't have time to teach us. I also went for Red Cross nursing classes for four hours, four times a week from 6-10 P.M., and I barely made it back home before the sirens went off. After that training, during the last two years of the war I worked as a Red Cross nurse.

For entertainment we went to nightclubs to listen to music; there was no dancing allowed during the war, but we had a lot of parties with friends. Everybody's living space was cramped, including our house with six kids and an old lady living with us because we had to rent out one room. Too many people without a place to live. We had a curfew, so when we had parties, we had to stay over, sleep in the bath tub, on the floor, wherever you could find a place to lie down.

But we had a great time playing American music (and dancing privately). When we would go to the theater, we would often end up in a different shelter. Most theaters had big basement shelters for the crowds. Night clubbing you just went for the music and drinks. There was no age limit for drinking. They had beautiful bands but no dancing. We weren't allowed to dance because it was wartime; soldiers were fighting and dying, and such "gaiety" was inappropriate. We used to go to the balconies where they stored extra chairs and tables, and one person was a lookout for police coming and checking, and we would dance there.

We had good times until two years before the war was over, and things started to go bad. We grew up with clean streets and houses, and good food. Hitler was an admirer of Grecian things; he built buildings, beautiful great highways. He sponsored sporting events and built facilities for them, and he felt that everyone should be able to afford to go to the theater.

Jerry and Ursula, Mother and stepdad, with half sister Gigi

But he was also a stickler for a pure race; that's when the trouble started for the Jews. I remember my mom getting mad; she lost her lawyer, her doctor, and one of the store owners where she shopped. They were Jewish and were gone. I lost my best friend, Stephanie Hirsch. Her parents sent her to South America to family they had there. Before I knew it, her parents were gone too. After the war I went out to eat, and there was Mr. Hirsch! When I played with his daughter he was disabled, in a wheel chair. Now after the concentration camp he walked with a cane, but he lost his wife; she didn't make it.

But the war years were tough. Constant alert for bombing. While I was working learning a trade in tailoring I never knew if the next morning the street car would take me to work or if there was enough damage that I would have to walk for two hours to work. Food was rationed, but with a big family, we had plenty. We used to carry our holiday roast and all our butter down to the shelter with us. The last two years we had bombing at 10 A.M. and at 10 P.M. We were happy when the weather was bad; then the Americans couldn't fly. We never got undressed until after midnight because there was no time to get dressed when the sirens went off. So we went to sleep with our clothes on and suitcases packed. When the siren went off, everyone grabbed a suitcase and off we went to the shelter. The suitcases had our important papers and pictures in them. In the shelter you would sit and knit or read or visit with your neighbors, hoping and praying your home was still there. My mom used to say, "How can anyone make war with a country like America?" I remember my mom sitting like a mother hen with five kids in front of her, huddling over them when we heard the bombs fall.

They always told us that the one that hit, you won't hear. When you hear the sound of all the planes humming coming in for the bombing, it was awesome. Kids were tired in school because they didn't get enough sleep. I remember the one that hit shortly before the war was over. It must have been the last one to destroy anything because most of Berlin was already destroyed. Where I worked was gone, our school was hit, and we were stuck in the shelter. The doors would not open, and the lights were out. I checked that my mom and the kids were OK and went with a candle to some of the other rooms to see that everyone was all right.

The bombing continued for three years. We laughed at the English bombings; they were just phosphor fire bombs. They were very dangerous; you couldn't get them out with water, just with sand. But they were not as damaging as the other bombs. We always said that the Americans still let our house stay when everything around us was bombed out. The back of our apartment building was bombed out by German planes trying to get the Russians out.

When my brother was here visiting, he reminded me of some things, some of which if my mother had known, she wouldn't have let me do many things. My brother reminded me of the woman who slapped me and screamed at me "Sister, how can you be so calm?" (German Red Cross nurses were called "sister.") A lot came back to me when I saw the Oklahoma bombing. I broke out crying, remembering things like standing and waiting for men to dig to get people out of a bombed-out house. We could hear sounds, and when they got closer more debris would fall, and some we could never get to. Another time we got them out, and one girl was stuck under a beam with her arm, and we had to stop the guys from removing the beam because she was under it too long, and we needed a doctor to amputate her arm.

The job I got paid for as a Red Cross employee was on duty at a train station. No trains were going from that part of town except the one to Hitler's house outside of Berlin. I was never on duty when he left there, but Goebbels and Goering went a lot.

When trains came in, we had to go over to the train and check wounded soldiers: examine wounds, put on new bandages, take care of boils, or help get them off the train. I used to like to kick officers who were not injured off their seats to make a place for a wounded soldier. We were allowed to do that.

When I was on night duty, I would come home in the morning and lie down to sleep in my uniform. At 10:30 A.M. the sirens went off, and we went to the shelter. Sometimes I had to keep on working after the bombing if I was needed and just had enough time to get home to clean up and put on a clean uniform and go back to work.

Later I was transferred to be a nurse in an ambulance. There was a driver, an intern, and a nurse. The ambulances we had were like those you would see in a WWI movie—a big box on wheels. After the bombing we would go out, both sides of the streets on fire, dust and smoke everywhere, and sometimes just enough space for the ambulance to go through, both sides of the streets with big holes and the smell of gas. After a bombing, the Women's Association would come out and offer sandwiches and hot soup and drinks for the people who were bombed out. I remember one time I had four people with concussions in our shelter, and I was the only nurse. They were getting sick to their stomachs, and I was holding a bucket for them. One of the women came and asked if I wanted a sandwich. I had just come off night duty; I was so hungry I said "Yes." Our Field First came in and said, "WHAT ARE YOU DOING?" I had no other help and was so hungry—what are you to do?

A bombed-out church served as a hospital. When the Russian army entered Berlin in April of 1945, they were anxious to use the local medical personnel for their own purposes. I removed my Red Cross nurse's uniform to avoid being taken. When troops entered my apartment, I hid under a mattress. Other women were not so lucky. An elderly Red Cross nurse in the building was raped. Others were taken and never seen again.

My family had no relatives outside of Berlin where they could seek refuge during or after the war. As some neighbors in our building fled to the West, even to America, they gave the keys to their basement storage cubicles (which also served as bomb shelter) to other residents in case they didn't come back. The store of potatoes and coal they left behind were very welcome in those bleak postwar times.

After everything settled down, I went to the west side of Berlin (the American zone) to find a job working for a diplomat's family. I could no longer work as a tailor. Somehow I was allergic to the things they used in the material, and I kept breaking out in a rash. So, I became a maid. It was a great job; I learned a lot of American cooking, and they told me they would take me to the States. Mrs. Collins, my employer, had all her household goods shipped out of Berlin just one day before the airlift started, and everything closed up around Berlin. Then they got transferred to Russia, and there was NO NO NO way I was going to Russia. Not even with a diplomat's family. So I put in for a visa to go to the U.S. I could go as a tailor, or a nurse trainee, or maid, or cook.

The second American family I worked for in Berlin had fired their cook and asked me to cook until they hired a new one. They liked my cooking and hired a maid instead, so I stayed as a cook. There were many things I could do.

One thing was sure, in Berlin you didn't know when you woke up if the Russians had taken over again, so you lived it up as you could—dating a GI, going to the club, you had peanuts to eat, cigarettes to smoke, and a clean, good-looking American soldier. We used to be so strict, but with what happened with the Russians, my family—mother, sisters, and I—we had a guardian angel with us that nothing happened to us. But I thought that after being so good all those years with my real nice friends, maybe now a Russian would get me; I hated the idea. My mom said I was just waiting for the Americans to come.

The Russians came in April; I turned eighteen in May. The Americans stopped bombing when the Russians came in. The Americans were on the Elbe River waiting because the Russians were going into Berlin. In our apartment building we had red

Postwar Berliners looking at life-saving American Airlift planes

carpet going up the stairs and in the hallway. The Russians put their horses in there, in the hallway where you first came in on the red carpet, and that carpet went up the four-story building. They took mattresses out of apartments and put them down there and had horses on them.

Since my mother was divorced, we were alone, and that was our luck. My dad was a big shot, and they were looking for him. That is why I never looked for my dad. I was afraid that he would think someone was looking for him. I loved my dad; I was his favorite. The last time I saw him was after the Russians came in. He was standing downstairs, and my mother said, "Your father is down there; you better go see him." He always came by to see if we were OK after the bombings. On this last meeting, he explained that he was a hunted man because of his political affiliations as a Nazi (*and Gestapo*); then he disappeared and was never seen or heard from again.

I met my husband Jerry in a funny way. He came to the house with some friends. I was sick, and a girlfriend of mine and her boyfriend came to see how I was doing. I was really sick; I had brain fever. After all those things going on during the war, finally I folded up. I had a high fever and was in and out of consciousness. Jerry came along with them, and I didn't even know they were there. They told me he wouldn't date anyone; they couldn't get him a date for anything. Then one day the doorbell rang, and my landlady came and said that there was a GI who said he wanted to see how I was doing; he knew I was so sick. I thought it was such a nice thing that a stranger would come to see how I was doing. I was getting better. Then he came on Saturday and asked if he could come by the next weekend. I said OK, and he came by on Wednesday, Saturday, and Sunday.

We weren't allowed to get married until about ten months before we went to the States. The military wouldn't allow it. The reason for the wait was to keep too many GIs from marrying German girls. The Army figured if they were made to wait long enough, they would get discouraged and not get married. From 1945-1948 it was that way. They would ship the bride back to the States and the guy to Korea. We met in 1948 and didn't get married by the church until 1954. Our daughter, born in 1949, was four years old by that time! We actually got married three times: first by a German lawyer, then by the German Civil Court, then by the Catholic Church in Berlin in 1954.

When my daughter was born in 1949, it was airlift time. I nursed her, but my sister in East Berlin lost two babies because there was no milk and her babies died. Jerry could not get food for us either. Once in a while he smuggled oranges or apples out, but their uniforms were so tight they couldn't carry anything out in their pockets. There wasn't much food at the PX, where military families shopped. I had only six diapers, so I was constantly washing, rinsing, boiling, and drying diapers. It was impossible to get blankets and clothes. Jerry waited for months for clothes for the baby to come in. When the airlift finally lifted and they got things in, he bought everything they had.

We were rationed one loaf of bread a week, vegetables were dehydrated, and Canadian flour that was great to make hot cereal, with milk powder. It is amazing what a human being can live on. The airlift was a wonderful thing; it brought in food and coal. In the East sector, my mom and the kids didn't have much.

After my daughter was born, we rented a room from a lady who had a big yard full of vegetables and fruit, and we had all we could eat.

My family loved Jerry. He loved kids, and the kids all came to him. His family was all right with him bringing me home. His mom said, "He loves her and he's happy; she must be all right." German families were generally glad the GIs were there for their daughters instead of the Russians. But they knew you would leave Germany.

We had four months to get ready to get married. Jerry was supposed to leave in January, and the paperwork takes a long time. There were seven of us girls getting married, and we all ended up in Fort Carson, Colorado, at the same time. I didn't have to wait long for my papers because they got clearance from the investigation when I worked for the diplomat's family. I also found out that I had a visa waiting that I would no longer need.

After our wedding they kept Jerry in Germany, saying he was sick and all kinds of excuses so the three of us could travel to the States together. He was supposed to leave in January, but we didn't leave until March. It was quite a trip on that ship. It was nothing like a cruise ship! When we got to the U.S. I was so disappointed not to see the Statue of Liberty. We checked in after we got off the ship, and we left in buses to the train station. As we crossed one of the bridges, I screamed "There She is!" Everyone was so tired, and they all fell to sleep on the bus. My screaming woke them up, but they missed it. But I saw my Lady Liberty, and I was happy. My husband told me he had crossed three different times and had never seen her.

When we got to St. Louis, Jerry's family was so great. They lived in an apartment over a tavern that his dad used to own, and they had a party for me with German music. His dad was dead, but his mom and sisters and family still lived there.

By May we were in Colorado Springs and no apartment to rent. It was hard, but after a few weeks we rented a little cottage and have been Coloradoans since.

My mother told me that when I was four years old, I said to my father, "When I grow up, I'm going to be a secretary." To me a secretary meant making a lot of money, and I'd buy a car and drive to America. Now, where in the world did I get that idea, to go to America? My father said to me the last time when he came to see me, "Don't stay here; go to America. Get out of here." He is the one who put that idea of America into me from little on. Where did he know it from? I never got to find out.

I love the States. Everyone has been so nice to me, Jerry's family and friends, then my landlady in Colorado Springs. I made my citizenship in March, 1956, and for me this is home.

I wish I had pictures of things. I have them with me in my head, but at the time I was growing up, there wasn't much picture-taking, and the ones I did have were with my autographs in a suitcase. The Russians took the suitcase. I would give anything if I could look at them now. The younger generation doesn't want to keep anything, but when you get older, you want to look at all those great memories, and you wish you had them.

Eric

Eric Brettschneider

"Ulli has on lady shoes! Ulli has on lady shoes!"

———————————●———————————

A Child's Remembrance of a Grown-up War
For Eric Brettschneider by Margaret Brettschneider

An excerpt from Eric's story as told by MJ Brett from interviews that lead to her book, <u>Mutti's War</u>.

After reading the very gripping <u>Mutti's War</u>, I was astonished to learn that the author, Margaret Brettschneider, is a resident of Colorado Springs, Mutti's daughter-in-law, and married to one of the young sons in the narrative. She also lives in my old CS neighborhood. Margaret has interviewed her husband Eric (Ulrich) and effectively recounted his experiences in war-torn Germany—a very unusual perspective, from a child growing up in an environment that initially honored Adolf Hitler.

❚ ❚ ❚

War came to Konigsberg, East Prussia, in 1938, when I was only a boy of four, so I didn't understand much about it. The war was only a topic of grown-up conversation, but nothing war-like seemed to be happening. I later realized it was happening someplace else. Konigsberg was way out on the east side of the Baltic, next to Russia and Lithuania, and it was isolated from the rest of Germany by the Danzig Corridor of Poland, given to the Poles after World War I. With a war going on, it became even more isolated, so that most goods came in by ship.

Except for my Vati being drafted into reserve military training, nothing changed for a while. When Vati came home from reserves, Mutti was all happy and would fix his favorite dishes, which were also my own, like Klopse, a sort of meat ball, and Rouladen, which is meat rolled up around pickles. My younger brother Juergan and I would sing songs for him. and he would bounce us on his knee singing "Hoppe,

Opa and Oma

Hoope Reiter."

    What I remember from that time was that life was full of excitement. There were parades and flags, bomb shelters and bunkers being built, and new airplanes flying overhead. I was most preoccupied with bunkers, and they later became quite important in our lives, but in 1938, we knew nothing of that. There was a great day when we went to Oma and Opa's (*Grandma and Grandpa*) apartment because there was to be a parade and the Fuhrer would be in it. I was excited because all my little friends were. I knew that their parents called Hitler a great man, so I believed it was so. Mutti didn't seem as impressed as the rest of the family, but it was a little child's paradise. Who doesn't love a parade? So, we all stood on the balcony and watched as people with huge red flags and torches went by for hours, and thousands of brown-shirted men walked all in unison with high kicks my two-year old brother and I tried to imitate with little success. About all we managed with our exertions was to accidentally kick over Oma's favorite vase, so we had to go to bed with no dinner and even worse, no further chance to practice.

    I remember that my Opa had little red and white flags with what he called the "swastika" in the middle in black. Whenever I tried to copy the swastika on a piece of scrap paper, Opa would scold me for getting it backwards. I tried to wave my flag faster when the Fuhrer rode by, standing up in his long auto. Little else about that day impressed my young mind, except that my Oma made a strange statement and Opa agreed wildly and kissed her, which I had never seen him do before. She said something about how the Fuhrer was so handsome that he *must* be a great leader. My Opa and Vati both grinned, while my Mutti left the room angrily. It was only later in life that I realized the repressed role of women in those years. They listened only to their husband and voted as their husband said. So Opa was pleased because "handsome" was good enough. He apparently didn't think she needed to know more than that to ensure her loyalty to the Nazi cause.

A year later, when it was time for me to go to my first day of school, my Mutti put my pack on my back along with the customary *Zuckertute* or cone of treats. I was so proud to go. But when we reached the classroom, the teacher looked sternly at my face and said to Mutti, "He doesn't look Aryan enough," and I could feel my Mutti bristle with anger. "We've all been born and raised in Konigsberg," she said, and she marched me right back home. We waited another year to try again. It was only years later that I found out Hitler replaced all the teachers and professors in our town with Nazi Party members. In our family, all the men have a slightly eastern look in the eyes, a bit almond-shaped. There was a family joke that there must have been a Ghengis Kahn in the woodpile somewhere centuries ago, but I had inherited my father's eyes. This episode is memorable only in the fact that I became a bit shy about going back to school. I hadn't thought of myself as "different" in any way, and that teacher taught me the lesson that it wasn't a good thing to be different during that time.

A couple of years after that, I was old enough to notice that people didn't talk much any more at the *Metskerei* (butcher shop) or the *Bakerei*. These places used to be filled with constant chatter. But now, the pleasant hum of mothers talking to their neighbors while holding the hands of their children and juggling their daily rations of food petered out. It was now just greetings or nods, with a perfunctory "*Heil Hitler*" when we left the shops. "*Heil Hitler*" had taken the place of "*Gruss Gott*" as a greeting in the South and "*Guten Tag*" in the North.

At school we had to practice giving a hearty, loud "*Heil Hitler!*" and little boys do well with shouting, but it puzzled me that my Mutti's was barely audible. It's funny what a child might remember, but I became aware that people seemed frightened of each other, and no one complained about politics or economics, or anything at all. I thought it strange that conversation could change so suddenly. But when I asked, it was explained that the Fuhrer didn't want anyone to complain. He wanted everyone to be happy.

By 1940, when I was six, there were angry scenes in the streets. Black *Politzei* wagons took people away, and their apartments were empty until new people came

Eric "Ulli"

to move in. When I asked about it, my Mutti put her finger to her lips to shush my loud voice and whispered, "I don't understand either, but Vati said many people are needed to work in industries in Poland and Czechoslovakia, so I think they're taking the workers whether they want to go work for the Reich or not. It's dreadful, but you mustn't talk about it or they might take us too. Of course, my next questions were "Why?" and "Why didn't they fight the men who were pushing them into the trucks?" And my Mutti said, "I think I would, but you can see in their faces that they're too frightened."

"Why don't they take only the men workers, then?" I asked. "Why are they taking that little girl?" She was about my age, and I waved at her as a man put her up in the back of a truck. She was crying and she didn't wave back.

Mutti turned me away, grabbed my hand, and took me home. She was silent; I saw her lips pursed like when she was mad, but tears were running out of her eyes the whole way home. Mutti didn't have to tell me after that day to keep my mouth shut and not ask so many questions. I had nightmares for weeks of someone coming and taking my family away, putting us into the back of a black van, all to the horrible "nee-ner, nee-ner" sound of the siren. I wanted to ask my Vati so many things, but he was called up to go to the Army full time in the East. He was gone most all the time after that, and I know my Mutti was very lonely. I could hear her crying at night in the next bedroom when I was supposed to be asleep.

But there were happy times, too. When Vati came home on leave, he brought presents from all the places the German Army had conquered. He brought us fur boots from Russia, and some beautiful big green medals on a ribbon that went around the neck, with shiny stones and pearls. Juergan and I played with them. Vati had visited the camp at Riga and paid a Russian POW artist to paint a portrait of me, using the miniature he always carried in his wallet, and he had paid another man, a Russian shoemaker, to make Juergan and me those wonderfully warm felt boots. The man had asked my Vati to give the Russian medals to the little boy in the picture, since he said sadly that he thought he would never again be allowed to go home to see his own little boy in St. Petersburg.

When Vati told me how sad the man was, I felt sorry for a man not being able to go home to his son. But I was delighted that he wanted me to have his medals, and the boots kept me warm through another cold Baltic winter before I outgrew them and passed them on to Juergan..

While Vati was home on leave, I remember that my Opa threw a big party, and my brother and I sat in the middle of the floor and played with the medals, much to the amusement of all these German officers in the room. Our play medals were even bigger than all the German ones they wore. One officer told me that the people who had owned them were now merely prisoners of war in Riga, not worth the powder to

Eric and Juergan

blow them away. Of course, it didn't register with me at that age that prisoners of war were not criminals. I thought anyone who was in jail was a bad person and deserved it.

And it seemed strange that Opa would entertain these soldiers. It was only many years later that I knew enough about the military to wonder why my Opa might have had a big party for all these high-ranking officers. Opa was a civilian pharmacist and he was very old. What had been going on that he was involved at all? Why would they have bothered to come to his party? But, as a small child, I only remembered that they talked about all kinds of war things. And I saw the same expression of anger on my mother's face as she helped Oma prepare food in the kitchen for all these men. "Food is scarce enough without us feeding all these Nazi officers," she said. Oma said, "Hush, Liebling. The officers brought us enough food for a big feast."

I was quiet in the corner of the kitchen, hoping Mutti and Oma would not see me and would keep talking. But they didn't talk about it anymore, so I built a lovely scenario in my head of my brave Opa, whom everybody loved, dashing off to the rescue of these soldiers when they lay dying. In actuality, my Opa seemed more bent on political talk than dashing off to rescue anyone—even though he did rescue my Oma when the firestorm bombs fell on Konigsberg later in 1944, and then he was killed by the fire right afterward. I never had any answers to my questions, because by the time I was old enough to think something about this party was odd, Opa was gone.

Soon after Vati' s furlough, Russian prisoners showed up in our back garden to dig a bomb shelter. I suppose Vati arranged to have the bunker built with prison labor. The men dug under the garden furniture and made a deep hole. Then later they closed it back in as best as I could see from my upstairs bedroom. I wanted to watch up close, but Mutti and Nanny said we boys had to stay in the house and not go near the prisoners. Food was becoming quite scarce by then, but I noticed that Mutti used our last potatoes to make soup and took it out in great steaming bowls to the men for their noon meal. I was surprised she would feed "our enemies," but she said that they looked so sad and thin, that she couldn't eat a bite while they were out there in our garden working so hard.

Of course, we children didn't fully understand, and we protested that we didn't have enough soup left for ourselves, and that we were still hungry. I'll never forget my Mutti's reaction. She abruptly poured her soup into our two bowls and then said, "I only hope that when Vati is taken prisoner, someone will try to give food to him." I felt embarrassed then, and prayed my Vati would never be a prisoner, but I couldn't understand how he could ever be, because my Vati was a good man who would never commit a crime. When I said so, my Mutti shushed me and said, "Son, there are many things happening that you can't understand, but we must do as Vati told us and use this bunker. If sirens go off, you are to grab your new baby brother, make sure Juergan follows, and get in the bunker and close the door, even if Nanny or I are not there. Do you understand? I'm counting on you to take care of your brothers no matter what happens to anyone else. Don't stop for anything—just run with your brothers and get inside and stay there until someone comes to get you out."

Of course, being curious little boys, we thought it a great adventure to go out after the prisoners of war had left and stare down into the hole. And once it was finished, we played in the bunker every day, finding bugs and pretending bombs were falling, even though we had no idea yet what bombs were. By the time bombs really were falling, it was not so much fun. We couldn't imagine why anyone would drop bombs on us. We hadn't done anything to make anybody mad at us, but it wasn't long to where big bombers appeared mostly during the night, and we'd have to sleep in the bunker until the "all clear." Later in the war, we got raids both by day and by night.

The bombings may have been mostly the British and Americans dropping whatever bombs they had left before they headed back to Britain, because at that time, I didn't think there was much of military value in our town. I later found that Konigsberg had a large harbor, equipped for all kinds of shipping. As an adult, a pilot for thirty years in the U.S. Army, I later learned the Norton bombsights that were the best available to the Allies in the 1940s were not very accurate, so the bombs on us could've been intended for the harbor and simply went astray.

Our Nanny hated the bunker because of the bugs, and she was glad when it eventually flooded underground, as that was an excuse to move our almost nightly siren-roused sleep into the braced-up section of our keller under the house.

I don't think I truly understood all the "boom boom booms" that we boys tried to count, or sing louder than, or make fun of. Though at first they meant little to us, they surely panicked Mutti and Nanny. I could always tell because they held us much too tightly as the booms got louder. I guess we sensed their fear because Juergan would start crying, and I felt alarmed that Mutti was alarmed. Then one night we also heard huge whistling noises that seemed very close, somewhere in our neighborhood, and we were bumped up and down when this boom arrived—close, it seemed. Then, I was scared too, but perhaps just beginning to realize the intensity of bombing and that the bombs actually landed on things. Suddenly I was glad for the bunker in our keller. My Mutti made Nanny hold us boys while she ran outside to see what was hit. The house next door was burning and our neighbors, Frau Schmidt and her teen-aged daughter, could not get their bunker door open to get out, because lots of beams had fallen and blocked their exit.

We all cried when Mutti didn't come back for a long time. When she did come back, our neighbors were with her. They were burned and terribly frightened. Mutti's hands were all black, burned, and torn, so I realized she had dug them out with her bare hands. When the all-clear sounded, Mutti took the neighbors upstairs and made us boys sleep on the floor so Frau Schmidt and her daughter could have our bed for the night.

The next day, they tearfully went away to an aunt's house in the country, and said they hoped it would still be intact and their aunt would be willing to take them in. We never saw them again.

There were no more furloughs for our Vati, and we missed him dreadfully. I now convinced myself I was too big for "Hoppe Hoope Reiter" and other musical games Juergan wanted me to play with him. I wasn't big enough though, because I always seemed to drop him off my crossed knee, even though I tried to bounce him properly. Vati had not been able to come home since right after our baby brother Wolfgang was born. Mutti still cried at night, even when we had to go into the bunker, but she hustled us boys around in the daytime as though she had slept well. I was big enough by eight to notice that Mutti and Nanny were getting really thin. What clothes they still had hung loosely around their bodies and when Mutti hugged us, she felt all bony. I began to realize that Juergan, Wolfgang, and I always had more in our bowls that she did, and reality began to dawn on me. She was giving us her portion. After that, I watched her a lot and worried that she would get skinny and just disappear one day. I tried to make her keep more of my soup, because that was all we had by then, but she wouldn't. I could not, of course, give voice to any of these fears, but they haunted my dreams and turned them into nightmares. It hurts to imagine Mutti's fear that she could not feed her boys, and I imagine three hungry little boys were a tribulation for her. It was so bad that Juergan and I talked about food a lot when we were in bed at night. "What will you want to eat after the war, when there is plenty?" It became a warped little game, but I tried to imagine that I would first make sure our Mutti got to eat her fill.

Money is a funny thing. After World War I, Mutti said it took thousands of marks to buy food in the "inflation times." My Vati was a wealthy businessman, but it took most of his money just to buy food and clothing. Then, after that came a terrible depression, and no one had jobs *or* money. Vati had his business down on the waterfront. He was a wholesaler, but there was almost no shipping or trade at all, hence times were terrible for everyone, even those who had once had money.

Then Hitler came, and he put 350,000 men to work building the Autobahn, Volkswagens, and aircraft, and Vati's business grew and grew. Big ships again came into the harbor and cranes grew all over the dockside. My favorite days had been when my Mutti and Vati took us walking down on the wharves. Vati had said that increased business, a returned busy seaport, and jobs for everyone were the reasons why he and Opa thought Hitler was a great man, but now Vati was gone, and we had not heard from him in a long time. Once he went away, though, Mutti's true feelings came out. I could see that Mutti saw Hitler and the war quite differently than had Vati and Opa, but she refused to talk in front of us. Even a child could sense a change, as Hitler began to do rather "funny" things and friends began to disappear. My Opa would say, "Hitler doesn't know about this or that event, or he would stop it." But I don't think my Mutti believed that anymore by 1944.

I think Vati had given Mutti a lot of money before he left, but soon after the war with the Soviets started, money wouldn't buy anything. There was simply nothing to buy, whether one had money or not. Clothes were recycled between family members, and later even to other families. Prussians had always been too proud to do that before the war. We passed clothes down to the next boy, which Mutti thought quite practical, and it didn't bother us a bit because Mutti would always buy me more clothes. But soon, there was nothing to pass down. There was no more to buy, and I had less and less to wear and, with my growth spurt, my shoes no longer fit either. Mutti and Nanny cut down one of my father's business suits to make me a suit for school, but shoes were a problem. Unfortunately, it was winter and snow was on the ground, so Mutti could not be persuaded to allow me to run barefoot. There seemed to be no one who was my size who could pass on their shoes, and certainly none to buy. Finally, Mutti gave me her old gardening shoes to wear to school.

I might have been all right had the other children not noticed. I still remember the feeling of humiliation as Gerte and Hilde pointed their fingers and giggled until the other kids noticed, too, and they all made fun of me. "Why, Ulli has on lady shoes!" Hilde said, and everyone repeated the phrase in unison, "Ulli has on lady shoes! Ulli has on lady shoes!"

I did the only thing that made sense to me at the time, I ran away. After that, I walked to school, attended all day, avoiding other children of course, and walked home in the snow barefoot. I carried Mutti's shoes in my knapsack and put them on just as I got on our street, so she wouldn't see me without them. The truth came out when I became very ill, and Mutti and Nanny tsk-tsked over my blue, blistered, frost-bitten feet and scolded me continually. I cried and said I wouldn't wear lady shoes no matter how much they punished me. Three days of bread and water did nothing to change my mind, so Mutti kept me home from school until we could trade for a pair of worn-out shoes from an older boy, who only had a younger sister, so they could not be passed down. The younger sister got Mutti's gardening shoes, and I got the boy's rundown-at-the-heels shoes. But they were far better than wearing my mother's, so I never complained that they hurt my feet.

I realize now how hard it was for Mutti with three hungry boys who grew taller every day and whose feet kept growing. But at the time, those shoes of Mutti's sort of marked the time when I realized that Germany was losing the war, and I then had the new worry of wondering what would happen when the Russians or the Americans came. Would we all be prisoners of war, dependent on soup from some kind Russian lady, or would we be taken to the East to be workers whether we wanted to go or not? The enemy soldiers were cannibals. All the posters and radio broadcasts said so, and I still thought that anything written down had to be true. Everyone feared the Americans, but they feared the Russians more, so whole families, or what was left of them, began moving west.

Mutti didn't want to leave because Vati had been missing for over two years with no word, and she was afraid he would finally return home, and we would be gone, and he wouldn't be able to find us. It was enough of a fear that she waited until the Russians were practically at the gates of the city to run. Of course, it was *not legal* to run. Hitler had issued express orders that the people of the Eastern regions had to stay put, and fight and die to the last man, woman, and child, but many people hadn't been listening to him for some time. Mutti could not have told her father or mother when she decided to smuggle us boys out of town, because it would involve going against Hitler's orders. Opa still believed Hitler would come out with the great secret weapon that would win the war for Germany, and of course, Oma had to believe whatever Opa believed. He would have brooked no insubordination from his daughter, who no longer believed that pipe dream.

Mutti found a way to smuggle us children out of the city on a train, and I still remember our Nanny boosting us up into the shot-out windows of the train---Wolfgang howling, Juergan shaking with fright, and I was trying to pretend to be brave. Mutti didn't tell us that we would never see our home again. She only told us the day we left, when she and Nanny buckled us into layers of our clothing and donned the backpacks, that we were "going to find Vati." Of course, Juergan and I were thrilled to think we were on our way to find our Vati, but Wolfgang had been a tiny baby when Vati left, so he didn't know him enough to have remembered him, nor to have missed him like Mutti and Juergan and I did.

The trains hadn't lasted long. Bombing raids had made many rail lines and bridges impassible, and soon we had joined the great exodus of peasants and property owners, business people, and kitchen maids. Prams, handcarts, children's wagons, farm wagons and even old cars without petrol were pushed or pulled along the crowded road. Every vehicle was piled high with belongings of a family, whose members took turns with the pushing. Soon, half the items, and even the vehicles, were left at the side of the road to lighten the load. After a few days, people were reduced to their knapsacks like us, and many left without the more feeble family members who were left behind as well. When I became ill with dysentery, a new fear was born. How long before Mutti would have to leave me behind so she could continue to carry Wolfgang? But Mutti prodded us all along. She put me in charge of keeping Juergan from getting lost, or scared, or run over in the panicky crowd. At some point I realized this was a real fear, when we saw more and more children lost in the melee, crying for their mothers.

By the time of this journey across Europe in late 1944, I was nine, going on ten, Juergan was seven, and tantrum throwing "Baby Wolfgang" was barely four. He hated the name, but that made it even more likely that Juergan and I would call him that.

What does a child remember of that terrible race to stay ahead of the marauding Soviets, stay alive, and find Vati? Mostly it was the physical things like being too tired to go on, but then the Russian planes would strafe everyone on the ground, so we had a powerful incentive to take cover and then keep moving. I could never again see the

Russian red star on a plane and not remember the gut-wrenching fear of thousands of people scrambling over anything in their way to get to the ditches, and watching the planes diving. It always felt as though they were aiming just for you.

For three growing little boys, the worst part of the journey was being hungry all the time. Poor Mutti tried hard to find us food in the woods: berries, mushrooms, gleaned potatoes or turnips from already harvested fields. The gleaners were like locusts, so there was little to find. Most of the gleaned vegetables were moldy and rot-

Vati, Ulli (Eric), Juergan, and Mutti

ten, but we ate them anyway. One time, Mutti made "bark soup" in the little cooking can. We didn't keep it down very long, but it salved our hunger for a couple of hours before Juergan and Wolfgang were crying, and my mother cried, too, because she could find nothing to give them. I made up my mind I would not cry from that day on, not for anything.

I had learned to read my mother's eyes for whatever needed to be done, whether to capture the baby, gather firewood, or drag Juergan with me to run from the Russian planes. She rarely had to tell me what to do anymore. I usually knew, and I had to grow older—fast.

It seemed that from town to town, I mostly remember the bunkers. I never remembered the people. I think that was because they somehow all looked the same—frightened. When we entered a strange village after walking all day, Mutti would find the nearest bomb shelter and bed us down there to keep from having to wake and move us when the bombers came. My little brothers thought the far away booming was like fireworks, but I already knew better. Somebody was having their home taken away, like ours had been, and somebody in a plane in the sky was often seen to be shot down. My Mutti and I sadly talked of both the people on the ground and the enemy in the sky being shot down. "They are all together in death," she said

One night in Chemnitz, it was a memorable bunker whose ventilation system didn't work, and the people sheltered there were faced with a horrible choice of suffocating inside, or being killed by the bombs outside. We took our chances with the bombs, and I still remember the bomb's hot breath as it seemed to pursue us by rolling up the street behind us as we ran. Was it malevolent enough that it could find and follow us? It seemed so, as our clothes were pitted with burned holes by the time we found shelter in an open spot in a park. I remember the quiet after we could run no further, collapsing on the grass, and how my baby brother sang a Christmas song he said would "make the bombs go away." Tired people who had also found their way to the open spot began to join in, and soon the voices really did seem loud enough, because the bombers flew away to the north and it was again silent.

As bunkers go, though, I remember most of all the one that sheltered us in Weida, where we stayed until the Americans burst through the door offering the children candy and the new mystery of chewing gum. The mothers were frightened that the American soldiers, being "cannibals" of course, were just trying to fatten the children up so they could eat them. It took a little while for this distrust to be resolved, but everyone soon began to appreciate the kind Americans who fed everyone in their "mess tent" and helped to rebuild homes that could be salvaged. But one day, with no warning, because of the division of Germany by the Yalta Conference, our new American friends moved away in their jeeps, and the Soviet troops took over in their horse carts. That was when even we little boys realized *why* our Mutti had been afraid enough of the Russians to smuggle us out of Konigsberg to save us. But now, they had caught us.

After the Russians came, my Oma, who had followed us to Weida after my Opa died in the firestorm bombing in Konigsberg, made me bury my beautiful medals in the back yard before the Russian soldiers could find them. She kept insisting that the "Bolsheviks" might think we got the medals by hurting some Russian, and they would take us prisoner. I did ask Mutti about it. She just threw up her hands and said, "I wish you were old enough to understand where we've been, and why we left. Your medals are not as important as keeping the family safe."

In no time at all, the Soviet soldiers took away all the food the Americans had given us. Even though the war had officially ended with the death of Hitler and the capturing of Berlin, it was still a war for Mutti—to find food for us children, and to try to find a way to smuggle us boys to the West Zone, even though it meant illegally crossing an increasingly fortified border across Europe.

I was beginning by then, at ten years old, to realize that Germany had made some kind of terrible mistake in its choice of leaders. Hitler led us out of the depression, but right into war. The first action endeared him in the hearts of the German people, for a while. But the second action, once his methods were discovered by both Germans and the rest of the world, made him, and by extension, us, the most hated people of the twentieth century.

For the complete adventure of this family's physical, emotional, and political journey to find their mysterious Vati and escape to the West, read <u>Mutti 's War</u> *by M.J. Brett (also known as Margaret Brettschneider). The ending of the episode will blow you away. The book is available on Amazon.com and on the author's website at www.mjbrett.com.*

Also by M.J. Brett is another fascinating thriller based on her own postwar experiences in Germany, <u>Shadows on an Iron Curtain</u>. *It describes life on the "Border," that very security-sensitive area along the Iron Curtain where American military forces faced their Russian counterparts in a powder keg situation for several years, trying to avoid starting World War III.*

Elsie's father—a German soldier who would not shoot a gun

Elsie Streeb

"If I see on the other end of the rifle another man, that man has a family and a life. I can't shoot him."

———————————●———————————

Elsie Streeb's memoir runs the gamut from life in Germany during the war to coming to the U.S. as bride of an American serviceman—and everything in between. Nothing was easy or routine for this young couple, who only wanted to be together in America after the war in Europe ended in May of 1945. It is another unique story—of patience, courage, perseverance, and yes, even love. She tells it best herself, in her own words.

◗ ◗ ◗

A Special Soldier Father

I was born in 1928 in Darmstadt; that's south of Frankfurt. I didn't go to kindergarten but started school in the first grade when I was six, in 1934. That was about the time when Hitler came in.

The war started in 1939 when I was ten. The only way it affected us at first was we had blackouts. We lived in an apartment in a building owned by the city. We had to have sheets made for the windows, and we had shades to pull down. At six o'clock or so in the evening when the sun went down, we had to black out our windows. The whole city was always dark at night.

My father was drafted right after the war started. He was born in 1905. He first went to Poland and was in the city of Posen. He was part of the German occupation; he wasn't in the firing line. My mother went there on a vacation to join him.

Did she take you with her?

Oh no. I took care of my younger brother and sister for six weeks while she was gone. I was twelve. There was no babysitter or anything like that then.

Elsie at six

My father would never have shot a gun. He was a shoemaker. This is how he stayed in the army without having to shoot, because he made boots and shoes for the officers. He made shoes that fit like a glove. He made all my mother's shoes and shoes for the family. He could make new shoes from old ones. In Europe you had to go to an apprenticeship and then a yeomanship and then you became a Master. My father was a Master shoemaker. After the war, he and another man had a shoe repair shop. I came over here with a pair of boots he made. I don't have them anymore; I'm sorry I gave them away. In this country, there's nobody that can do like that.

My father could have been an officer. They offered him training, but he never accepted it. He always saw to it that he didn't have to shoot. He said, "If I see on the other end of the rifle another man, that man has a family and a life. I can't shoot him."

In June of 1940, the German troops entered France, and my father was right away transferred to France, and my mother came home from Posen. From France he was sent to Smolensk in Russia. Also in Russia were two brothers of my father. His brothers died in Russia. One was in Kiev. He died when he was shot in the stomach. His officers sent us a picture of his stuff hanging out; that's how cruel they were. An older brother was at Stalingrad, and he was on a ship that left Stalingrad and it was sunk.

He never came back.

Our city wasn't bombed seriously until the 16th of September, 1944. The British did the main bombings at night, and then the Americans did the cleanup next day. We had two bombings in one night, and that was it; that just wiped everything out. The city was completely gone in the center of it; only a few houses were left on the outskirts.

There were forty units in our apartment block. My father was stationed temporarily at a military camp just up the street. When bombs fell through the roof of our building, he could see the building burning. He came, and we were already in the cellar. On the roof they had sacks of sand lying all over the attic. He took me and a neighbor boy, and he said, "Our house is burning; let's go up there."

The bombs that came onto the roof were incendiary bombs. They looked like a grenade with a handle. When they hit, they crawled along like a snake and set everything on fire. So we watered those sacks of sand with buckets we took up there. By the time we finished, everything was wet, the flames were out, and we were out of water.

Often when the sirens blew that the planes were on their way, I wouldn't get up out of bed. My mother just had a fit. That night I did get up. I was looking out the door and saw bombers that had reached their goal, and they began bombing. They dropped a flare, and that flare stuck in the sky. It was shaped like a Christmas tree covered with green lights. It was a signal to the other planes that that was the place to bomb. I went into the cellar. That night I could have stayed in bed though, because when the bombing was over and we went up to see what was left of our apartment, my bed was not touched with one splinter. Everything else was a mess.

The next day my mother sent me across the city to find her sister and her family and see if they were still alive. I had to wear my gas mask, because everything was still smoking and burning. You have no idea what I saw. There were houses that were still burning and buckets standing around with bones in them. There were signs on the buckets saying, "Eleven people"—"Twelve people"—those were the bones of those people. There were piles of trash everywhere. There were bones sticking out, arms and legs sticking out. There was not one house left, not a hospital standing. The schools got bombed, too.

Before, we were able to continue living in our apartment. We had to have the windows and doors repaired because the pressure from the bombs blew them out. We covered the windows with cardboard. Now there was nothing left of the city and we had to leave.

Why were they bombing Darmstadt? Factories, strategic targets?

No, none of that. It was a maneuvering area, with several camps in the area. They just bombed everything. Our town was completely bombed out. There were 120,000 people living in that town. Several thousand people were killed; many more left town. We left too and went into the country where my mother had a brother. He lived on a farm but didn't farm it himself. We stayed until everything was repaired and the war was over.

When we moved into the country, the family didn't have to worry about bombing anymore, but there were shortages of everything. Fortunately, we were able to raise some vegetables when we lived in the apartment. The city would rent allotments; that is a plot in back of the building where we could grow potatoes and other vegetables.

But elsewhere, malnutrition was a problem and TB was rampant. For example, for our family of four—mother, brother, sister and me—we received a ration of an eighth pound of butter for a month, one loaf of bread per week, one pound of meat per week, and one egg per person per month. Milk was literally blue, with every bit of butterfat removed.

For baking cakes, cream of wheat substituted for flour. My mother saved coupons for a year so she could bake a cake. We had bread for breakfast, coffee (instead of milk) mid-morning, and our main meal was at noon. We had potatoes and vegetables that we grew in our little garden plot. Supper was more of the same. Coffee wasn't real coffee; it was made from ground up wheat kernels.

Elsie as a young nanny in Darmstadt. These two little boys were killed with the rest of their family in the Allied bombing of Dresden in February, 1945.

My mother cried a lot. She was worried because we were so hungry, and she couldn't feed us. I gave some of my bread to my brother because he was always hungry.

I was working at the time for the Army. I worked for an administrative center that took care of all the camps in the area and kept their records. I did clerical work as a civilian employee, until the Americans came. They were all officers working there. In the morning I had to get to work at that camp, which was on a hill outside the city. I went there by bus from my relatives in the country. It took about a half hour.

The way I got that job was this: When I was fourteen years old, I was in training for two years in a Nazi officer's household to take care of his two little boys, to be a nanny. But when my two years were up, I wanted to quit and get a job at a bank, because I wanted to train to be a journalist/foreign correspondent, and I wanted to learn another language. I could learn English better at the bank. I was allowed to go to the English school or to the higher school, but my mother wouldn't buy my books. My father said, "No way! You're going to train to work as a civilian for the Army so they can't draft you." I was seventeen then. In a year, I would have been old enough and they would have drafted me.

Toward the end of the war, my father came back from Russia as the German troops retreated from there. He was put in charge of a prison camp for French soldiers in the western part of Germany, close to the French border. That was his last post. He was most of those soldiers' friend, not their keeper. They helped him escape when the war ended. When he came home, he came on a bicycle. Those French soldiers who were his friends got him a net filled with apples so he looked like a shopper and wouldn't be stopped by the American troops. Then they wouldn't know he was in the German Army.

Europeans commonly shop with a fiber net, which they take on their almost daily shopping trips for groceries. We looked at one sent to Elsie as a souvenir. It was surprisingly sturdy and could have fit easily into a coat pocket.

During research, I have found references in different memoirs about German soldiers being made POWs after the war. Elsie had this to say:

Yes, my father was too. He came home, and then there came an edict around that everyone who had been a soldier had to report to the post, to the American authorities. They were trying to find out who was a Nazi. They just hauled them off in trucks. When my father came to that camp off the trucks, there were Negroes there. They whipped them with a whip off the trucks. That was so humiliating. But that was the only time they were mistreated, except for the food. They had no food for them; there were no trains, no transportation. The Americans couldn't get food to them fast enough. They fed them soup and crackers almost every day. When my father came home, he had the figure of a little girl, he had lost so much weight. They kept him in a compound where they lived in holes, like foxholes. No protection from the weather. The Americans dug holes for them because they had no other facilities for them. Everyone in that camp was German for their affiliations in the war. My father had no Nazi affiliation, so finally in August of 1945, he came home.

After the German surrender, our top officer at work said we had our choice to retreat with the Army or quit and stay in Darmstadt. I didn't go with the Army and stayed home, but there was no other employment.

My mother didn't have a job. She never worked. Hitler didn't want women to work; he wanted them to stay at home and raise families. During the war we got our income from my dad's army pay. I suppose that continued until he was discharged.

When we went back to the city after the war, our apartment was still there. The doors and windows were blown out, the furniture was in disarray, but we put all that back. Nobody stole anything. Then a lot of the people in my neighborhood were living in the cellar. All they had left was their papers. We never went into the bunker without our papers. We always had our papers with us to prove who we were.

The only things stolen was after the war. We had Russian soldiers in the neighborhood. They used to steal in the cellars. We had French in another camp; we had all kinds of people from all over. They were prisoners of war. When the Americans came, they let them all out, and they had no place to go. So they stole. You have no idea what a mess that was. The government in Darmstadt was taken over by the French and by the Americans. We were living in the American zone. In the camps, the prisoners were living in tents and some in the woods, waiting to be shipped home. And they stole like you wouldn't believe. You couldn't go out on a bike or anything. They would come out of the woods with long knives and steal it. One day they were all loaded onto a train and shipped out.

Were you afraid of the American troops? Did they brutalize you or mistreat people?

No, not at all. There was a Negro unit across the street, and they kept shooting at each other but they didn't bother us.

I was in a section of town in the outskirts of Darmstadt to see my godmother, to congratulate her on her anniversary. On the way home I had to cross a bridge over the railroad, and an American GI was leaning on that bridge, and I had to pass him.

He stopped me there and asked me for a date! He spoke German, but brokenly.

He had seen me before with my cousin, when he was on patrol and my cousin and I had been down in the woods. He said "Hello" to me, and I said "Hello." He asked where we were going; we said we were going home.

Did you recognize him on the bridge?

Yes. Then he said, "I'd like to see you again." I said I couldn't do that because my mother wouldn't like it.

He laughed and said, "If you don't come to my date, I will go see your mother." He was twenty years older than me, about the age of my mother!

I said OK and made a date with him, but we weren't allowed to fraternize or even speak to each other. His name was Otto.

The whole city was surrounded by woods. He walked ahead when we met at the base. I had to walk behind him and pretend not to know him. I had to follow him until we got into the woods where nobody could see us, because we weren't supposed to be seeing each other. It was an American edict that nobody was allowed to fraternize.

This was in May of 1945, right after the war ended. Otto went back to America in October. We were engaged by the time he went back, but we weren't allowed to write to each other. Not until he met a German soldier who was in the U.S. and going home through England and brought that letter to me on New Years Eve, 1947. Then we started to write each other.

He must have been pretty intent on marrying you to wait so long!

When Otto first got out of the service he moved to Wisconsin, near Madison. His aunt had a farm there, and he farmed with her, but that didn't work out.

His parents were Lutheran pastors. They worked in several places. They had ten children, and every child was born in a different state. My father-in-law came to the U.S. from Germany in 1900 as a missionary and married a missionary from Germany. They took over several churches around the U.S.

I went to Frankfurt to get my visa. I had to go to the American consulate to get my papers. Then when they gave me a physical examination, they found I had TB and said I had it a year before it was discovered. I had no symptoms, no cough, no weight loss, and I didn't suspect that. Of course they wouldn't let me come then. Otto first tried to get me over here through the church. And that didn't work out. I have all the letters from that. Then Otto told his sister, "If I can't get her, I won't get married."

Otto and Elsie

His sister lived in Denver and worked as the secretary for the head of the Annuity League in Denver. She went to her boss, Mr. Bloedorn, who was a friend of Senator Ed Johnson of Colorado. Mr. Bloedorn wrote to Johnson in Washington, and by pulling some strings in high places, I was given permission to come. When I got married, my sister-in-law gave me an album with all those letters. I haven't thought about that in fifty years!

I got to the U.S. on New Year's Eve, 1948, on a KLM flight. The stewardess made me sit off by myself, because she was informed I had TB. I stopped in New York, and when they were going through my luggage and found my x-rays from the German doctors, they wanted to ship me right back. So, a man came where I was waiting in a waiting room to be shipped back. I don't know where he was coming from, but he was an official, and he said, "How would you like to be in Denver at four o'clock in the morning?" So they put me on that flight, and I got to Denver on United from New York. Otto was waiting for me. It was 3 A.M. Mountain Standard Time.

Then when I got over here, they demanded that we get married by the fifth of January, and I had just arrived on January first. They had to find a doctor who would attest that there was nothing else wrong with me except TB, and that doctor had to be found within three days because we had to get married on the fourth or I would be sent back. I had no visa, only temporary permission to be here for five days. That gave us four days to get married.

Soon after we were married, I had to go to Denver General Hospital to have a checkup. They took my x-rays I had brought with me and took more x-rays and examined me. They said right away that you have to go to a sanitarium or we send you back. So by the end of the month I was in a sanitarium. I was twenty years old.

At first they wanted to take me to the Jewish hospital, but I was just coming from Germany, and I was scared to go to the Jewish hospital. I went to a hospital in Wheat Ridge. It's now Wheat Ridge General Hospital; at that time it was a tubercular hospital. Otto came to see me every Thursday and Sunday. I was there a whole year.

Then when I came home, in no time I broke down again and had to go back to the hospital. I was there for two years the second time. I had a tonsillectomy there, and they also took out five ribs and collapsed one lung. I only have one lung, on my right side. At that time they insisted on complete bed-rest, and I took a lot of medications—fifty pills every day. After those two years I had to learn to walk again.

Otto was really put through a lot. I felt so sorry for him. More than myself, I felt sorry for him, because he tried so hard to get me here and to get married. Something happened all the time.

Why did Otto choose to settle in Colorado? This was pretty German country around Windsor, but perhaps you didn't know that.

Well, he knew I had TB, and he had to go to a climate that was right for me. We couldn't live in Wisconsin. Otto got a job with his brother-in-law, crop-sharing on a farm in Windsor.

Did you have any fear of coming to what had been "enemy" country?

Heavens no! Everybody was so thoughtful and so nice. Why should I fear anything?

I wonder if you had gone to Tennessee or Alabama where there wasn't such a German population, would it have been any different?

I don't think so. The only thing I was fearful of was to go to the Jewish hospital. I had heard what they had done to the Jews, and I was afraid they wouldn't be kind to me, that they would abuse me or something. I said, "Whatever you do to me, I'll go anywhere but to the Jewish hospital."

Did you have any friends at school who were Jewish?

No, if there were any there, I didn't know them. They were only Catholics, Methodists, and Lutherans. I had known other Jews in Germany. My mother bought most of her stuff from Jews. These were Jewish stores I had known as a child. There was a Jewish building called Rosen Haus. It was a big building with lots of people living there, an apartment building. And the people were always looking out from there. One day I was on my way to school where I was training as a nanny. Twice a week I had to go by there on my way to those classes. I always saw people looking out their windows, and one day they were gone. There were just curtains blowing through open windows. There was nobody there.

They had to wear that Jewish star on their sleeve. There were many stores where it said on the window a sign that said "No Jews Served Here." When they were putting them away, we didn't know what happened to them. We just knew they disappeared. Where I lived there were very few Jews. But the stores where we used to buy things, they were owned by Jews, so we did know Jews. My mother had a favorite store where he used to deliver. He was a Jew. Before the war, the Jews were the only ones who were giving anybody credit. There was no credit anywhere else. Credit cards were something unknown. So if you wanted to buy something on time, you had to do business with the Jews. My mother bought our clothing and a lot of things we needed through the Jews.

I returned finally to Windsor in 1954. Our farm was across the road from Otto's brother's place. We farmed 70 acres on the west edge of Windsor on the north side of the road, where the medical center is now. In 1955 I became a citizen.

**Brother Heinrich in his Hitler Youth uniform, 1944.
Notice the very pensive expression on this young face.**

Reinhard Rosin

"The Russian troops were coming closer and closer, so there was no time for a funeral or burial."

———————⬤———————

Our family history had a dramatic beginning when my mother, at the approximate age of thirteen, left Germany with her mother and four of the younger siblings, plus her mother, my grandmother, to live in Siberia for three years while my grandfather was in the Russian army during World War I.

I was born in 1931, the middle child in a family of ten children. Two additional babies died in infancy. Mom's first child died five days old after five days of hard labor. No one remembers exactly when the other died, also soon after it was born; both were boys. My mother was given a medal called *Mutter Kruez* (mother's cross), for bearing seven sons for the Fatherland.

My father was a farmer, and our home village was Kultschin, about 100 miles south and east of Warsaw. Although geographically located in Poland, the area was heavily populated with Germans, living under Polish government rule, naturally. They were Lutheran. The German language was spoken at home and among the villagers, but school was a Polish entity, where only Polish was spoken. Our churches and businesses were completely German. (*Reinhard is trilingual, and he speaks English with hardly a trace of accent.*)

When war came to Poland in 1939, German occupation was not a hostile environment for the German segment of the population. Then in 1940 Hitler forced these "colonists" to abandon their Polish farms to resettle farther west, in Wartheland. It was then Germany but is currently Polish territory. They exchanged their Polish farms for reassigned sites in Germany. Reinhard recalls that his parents were actually ready and willing to leave Poland. Like the Japanese in California and the Jews in Germany, they were fearful of growing discrimination and worse. They were living in an intimidating environment, which, at the time, they were glad to replace.

Living in Nazi Germany presented some issues to the Rosin children. At ten, Reinhard was required to enter the German Youth, as all boys ages ten to fourteen were required to be part of the "Deutsche Jugend" (German Youth). He describes it as primarily a discipline-training regimen. Other accounts have compared it to Boy Scouts; perhaps among different troops there was a difference in leadership. Reinhard's experience involved leaders who seemed to enjoy their unqualified authority over these young boys, and their goal was to instill a knee-jerk devotion to obeying orders. Troops met three times each week for training, and Reinhard did not enjoy his four years attached to the group. At fourteen he would have been required to move up to the "Hitler Jugend" (Hitler Youth), which involved even more military-like activities. But by then the war was over.

By January 1945, Reinhard was attending a middle school twelve miles from home, which required a commute by train. As the outlook for German victory weakened, the population grew uneasy about the prospect of a Russian invasion. However, authorities didn't share with the public how badly the war was going and how critical the situation was for the immediate area.

My oldest brother Arnold, age sixteen, was notified to report for military duty. The following day police officers came and took our best horse. The next day they came after our second-best horse, leaving us with an old nag and one young horse that had not been broken.

My parents went to town to shop one Saturday afternoon. While they were gone, about two o'clock in the afternoon the mayor came to advise us to pack up and be ready to move out by eight o'clock. The oldest brothers and sisters at home began to pack as best we could. Our parents didn't get back until four or four-thirty in the afternoon.

The family depended upon horse-drawn wagon for transportation. There was no gas for private autos, and the other alternative was bicycles. The government had already confiscated our best horses. The younger horse died from stress a few days later on the trek.

Our family then consisted of Father, Mother, very ill paternal grandfather, and nine children ranging in age from eighteen to a year and a half. It was extremely cold, so our neighbors took Granddad on their wagon with them, as they had a covered wagon. There was no medical attention available, and he died on the third day out. The Russian troops were coming closer and closer, so there was no time for a funeral or burial. He was wrapped in one of our precious blankets and left beside the road. Also on that third day of our flight, it began to snow and turned bitter cold. Only the youngest of the children could ride on the wagon, so many of us had frost-bitten fingers and toes. Our toddler brother Adolf also had frost-bitten toes.

Reinhard

What followed was a two months' flight as refugees; some of the family walked, some rode in the wagon with their few possessions. They camped wherever they could and lived in considerable discomfort, with a high degree of anxiety. On one occasion, as they broke camp in the morning, three-and-a-half-year-old Irma took an armful of caps and mittens to load onto the wagon. She became disoriented and simply disappeared from the site. A frantic, two-hour search back in the dangerous direction from which they had come finally located her in the comforting arms of a concerned man who found her and was trying to locate her parents. A similar story, which didn't get resolved as easily, involved a three-year-old girl who got separated in a similar situation. The lady who found her knew who she was, knew her mother, but it took three more years to locate that mother.

Once safety was reached in March of '45, the family was assigned by the German authorities to a farmer who also operated a brick yard. Lodging was provided, and the family moved into a small two-bedroom house on the premises,

Eight of the nine Rosin children, Mother and Father, plus Grandpa who did not survive the evacuation. Reinhard is second from the left, front row.

where the farmer's workers had lived. In fact the workers were forced to leave so the Rosins could move in.

The older children found employment on the farm, in the brickyard, and neigh-

In a photo taken shortly after the war, the Rosin family harvesting potatoes at the farm in West Germany where they were staying temporarily. Potatoes will be gathered in the baskets pictured then loaded onto the wagon and taken to the distribution center for market. Reinhard is the worker at far right.

boring towns. The war ended shortly after.

Reinhard's brother Arnold survived the war but had been taken prisoner by the Americans. The family was reunited when Red Cross registration procedures located the parties, helped by an aunt who had kept in touch with the family. At the end of the war, as millions of displaced persons crisscrossed Europe, the Red Cross set up periodic stations to register refugees looking for lost family members. By this system, many friends and family members were identified and reunited. These people might otherwise have remained separated indefinitely.

By 1947, Reinhard's father initiated the procedures to resettle in America. However, he died in 1949, and it was 1952 before the move was made, because the application process had to be repeated. Then they had to spend a few months in a Displaced Persons camp at Hamburg. Reinhard's maternal grandmother had a suspected eye infection, and authorities wouldn't let her emigrate. Finally the family left her there, with her blessing and assurance that she would join them later in America, which she did.

Lutheran Immigration Services found sponsors for them---three Millikin farmers who happened to be brothers. And so, Mother Rosin with her nine offspring, some of whom were still children, emigrated to Colorado. Reinhard was twenty-one.

We were often asked, "How could a widow lady age forty-nine with nine children at home leave for a foreign country where they knew no one or the language?" The family had a meeting and came to the conclusion that as terrible as life was for them in postwar Germany, if the Lutheran World Federation of Churches was willing to sponsor them to America, they had better go. It couldn't possibly be worse there. If we can't tolerate life in the U.S., surely they would be willing to send us back if need be.

Our faith and endurance helped overcome all the problems and prejudices we encountered. The three original farmer sponsors were not very kind; another substandard housing accommodation was provided. It was an old, decrepit, bedbug-ridden laborers' shack for ten people. So at our first opportunity, we looked for other jobs. The family pulled together, saved every cent we could, and kind people befriended us. Later we found sponsors for several other relatives to emigrate to America. All have married, have families, are homeowners, businessmen and women, and all are definitely survivors.

Reinhard first worked as a custodian for the Greeley school district. Fellow co-workers and teachers took him under their wing to help him learn the English language and prepare for American citizenship.

Toward the end of 1954, I met Freida, the young lady that became my wife in August of '56. Her parents had been immigrants themselves as part of the Germans from Russia.

They taught her how to be independent.

In 1962, with the encouragement of his wife and father-in-law to use his talents, Reinhard struck out to be a self-employed interior/exterior painter. In 2008 at age seventy-seven, he is still at work climbing ladders, in business with brothers Heinrich (now Henry) and Adolf. This hopeful, hard-working, and courageous immigrant family has added much to Weld County's diverse population. And they never saw fit to return to their former homeland.

Looking like twin dolls, Suzette on left, and sister Laure

Suzette Erbel Von Riesen

"German planes flew over us, intermittently dropping bombs."

———————————●———————————

There needs to be a word stronger than "gutsy" and "spunky" to describe Suzette Von Riesen, as you will see. Small wonder she has so many friends and a family that worships her. At eighty she is lively, stylish, positive about life, proud of her family, and has a great sense of humor. Despite the tragedies she has experienced, she seemed to genuinely enjoy recounting her life story for you to read. She is inspiring, to say the least; you don't realize until she gets up to walk that she is "mobility-challenged."

As Suzette writes this memoir so competently, keep in mind that English is a second language for her, and she speaks French and German in addition to her native Luxembourgisch.

I was born early on Christmas morning in 1927. I don't think Santa Claus brought me because Luxembourg, the country where I was born, celebrated St. Nick's Day on December 6th. That is when the gifts appeared, which contained candy, nuts, and chocolate, and maybe a doll or teddy bear. Christmas was a holy day, spent in church and around the table at home with the family. I remember how my grandmother baked pies and cakes and made the best roast duck dinners.

Luxembourg is the size of Rhode Island, very beautiful, and rich in iron and agriculture. Our family lived in a town called Esch Alzette, not far from the French border and eighteen kilometers from Luxembourg City, the capital. My father was an electrician at the steel mill; my mother was a stay-at-home mom, a wonderful mother. My sister Laure was fourteen months older than I, looked like a little doll, and I knew I had her wrapped around my finger.

When Laure and I were about three or four years old, we started to spoil Dad, brought his slippers when he came home, and anything else we could do for him. At the same time, he became ill and was sent to a sanatorium at Vianden in northeastern Luxembourg, to be treated for tuberculosis. On Sundays we got up early, Mother would dress us in our best, and we would take a long walk to the railroad station to take two trains to Vianden. After arriving there, we still had to walk up a steep cobblestone street to a big building. These visits were happy times for Laure and me, although we could not have direct contact with our dad. We returned to Esch the same way we came. It was dark when we left home and dark when we returned.

This went on for several months until our father came home. He wasn't cured, but there was nothing more that could be done for him at the sanatorium. At that time Laure and I were taken to an orphanage, where we lived for nine months and went to school. The nuns were very strict. I can remember standing by the wrought iron fence waiting each week for Mother's visit and hoping she would take us home. Since she had a job, she could only visit us on weekends.

One day my father's sister came to see us and asked the nun to take us to the chapel to pray. We were told that our dad had died; he was thirty-four years old. When the three of us arrived at home, Mother took us to the living room where my father was laid out in a coffin with a glass top. Family and friends came to view and pay their respects.

The day of the funeral was a cold January day. The hearse was drawn by two black horses; they had black bows around their necks. The hearse had black bows too, and there were lanterns on the sides of the hearse. My mother and all the family and friends were dressed in black. Mother had a black veil over her face. The cortege headed for a brand new cemetery, where my father's grave was ready to receive him. There were few trees, since this cemetery was new, but there was a weeping willow close to my father's grave, which I watched grow through the years. It is still standing.

Now there was not enough income for my mother, since my dad had not been employed long enough. The solution was for her to get full-time work, but what would she do with her children? I was six years old and Laure was seven. We would either have to go back to the orphanage or have my mother's parents, who also lived in Esch, take care of us. They were getting up in age at sixty-six and sixty-eight, and even though it was a hardship for them, they wanted us all to live with them.

Mother found a job in a ladies' boutique. She could sew, and she loved pretty clothes. We went to school and helped at home. Grandmother was a seamstress and Grandfather was a shoemaker. They each had their atelier (workshop) at home.

Grandfather took us to the library, to the park, and to see Shirley Temple and Laurel and Hardy movies. We were loved, and Mother was content that we were in good hands. We never saw her sad, but we knew better.

My grandfather's nephew Emil was living in Charleville, France, not far from Rheims. He and his wife had no children. They would drive to Esch and take us back to their home, not by train but in a beautiful big car. We guessed that he had struck it rich; such an automobile was not common on our streets. They were the kindest,

Map of the frantic journey of Suzette's family fleeing Luxembourg into the safety of France

most gentle people, and they liked to spoil us. We truly hated to have our visits to their house end.

A page from Suzette's mother's diary of the evacuation from Esch beginning May 10, 1940

The warning signs of impending war came in 1939 when my grandfather told us the Germans were restless and would probably attack again, as they had during the first World War. That meant Belgium, Luxembourg, and France would be targeted. And so they did, early in the morning on May 10, 1940.

EVACUATION

In the early hours of that day we were awakened by cannon fire. My grandfather announced that German soldiers were in the forest near our house and heading our way. French soldiers were seen ducking behind buildings and shooting at the Germans. By eight o'clock that night we were told by the authorities to evacuate immediately. Older people, including our grandparents, were assembled in trucks and taken southwest toward France. My mother, sister Laure and I, along with my mother's sister Manny, Manny's husband, and their two children Irene and Gasty, started walking with all the other people towards France. We left our house exactly as it was, including food on the table.

We each had a rucksack packed with only the bare necessities. These had been packed since 1939 when Hitler had ruthlessly invaded Poland and other eastern European countries. We walked at good speed towards Audun le Tiche, a small French town on the Luxembourg border, about three kilometers away. It was dark and cold, and by the time we arrived in Villerupt , about three kilometers further, the gunfire seemed to be following us too closely. We stopped for the night in the Cantebonne forest and cowered under brush while cannons and bombs were blasting away. My mother held Laure and me tightly, and we were terribly frightened. The forest was full of people who had left their homes, but you heard no human voices, only bombs and cannons.

When the fighting subsided, we continued on a country road. I do not know if there was a leader or how and why we went as we did. By now it seemed that the whole world was with us in this caravan. There was no motor traffic, only refugees on foot. People began leaving their belongings on the side of the road, unable to carry them any longer. German planes flew over us, intermittently dropping bombs. In all this confusion, my mother spotted her cousin Eugene carrying his eleven-month-old daughter. He was desperate, having lost his wife and the baby's buggy in all the turmoil. Eugene tagged along with us, and we all took turns carrying the baby.

In Jopecourt some of us, including our family party, got on a train and ended up in Damviller late in the afternoon of May 11th. We were handed some food, the first since we left home. All along the route south, as we passed through villages and past farms, people sometimes gave us food. They must not have had much to share, and there were so many of us, but we were very grateful for their generosity and sensitivity to our ordeal. The war was catching up with us. Planes were overhead constantly; the sky was full of parachutes, and there was a lot of gunfire on the ground.

In the early morning hours of the next day, we headed toward Verdun. Again, the roads were packed with refugees. We heard languages we had never heard before. We managed to get almost to Verdun and spent the night in a Villa Bozo. (These details are written in my mother's diary, which I still have in my possession.) The next day we continued toward Verdun and ended up staying in the Casernes barracks, a camp where French soldiers and horses had been stationed before we arrived. They had already deserted this part of France. There were still occasional French soldiers seen along the route. They were not with an organized unit and seemed to be quite casual about the situation. My mother writes: "We walked so far and are so exhausted, again nothing to eat." Gasty found some dark chocolate in one part of the barracks and shared it with everyone. I remember clearly it was the worst chocolate I ever ate.

The barracks were large and lonely. We gathered straw for beds and tried to make ourselves as comfortable as possible. I remember Aunt Manny began to show the stress of this ordeal, remembering that the worst battle in World War I had occurred at Verdun. Planes continued to roam the sky off and on during the night.

On May 14, we gathered up our few belongings and headed south again toward

Dieu, about eleven kilometers away. The bombing around us never ceased. We saw dead cows in the pastures. We picked cherries off trees that were lining the road, welcome refreshment since there was no other regular nourishment. We slept that night in an open field. At dawn the next day we left by bus but were let out in Apremont la Foret, just a short distance from where we had started at Dieu. We continued on foot to St. Agnant-sur-les-Cotes, where we found shelter with a French lady. We had little rest until now and were happy to stay with her for a few days until we again headed south.

My mother's diary stops here. I was twelve and Laure was thirteen, and between us we remember a lot, with the help of French road maps. Of course all this was discussed many times after we returned home.

We continued our journey, sometimes on foot or by bus, sleeping in a barn, sometimes in a field. At Bar-le-Duc we took a train south toward St. Dizier. We didn't care at this point where we were going, as long as we didn't have to walk. The train was packed, and by now there were a few familiar faces. Mother's cousin Eugene and his baby girl were still with us, but by now he had lost hope of seeing his wife again.

We rode all day and arrived that same night back at Bar-le-Duc where we had started. There had been a bombing attack which destroyed the tracks and station ahead as well as at Bar-le-Duc. Dead bodies covered the area at the station. Once again, we defeated death. By now the refugee group contained a lot of French people who were evacuated shortly after we passed through their villages. We all headed northwest now toward Chalon-sur-Marne, only to be told by the Red Cross when we arrived to move on because it was getting too dangerous there, and the town itself might have to be evacuated. Somehow we managed to get on one of the few buses, which took us south to Dijon. It was packed with refugees taking shelter wherever they could from the constant bombing overhead.

Authorities of the city tried with loudspeakers to gather us into small groups so busses could take us to safe places. Our family was driven to Saulx-le-Duc, about twenty-five kilometers north west. I still see us standing in the middle of this village, forlorn, tired, hungry, and confused, when a French Army captain approached us and offered us his home. My aunt and uncle, Irene, and Gasty were taken in by another family. The French captain, his wife and children were fleeing to western France. By this time the Germans were getting closer, and the French army was unable to stop their drive.

We watched the captain and family as they drove away. They had just given us their home to stay in as long as we wished. It had been quite a while since we had had any comfort. The house was beautiful. Its large yard was surrounded by an old stone wall on two levels—hence the name "Les Deux Terraces." Laure and I had one worry: who would do the cooking? My mother had been a career girl ever since my father's death in 1934, and we had never seen anyone by the kitchen stove except my grandmother. I still remember Mother laughing when we asked her about who is going to cook. We were well-rewarded. The pantry had been left well-stocked, and after a much-needed soak in the tub, the three of us sat down to some scrambled eggs and potatoes.

Our contentment did not last long, however. The Germans marched into Saulx-le-Duc a few days later. I had never seen Germans before and was surprised to see that they did not have square heads. My grandfather always referred to them as "squareheads." The remaining days in Saulx-le-Duc were worrisome. We tip-toed around the village, avoiding the soldiers. We were given permission to attend school, thus continuing our formal education, which had been neglected for a while. Language was no barrier, since the Luxembourg school system required learning German from the first grade and French in the second, carried all through the grades until college.

Aunt Manny was asked by a German officer to be his interpreter. This was a difficult task for her; to be helpful to the enemy was more than she could tolerate. However, she had seen violence used on a priest and on an older man from Saulx because they hadn't translated accurately and were assumed to be deceitful. In the end, the German did speak fluent French. We always wondered what would have happened to Aunt Manny had she misinterpreted in favor of the French people.

On June 13, Paris fell. The Germans had already occupied most of Western Europe. It was a sad time, and the future looked bleak for us. On June 27 we were ordered to be at the railroad station where we would be boarding a train for the trip back to our homeland. The train was a "40 & 8," an old WWI freight car that could hold forty men and eight horses. It was full of standing refugees, packed in like sardines, and there was very little room for our group.

I have no recollection of the beginning of that trip until July 1st when the train stopped in Beauraing and passengers were handed some loaves of bread. My uncle decided to get off and make a fast trip to town for some food. Gasty, his ten-year-old son, jumped off the train and followed him. It was an agonizing wait for them to return. As the train started slowly to move, we saw my uncle running toward us with something under his arm. Gasty was right behind him. Everyone cleared a space so they could get back onto the train. My uncle jumped on, but Gasty tried and couldn't make it. On his second try, my mother caught him by one arm and dragged him in. My mother forever remained his favorite aunt.

Needless to say, the stress of the previous seven weeks took hold. My mother and

Aunt Manny sobbed; Gasty stood quietly for hours with me by his side. The rest of the passengers were all subdued, probably wondering what we were going back to.

We arrived back in Luxembourg City in the afternoon of July 2, 1940. The railroad station seemed normal except that it was filled with German soldiers, SS and SA.*

SS (Schutzstaffel= defense echelon) were an elite, quasi-military unit of the Nazi party, pledged by oath to loyalty to Hitler and acting as his personal guard. They served as a special security force in Germany and the occupied countries. The SA, "Brown Shirts," were a thug group more involved with street brawling and doing the dirty work on "disloyal" citizens, particularly Jews. The two latter groups were justifiably feared by the populace wherever they were assigned and were the real hard-core Nazis.)

We boarded another train and arrived in Esch about an hour later. I will never forget the walk from the station through Avenue de la Gare toward home. The streets were full of glass, houses pitted from gunfire. Store windows were broken, and there was no sign of life. It truly looked like a ghost town, like a mini *Kristallnacht*. We were just eighteen kilometers from Luxembourg City where nothing had been touched by the attack of May 10. This street in Esch and the area around it had been full of elegant shops for clothing, jewelry, leather goods, restaurants, etc.—nothing strategic but all owned by Jews. We wondered if there was a connection. But some non-Jewish residences nearby were vandalized as well.

When we arrived at the house, my mother unlocked the door. The lock had been tampered with but no one had broken and entered. Everything was as we had left it so suddenly on May 10th. The table still had all the dishes, silverware, and glasses, as we left it on the "last supper." There was mold on everything, but to my mother it must have looked beautiful.

As the days went by, townspeople returned, a few families at a time. We were anxiously awaiting the return of my grandparents, but they did not arrive until late August or early September. They had been taken to Montpellier in France near the Spanish border, where they had spent four months with other refugees from Esch. The war hadn't touched that part of France because it was in the part called "Vichy" France, not occupied by the Germans at that point in the war. We were reunited, and the next weeks were spent telling about our long journey to nowhere and their journey by truck to Montpellier.

Then, what to do? Mother had to look for a new job. The store where she had worked no longer had an owner. The family was Jewish, and Mother was certain we would not see them again. We went back to school, a private school this time, the Lycée des Jeunes Filles. Mother thought we might be able to continue our French lessons. The Germans, however, did not permit any French in any schools, public or private. We learned a lot about German geography and history, learned their Nazi marching songs, and had to raise our hand to mumble "Heil Hitler." The brain-washing was not effective.

Hitler Youth (Hitler Jugend or HJ) meetings, which were mandatory, were poorly attended by Luxembourg youth. My mother told the HJ leader that Laure and I were needed at home because our grandparents were old and ill.

In 1942 all Luxembourg eighteen-year-old males were drafted into the German army. This outraged our people, and to show their contempt, the men in many cities went on strike. In retaliation, the Germans assembled several teachers in the northern town of Wiltz and shot them. That was the end of the revolt, and the young men were drafted. If they refused, their parents paid the price.

There was underground activity from the start. The long swastika flags that lined the main street seemed to disappear frequently. My downfall came in late 1942 when I took a large flag down at the school and in front of German dignitaries. That was the last day of my formal education, and perhaps I was lucky it was left at that. My mother was not happy with me for jeopardizing everyone's safety.

I was too young for the *Arbeitsdienst* (Work Program), so I was sent to the steel mill where I was to be an apprentice for three years in every sector of office work. A friend of Mother's was the secretary to the director of the mill. She started me in her office and kept an eye on me. I learned steno and typing and hated every minute of every day of every year. At night I had a tutor to keep me in touch with normal courses, which I was no longer privileged to take. I learned English in the two years I attended the Lycée. I kept up with that language and now was able to continue my French, which was forbidden to be taught in the schools. (French is actually the official language of Luxembourg.)

When my grandfather died in December, 1943, my mentor was gone. Laure and I grieved, as he had literally raised us—the "father" we knew best.

The occupation became increasingly harsh. With their strutting march, the Germans seemed more hostile as Allied troops started a push toward the east. After the Allies landed at Normandy, a young friend confiscated a radio from someplace. We didn't ask where he got it, as it was illegal to have a radio. We were able to listen to the BBC radio broadcasts and followed the American soldiers battling their way through France towards the Benelux countries. Our lives were consumed with anxiety, as the German troops and Gestapo were getting more short-tempered. The underground kept busy sabotaging the enemy.

By early September, 1944, Americans entered Esch. The Germans had disappeared during the night. The first American troops showed up in a tank, then more and more tanks came rumbling through town. It was the most exciting and happiest day of my life. The streets were full of people tearing down swastikas, destroying Hitler's photographs, cheering, dancing, and singing the Luxembourg national anthem. Laure and I, our friends, and the townspeople entered the churches to sing hymns of thanks.

Our jubilation was not to last long. The Germans pushed back to the west, and again we were under gunfire. Bombs were falling on us again, and to make it worse, it was the coldest winter in 100 years. The Battle of the Bulge, which took place in the Ardennes, was to be one of the bloodiest battles of WWII. Northern Luxembourg and eastern Belgium were demolished. In Esch, people locked themselves in their homes again, and underground fighters were not safe anymore. Some were shot; some made it back to safety in their hideouts.

We lived in our cellar for a week including Christmas Day, while bombs were falling from above. The cellar was like a dungeon. Darkness and cold, hunger, and fear from four and a half years of Nazi occupation had made us numb. I can't even remember being scared any more. The food situation was particularly critical. Laure and I walked five kilometers to Kayl to get eggs and meat from farmer friends. We didn't have adequate warm clothing, and it was at this time I froze my hands and feet. The doctor told my mother I would some day lose all four limbs. I was young and didn't worry about it then.

Allied forces finally pushed the Germans back, to end the war for us December 28 and 29, 1944.

THE TURNING POINT IN MY LIFE

After the war was over, the humdrum of my daily routine at age seventeen was giving me doubts about my future. I was preparing for exams in a field that was of no interest to me. I was being trained to continue working at the steel mill where I had been apprenticed to various departments for the last three years, learning shorthand, typing, and how to develop photographs. I was doing it out of pride and to please my mother. After being expelled from school for taking down the swastika in the school yard, I counted my blessings that I hadn't been sent to Germany to work in a munitions factory.

Our lives were gradually getting back to normal. American soldiers replaced the Nazi occupiers. Two American MPs were billeted in our home; one was a veteran of the first World War. They showered us with apples, fruitcake, and chocolate. The schools were full of soldiers, so we couldn't really continue our education at that point.

Then I met an American corporal at a Red Cross tea. It happened like this: the American Red Cross planned Sunday afternoon get-togethers in Luxembourg City for the GIs and young ladies

Suzette and Lyle

from surrounding towns. They needed chaperones, and my mother was asked to be one. Laure was eighteen and spoke English, so she was allowed to attend. I was younger and spoke English too, but I could join them only if I sat with a chaperone. The casino where the party was held was swarming with soldiers and Luxembourgers. Glenn Miller's recorded music provided music for dancing. It was my first social event, and I had to sit with the "old" people (my mother was only forty-three years old!) and watch. At one point I sneaked away in the crowd, saw my cousin Irene, and headed her way. She was talking to a soldier.

We were introduced and engaged in an awkward bit of dancing together. I had never danced before, and he wasn't much better. He was blond, blue-eyed, Protestant, and had a German name, Lyle von Riesen. After that first meeting he would show up at our front door regularly and at the most inopportune times, having hitch-hiked from Luxembourg City to Esch via jeep, ambulance, or whoever would give him a ride. Two and a half weeks after we met, he asked me to marry him. Marriage had been

Luxembourg brides ready to leave for America—Suzette at far left

the farthest from my mind; I hadn't even dated. I had my exams to consider and didn't really enjoy his visits. But after persistent proposals, I finally agreed to take the big step. The whole family liked him, except the thought of a Protestant in our Catholic family made my grandmother wince. The distance between Luxembourg and the USA naturally gave my mother second thoughts before finally giving her blessing.

I started to take the exams seriously. My tutor came back, and I was determined to do well. With everyone's cooperation I survived two grueling days of questioning and passed, to be certified as a "white collar woman."

In the meantime, Lyle was making arrangements with his chaplain. He also wrote his parents about me and asked them to send the legal papers necessary for the wedding (and also, would they please send some popcorn?). When I think of them now, I wonder what their reaction was. After all, their son was a level-headed boy, a scholar, president of his senior class. Before the war, he had worked for a year to earn money to enter Kansas University as a pre-med student. What powers did this young, foreign, CATHOLIC girl hold over him?

We were married on New Year's Eve, 1945. My sister Laure picked the date because she thought it would be romantic. Since Lyle was a Protestant, we could not be married in front of the altar in the Catholic church. Instead, the ceremony was performed behind the altar.

The next day we took a train south to spend our wonderful, fun-filled, ten-day honeymoon on the French Riviera, including a side trip to Monte Carlo. Upon our return to Esch, Lyle rejoined his unit and left for the States in March of '46; I followed three days later.

A group of English, French, and ten Luxembourg "war brides" gathered at Le Havre for the trip to the US. There was quite a bit of red tape to deal with, but we finally sailed, on the Italian liner *Vulcania*. The trip was not pleasant. Since it was March, the weather was cold, windy, cloudy, and rainy. The ship rolled a lot, making a number of passengers sick, including me.

Arriving in New York, there was still more red tape, and the Red Cross assisted us in many ways. Some of the girls didn't speak English well. I lost my luggage and had to continue on to Kansas City without it. Lyle's brother met me at the station, and soon Lyle, in civilian clothes, showed up as a surprise. Our final destination was Marysville, Kansas, Lyle's home town. His dad met us, speaking German, and he looked like a very happy father-in-law. Lyle's mother and sister sized me up carefully, and I felt accepted by the family.

Lyle, Suzette, and fellow Luxembourger Marcelle King

Lyle enrolled at Kansas University in Lawrence and graduated in 1955 with a Ph.D. in microbiology. By then we had two children. We moved to Kansas City when he was offered a position at the University of Kansas Medical Center in the bacteriology department. After four years we transferred to the University of Nebraska Medical Center where Lyle taught in the Department of Bacteriology for twenty-four years. Upon retirement, we moved to Fort Collins, where our son Matt had attended Colorado State University and continues to live with his family.

The retirement years were good to us. We enjoyed our hobbies and family. My family in Europe, Lyle and I and the kids, traveled back and forth almost every other year. They showed us Europe, and we showed them America from coast to coast.

Lyle died in 2006 after two years of illness. My left leg was amputated six months before that. Lyle left me knowing I could take care of myself, functioning adequately with a prosthesis. I even took him for a ride to demonstrate that I could still drive a car.

POSTSCRIPT

At writing in 2008, Suzette's doctors are urging her to have her right leg amputated. She refuses to consider that as an option, having turned a frisky eighty on Christmas Day. In addition, the health of her fingers is deteriorating. Her hands are reddened; fingers are stiffening and turning blue. She can no longer knit, a hobby at which she excelled and which has given her great satisfaction as well as a closetful of stunning, handknit garments. Yet, her conclusion to this memoir is unbelievably positive. Referring particularly to her sixty-year marriage but also to life in general, she writes:

I can say life has been good. No regrets; I would not change anything. I WAS LUCKY, and I miss him.

We should all be so lucky.

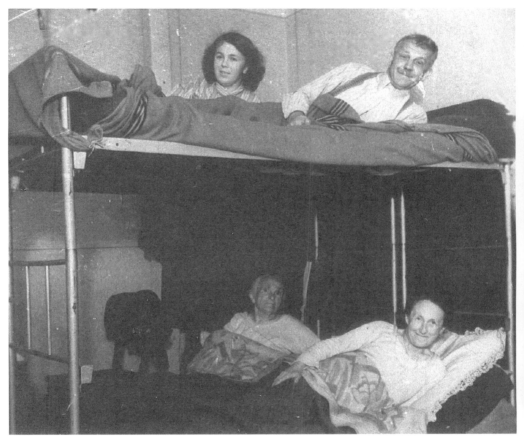

Living quarters at camp were crowded with two families sharing one room

Marcelle Abens-King

"Families that were strangers to each other had to live together."

———————————— ● ————————————

Marcelle's story is another unusual one in this collection of wartime narratives.

Many of our subjects are victims of situations over which they had no control, and Marcelle's family's predicament was also the result of no wrong-doing on their part.

Like Suzette, Marcelle is "quadri-lingual," and her accent is a charming combination of all four—German, French, Luxembourgisch, and English. Both their narratives show an admirable command of English.

I was born in the Grand-Duchy of Luxembourg, a tiny country of 999 square miles, surrounded by France, Belgium, and Germany. In 1839 we were given our independence, from the Netherlands, I think, according to the First Treaty of London. Vianden was my home city. It is close to the border with Germany, just across the river Our.

The joy of being called "Letzeburger" ended May 10, 1940, when Hitler's army invaded our country and proclaimed, "You are now Germans." Our national motto was, "We want to remain what we are." The Nazi rule was harsh. People died just for wanting to keep their Luxembourg nationality. Some died by firing squad after they had to dig their own graves and being beaten half to death while having to do so. Many ended up in concentration camps, and a lot died there from mistreatment, disease, and starvation.

My brother Victor was twenty-eight years old when he was arrested on September 1, 1942, for refusing to say "Heil Hitler!" to a Gestapo (secret state police). He was sent to a concentration camp in Hinzert, Germany and later on to a camp near Lublin, Poland, with a group of other Luxembourg prisoners. Two of them died during this long, sorrowful journey.

In March, 1944, he was sent back to Luxembourg on condition that he report to the Gestapo headquarters in Luxembourg City. He would have been executed there if it were found out that he had belonged to the Luxembourg underground. But the underground learned what was going to happen to him and got him off the train when he crossed into Luxembourg. They managed to get him to our hometown, Vianden, where he remained in hiding until the Americans liberated the

Marcelle on the left with sister Margot

town, the last city in Luxembourg to be freed by Americans from Nazi Germany.

My sister Clemy was 22 at that time and would have been forced to go to work in Germany, but she managed with the help of the Luxembourg and French underground to cross into France one night and ended up in Montpellier in the south of France, which was unoccupied *(by Germany)* at that time.

On December 2, 1942, at six o'clock in the morning, the SS knocked on our door and told us that we had two hours to pack, as we were going to be deported to Germany.

Our family at home then consisted of my maternal grandmother, my father, my mother, my sister Margot, age sixteen, and me, age ten. My 81-year-old grandmother asked the Gestapo guy if she had to go, too—at her age? He replied that of course she was going, too. My grandmother then looked at him and said, "And do you think you are going to win this war?" He did not like that remark and told her to shut up or she was going somewhere much worse than the deportation camp.

A bus picked up us and another family. We were the first to be deported from our town. At the Gare de Luxembourg (railway station), we, plus some more families, were put on a train while a lot of sad-looking people waved goodbye to us as we departed our beloved little country for an unknown future.

The third of December, after a twenty-four-hour train ride, we arrived at the train station in Leubus (now Lubiaz), where we were met by the SS Manschaft which was going to "take care of us." We had to walk a short distance from the depot to the Deportation Camp #158.

The camp was the monastery of Leubus, supposedly the largest in the world. That part of Germany, called Silesia, now belongs to Poland. I don't remember too much about our brief stay there. The monastery was huge, with big beautiful rooms and halls and a magnificent church that we could not enter. The monastery is just an empty shell of its former self now, which is very sad. There weren't monks there any more, and still to this day a lot of mystery surrounds it from before and during the war. From what little is known about that time, many prisoners from concentration camps had to work deep underground in horrible conditions and died there. We didn't know anything about that until many years later. From what I have read about it, by that time nobody was around anymore to shed light on what took place at one time in that beautiful monastery.

September 17, 1942, was the day the first Luxembourgers were deported. Later on in November, people in the country decided to collect toys for the deported children, as Christmas was approaching. It was quite a shock to the people at what the Nazis were doing to us. My mother and I bought a toy and sent it off, but I don't remember what it was.

Lo and behold, when Christmas came, we were in Leubus ourselves, and I received one of the gifts sent from home. I do remember a small wooden duck with four red wheels I pulled out of the box. I was a little too old for the little duck, so we put it back into the box and sent it to a cousin of ours at home who had some young kids.

On January 21, 1943, we left Leubus by train for Boberstein, also in Silesia and now called Bobrow. There were 510 of us that went there; 155 went to another camp. In all, 4386 Luxembourgers were deported to eighteen different camps during the war.

Boberstein was a small chateau surrounded by a little town called Schilbau, with a train station where the "political prisoners," as we were called, got off and walked to our new home on a very cold day.

There were some buildings on the grounds surrounding the chateau, with many small rooms which became our living quarters. Families that were strangers to each other had to live together. Of course there was no privacy whatsoever. We had triple bunk beds with straw mattresses and at the beginning, lots of bedbugs. We did have blankets and pillows. There was one small closet per family and a table and a bench

Schloß
Boberstein

Internees were not housed in the castle; they lived in out buildings on the castle grounds. Administrative offices were accommodated in the castle itself.

in the room.

My father had to take the train every morning for Hirschberg, now called Jelenia Gora, where he worked in an optic plant. There were some Russian POWs working there also. They made some glass paperweights for my father, behind the Germans' backs of course. I have one sitting in my bookcase, and I love and treasure it. My mother had to help peel potatoes in the camp kitchen. There were several hundred people there to cook for. Every day they took so many ladies to do that and to work in the kitchen. My sister Margot worked in a plant where they made military uniforms.

I went to school in the camp. At first we had some Luxembourg teachers from the camp, and we even learned some French, which was forbidden in Luxembourg during the Nazi occupation. In fact, French names were removed and changed. When the SS came to check on us at school, we had to hide the books. After a while we got some German teachers, and that was the end of our French lessons.

At Boberstein my grandmother had a congenial relationship with the "Lagerfuhrer," the top boss of the camp, named Korte. He was always respectful toward her and would come into our room and say, "Good morning, little mother, and how are you?" One time this young SS guard came into the room. He worked there and was supposed to look through all the rooms and make sure everything was OK. He had lost an arm in the war and sort of had a chip on his shoulder. He came in and my grandmother was sitting   there knitting. She was always knitting socks. He said to her,

Leaving Boberstein

"You're supposed to get up when I come in here!" She said, "That's no way to talk to an old lady. I'm not going to salute a young snapper like you." Then he started to yell at her. Somebody went to get Commandant Korte, and he came and told the guy off.

We managed to stay warm in the winter. It could get quite cold there in Silesia. The food was nothing to brag about, but we did not go hungry like the prisoners in the concentration camps. They just starved to death.

Liberation—and ready to return home to Luxembourg. Marcelle is holding the flag, second from left, front row.

We also didn't have much trouble with the SS who guarded us. Sometimes they would get mad at us for some reason and would close the iron gate to the camp. But most of the time they acted like decent human beings. We could leave the camp, go to church in Schildau, and walk to different little towns around there.

When we were in Leubus, one of the SS—his name was Willy Funk—developed a taste for "Quetch." This is a typical Luxembourg beverage, made from plums. It is very potent, something like Schnapps. You have a shot of it with a good glass of beer. When Willy would come around in the morning to check the rooms, he would be offered a glass of Quetch by those of us who had been sent some from home. By the time Willy got back to his office, he would feel no pain for the rest of the day.

Willy came to visit us once in Boberstein and got to taste his favorite beverage again. It was a nice visit. I don't know what ever happened to him, but I hope he made it through the war.

My grandmother was finally allowed to return home, due to her age; she was 82 or 83 at that time. There were these two old ladies; they were the oldest ones in the camp. This friend of my grandmother was a year or two older. She was going to be sent home, and she was anxious about it. The night before she was supposed to take off, she went in to the toilet and died right there. But my grandmother made it home. Not to our house, because other people had moved in there like squatters, people that had collaborated with the Germans. She moved in with relatives in another town; one of her nieces offered to take her in.

The seventh of May, 1945, we received the good news that Nazi Germany had capitulated. The SS had left a day or two before, so we were on our own. We raised our Luxembourg flag that someone in the camp had kept hidden for this special reason, singing our beloved national anthem *Ons Hemecht* (Our Homeland) and waited for the Russian soldiers to come and help us to get home again.

May 29 we left Boberstein by Russian trucks, sitting on top of our few belongings, headed for Liegnitz (now Legnica). We were there for three weeks, staying in apartments left vacant by the owners fleeing from the Russians. From there the Russians drove us to Risa where we slept on cement floors in hangers for two days. The third day, American soldiers showed up unexpectedly with their trucks to drive us to Leipzig. It was wonderful to see these men. We were given a tall tin can of American soldiers' rations. Some had helped liberate Luxembourg.

Marcelle's feisty grandmother on the right, pictured with her friend who died just before she was to be released to go home. Gentleman in the center was part of the family that occupied the room with Marcelle's family. Photographed at Boberstein

They took as many of us as they could and promised to come back the next days. But a little later, a bunch of French soldiers showed up with their trucks and drove the rest of us to Leipzig. There they put us on a long train of boxcars and we were finally on our way home. Of course there was no hygiene on this train, so we had to do the best we could. The train would have to stop in strange places, so there were usually some trees or hedges to hide behind. We rode through some of the big industrial German cities like Essen, Dortmund, Kasel, etc., and there wasn't much left of any of them. Leaving Germany, we rode through Holland and Belgium and the 25th of June, 1945, into Luxembourg. How this whole trip and who organized it came about so soon after the end of this horrible war, is still a mystery to me and always will be. After two and a half years we were finally home again, and very happy.

My whole family survived the war, but some of our neighbors perished in the concentration camps. Some of our young men, forced into the hated German Army, died in places like Russia. I lost three cousins there.

I went back to school, to high school (I got my GED after moving to America), and life returned to normal. I met my husband in 1954 at a dance; he was an American GI. Philip was in the Air Force, stationed at Bitburg, Germany. We came to America in November of 1957 with a baby boy named Donovan. We lived in Wyoming for several years, and our daughter Laurie was born in Cheyenne. In 1966 we moved to Colorado. Philip worked for IBM for twenty-five years. He has since passed away.

My sister Margot still lives in Luxembourg. We are the last two left of our family; my father died in 1966 and my mother in 1968. I have visited Luxembourg several times and am getting ready to go visit Margot this summer of 2008.

Victor Abens with some of his distinguished, official visitors which include Eleanor Rooselvelt and Ambassadress Pearl "Call Me Madam" Mesta, Queen Beatrix of Holland, Pope John Paul, and not pictured here, Queen Elizabeth of Great Britain

Victor Abens

My Experience in the Hinzert Concentration Camp, 1942-1943

On September 1, 1942, I refused to say "Heil Hitler" to a top Gestapo in Diekirch, Luxembourg. At that point, I was arrested and interrogated at the Villa Pauly in Luxembourg City. That was a bad place, and most of the people who were arrested were taken there. I was hit in the face and then put in the cellar of the villa, which had been converted into little dark cells. Kloecker, an SS officer, told me that he knew that I belonged to the L VL, a Luxembourg resistance organization to help young Luxembourgers from being forced to join the German army. (I had joined the organization at the beginning in 1941.) Kloecker told me that the Gestapo knew where the L VL and LPL (Luxembourg Patriot League) met every Sunday by the church in Diekirch. Kloecker was called away for half an hour and I was alone in the interrogation room, and I looked at a letter sitting on the desk. I could read the names of 5 of my colleagues who belonged to the L VL. Kloecker didn't bring up again my denial about not belonging to the L VL.

(A side note: When I got to Hinzert, I told a friend from Diekirch about the names on the letter and asked him, if he was released from Hinzert, to warn the 5 fellow colleagues. He was able to fulfill that promise, but in October 1943, the Gestapo arrested two of those 5 colleagues.)

I was taken to the Hinzert Concentration Camp with other strike prisoners. When we got to Hinzert, we got the terrible reception that hundreds of Luxembourgers had already been subjected to in the camp, and hundreds more were to follow.

Accompanied by their ferocious, biting dogs, the SS (one was called "Iwan the Terrible") started beating us up as soon as we got off of the trucks at Hinzert. The bellowing voices of the SS, the beatings, and the barking of the dogs was something no one who was there could ever forget. Some men just collapsed, but the SS just kept beating them up until they got up again, chased by the dogs. Completely exhausted, we were ordered to get out of our clothes. Our bodies were shaved. Thank God prison-

169

ers who had already been at the camp for some time did that task. These men did their best to help us out as much as they could.

After either an extremely hot shower or an ice-cold shower, we were taken to a quarantine barracks. The SS came inside, often unannounced, and threw the prisoners' beds around just to be nasty. After a certain time, we were ordered to leave the quarantine barracks and were assigned to different barracks. At the new barracks, I got acquainted with other Luxembourg colleagues. All prisoners were assigned jobs: laundry, sewing, cooking, or working outside. The prisoners were all ages, all social levels, and with different characters, but we were all united in the same solidarity.

The top "Kapo" (guard) was a man from Switzerland whose name was Wipf, a pliant tool for the SS. He mistreated the prisoners with sadistic brutality and beat some of the prisoners to death to the delight of the watching SS. Thank God some of our prisoner colleagues managed to get the job of room elders, and they were able to help the rest of us as much as possible. I'm sure a lot of the prisoners survived Hinzert only because of their help. In barracks three and four we had two communists as room elders— Heinrich and August. They were arrested in 1933 but still had a bit of humanity left. They were very strict, screamed just like the SS but seemed to get along with the SS pretty well. August was fairly nice to me. Every chance he got, he enjoyed explaining communism to me.

One little episode showed me how the SS and the room elders worked their way with the prisoners. We came back to the camp after working outside all day. We were taking a shower when we were called for inspection. About fifteen prisoners, me among them, were late to the inspection. Iwan the Terrible screamed that we had to stand in line in the room, and each one of us was to receive twenty-five lashes to the buttocks. Wipf usually administered the lashes. The men would scream with pain and couldn't sit down for weeks. We pleaded with room elder August to tell Iwan that we were late for inspection because we came back late from work. August said that he would see what he could do. Iwan and Wipf came in together—we were still standing in line. We were trembling and shaking all over. Iwan explained that if one of us would volunteer for the whipping, then the rest of us would not have to go through that. Right then, August looked at me and winked. And as if I were paralyzed (or more like hypnotized), I walked to the table and bent over. Wipf gave me only one lash, but I screamed like I had received at least ten lashes. Iwan kept his word; everyone else was okay.

The prisoners like me who worked outside had to be up and ready by 6:30 A.M. Because we worked outside the camp, we didn't have as much contact with the SS. But we heard all about the brutality from our colleagues who stayed behind. They were constantly looking for an excuse to mistreat or beat a prisoner to death. Prisoners that didn't speak German got the worst treatment. Some French prisoners who had been on the road for weeks were completely exhausted and starved to death when they got to Hinzert. I remember a young Frenchman we called "Bel Ami" who had a beautiful voice. He would sing us songs from his native Bretagne (Brittany), until his voice got thinner and weaker, until it was heard no more.

Next to me in barracks 3 was an old Russian man who had been at the camp for quite a while. He told me to put wrapping paper around my body; it was good protection from the beatings. I did that, and today I still think that advice saved my life. Since he was more starved than I was, I would sometimes try to share my meager rations with him, especially after we started receiving packages from home. He thanked me in such an unexpected manner that I never have forgotten. Every Sunday we had to clean our *gamelle* (our soup dish). We had to get our *gamelle* as clean as possible, otherwise we were beaten again or our watery soup was taken away. I had a metal *gamelle* that rusted immediately no matter how much I cleaned it. One Sunday, standing in line for an hour with our *gamelle*, the old Russian was ahead of me, holding his shiny aluminum *gamelle*. Iwan the Terrible did the inspection, and it started with lots of screaming and beatings. I tried desperately to get my dish clean. As Iwan got near to us, the old Russian put his shiny *gamelle* in my hand before I realized what he had done. Iwan beat the old man but thought that "my" *gamelle* (the old Russian's) looked good. The old Russian never said anything about this incident during the 5 weeks we were together. If he is still alive, he's probably long forgotten about the incident, but I will never forget about him.

I worked near a forest where the prisoners had to bring wood out and cut it up. Some had tools to do that but did not share the tools with the others. You weren't allowed to stand around and not do anything or you would be beaten by the SS. We were ordered to pick up a piece of wood, take it to a place, put it down, then pick up another piece of wood there, and then move that to another place. It was one of the worst things they did to demoralize the prisoners. I also remember that the Germans that lived around there could care less about us and showed no sympathy.

For Christmas, we were allowed to receive one CARE package. Later on, our families could send us clothes and food. But the SS always opened the boxes first and they took out whatever they wanted. The CARE package I received came from friends and neighbors because my parents and sisters had been deported to Boberstein, Silesia (now Poland) by then. The CARE package helped me to gain a little strength back.

Even on Christmas Eve, the SS showed their sadism. Kapos Wipf and Kleinhenn brought in a huge plate of wonderful-smelling sausages, put them on a long table, and then left the barracks. We were starved and were ready to attack the plate with the sausages, but our room elder August held us back. It was torture for all of us. Fifteen minutes later the two Kapos came back, looked at the plate very carefully to see if anything had been touched or eaten, and then took the plate away. Thanks to August, we had resisted the urge to eat the sausages and it saved us a long night out in the bitter cold that some of us would not have lived through.

January 13, 1943, we were told to pack up our belongings. We left Hinzert for a prison in Trier where we could rest up a little and the Kapos were more humane. Eight days later we began a long sorrowful trip. Two of our colleagues died on this trip. Through Cologne, Hannover, Berlin, Posen, Warsaw to Lublin, another concentration camp.

This personal account is from a chapter in the book, <u>Hommage `a Victor Abens, les Amis du Chateau de Vianden 1997</u> translated by his sister, Marcelle King.

Victor Abens is pictured here with his friend and fellow Luxembourger, Frankie Hansen. Victor and Frankie were interned together at the Polish camp at Lublin. Toward the end of the war, they both ended up in Vianden, Marcelle and Victor's home city, helping American military forces in their final efforts to rid Luxembourg of Nazi occupiers.

According to Marcelle, Frankie performed an extraordinary act of bravery to aid the U.S. 8th Infantry Division. The Roer bridge was strategically critical to American victory. The retreating German army had set charges of dynamite to blow up the bridge, and Frankie volunteered to enter the water and defuse that dynamite. For his heroic act, he was awarded the Silver Star by the American government, the first non-American to be so honored, accomplished by a special act of Congress enacted May 2, 1947.

Victor Abens also served his country with distinction. In addition to wartime activity with Luxembourg underground, he had a distinguished postwar career in public service. He was elected Vianden's mayor, then served for thirty-five years in the National Parliament as well as several years as a member of the European Parliament.

Frankie also served in the Luxembourg legislature and passed away in 1981.

Victory-In-Europe street party for London children. Notice boarded-up windows from bomb blasts during air raids.

Doris Alexander

"It was a huge relief to know we could sleep in our own beds again and not hear that awful siren."

It was Sunday morning, September 4, 1939, and my mother called upstairs to my sister Rose and me, "Come downstairs quickly. The war's broken out!" We were making our bed, and Rose carried on but I rushed downstairs. Prime Minister Chamberlain was on the radio announcing the dreaded news.

I was nineteen years old. For the next six years, our lives changed completely. We lived in London in a flat—my parents, four sisters, and I. We soon moved to a house though, because my mother was terrified of being in a top floor flat when bombs were falling. However, during the first year of the war, there were no bombing raids. The house had a small back garden, and my father dug a large hole in the ground for a shelter. He bent some corrugated metal into a cover, and during the Blitz we five girls, my parents, and later two infants, slept there every night. My dad slept in a kitchen chair in the entryway, and the rest of us somehow managed on the mattress of a double bed which was placed on the ground.

My eighteen-year-old sister Renée and I worked together in a men's tailoring factory. Soon after the outbreak of war our jobs changed, and we started sewing army officers' uniforms.

That first winter was bitterly cold and wet. None of us had a car; not many people in England did at that time, and public transportation soon stopped functioning. My sister and I used to pull on our dad's woolen socks over our shoes to walk to work every day. We had to walk two hours each direction.

Before long, the factory where we worked in London's East End was bombed, and we moved into another building. My sister was called up into the Women's Royal Air Force. I was called too, but because of ill health, I did not have to serve in a uniformed position. My job at the factory was considered war work though, and I continued until I was close to delivering my daughter.

My fiancé George enlisted in the RAF a few months after the war began. He was in the first class of mechanics trained to work on war planes—Spitfires, Hurricanes, plus Wellington and Lancaster bombers. One day he came home to his parents' house, dropped off his kit (duffle bag), and came over to my parents' house to visit me. That night his house took a direct hit from a German bomb. His mother, brothers, and sister were all down in an Underground tube station spending the night as they always did, sleeping on the platform. George's father worked as an air-raid warden and spent all night watching the skies for incoming planes. When he returned home in the morning, he found George's duffle bag but was told that no one had survived the bombing. He went berserk thinking that his son had been killed.

Corporal Alexander, Royal Air Force

George and I were married in February of 1941—my husband in uniform and I in a borrowed wedding dress. By that time, rationing was a part of our daily existence. Three of us sisters were married to men serving in the military, so we all stayed with our parents. My mother pooled all our ration cards and managed to put food on the table every day. She was magnificent! The weekly ration allowed each couple two ounces of lard, two of cheese, two of sugar, four ounces of bacon if and when it was available, two pints of milk, twelve ounces meat, two ounces loose tea leaves (which were used and re-used to get our necessary "cuppa"), and one egg. There was very little if any fruit and vegetables. My dad grew as much as he could himself. The government leased small plots of ground they called "allotments" to citizens who wanted to try and grow their own produce. There were signs proclaiming "Dig For Victory" everywhere. Dad also somehow managed to get some chickens and built a chicken coop in our tiny back yard. He kept his own chickens for years after the war, too. Rationing didn't end when the war was over but continued another nine years until 1954. Children in those times had never seen a banana!

Many women whose husbands were in the military joined what was called the Land Army and took over the jobs of farm workers in the country. Also, men who were too old or medically unfit for active duty joined what was called the Home Guard. They were to be Britain's last line of defense against the enemy should the English Channel ever be breached. There were no real weapons to be spared, but somehow these dear souls were going to do their bit for king and country.

In 1941, everyone including infants was issued a gas mask which we had to have with us at all times, or we would be fined. Wardens patrolled to make sure everyone was complying with the law. It was a nightmare to think of putting that awful thing on my baby girl!

About that same time, school age children four to thirteen years old were evacuated out of the cities being bombed to safer places in the countryside. My youngest sister was billeted with a family in the country. She was so scared and homesick. My mother actually went and brought her back after about six months. She firmly believed we should all be together! Expectant mothers too were evacuated when their delivery date drew near. I was sent to Hertfordshire, just outside London, where the country manor of a large whiskey manufacturer was being utilized as a maternity hospital. The grounds surrounding it were full of tents of troops bivouacked there. My baby was born in that house in 1942, and later I returned with her to London.

In London when the Luftwaffe began its night raids, all buildings were required to hang blackout curtains at the windows and doors. We had to buy black fabric and fashion hangings which would prevent even a chink of light to show through. Wardens patrolled the streets at night to catch any offenders. Most everyone carried a flashlight, because there were no streetlights, and what transport there was drove with dimmed headlights.

We all hurried home at the end of our day to make ready and go to our air raid shelters.

Our house had only cold running water, no bathroom, just a backyard toilet. Refrigerators were unheard of. There was no central heating—just a fireplace in each room. Coal was scarce, like everything else. When we got word our local coal yard had some, my sister Vi and I would push our prams to the yard and get a half sack of coal each. Only the living room fire was ever lit, so the rest of the house stayed cold all winter. We would heat kettles of water and fill hot water bottles to take to bed.

During those six years of war, sheer will power and love for their king and country kept Londoners going. Everybody helped their neighbours, and neighbours became just as close as families. Our Mr. Churchill's indomitable spirit was actually a national spirit. I think it was through his relationship with President Roosevelt that a programme called "Lease and Lend" came about. We started receiving powdered eggs from the U.S.A. and something called Spam, which we had never seen before. The Red Cross received packages from the U.S. too, and they once gave me a package containing a baby outfit and blanket made by some American lady. We couldn't get baby clothes in our shops, and what yarn we could get was only to knit things for our troops overseas.

When George finished his basic training, he was stationed at a base just outside London, so he was able to be billeted at home. The base was quite often bombed, and one of them hit the base hospital one night. Many patients were killed and many more injured.

In 1943, the year after our daughter was born and three years after George had enlisted, his squadron was transferred to India to prepare for the invasion of the Far East. The night before he left, there was an air raid in progress, but he came home to say goodbye and found me huddled with the baby under the kitchen table. We had been unable to get to the shelter in time, and bombs were falling. He had to leave us there and return to the base. Quite a lot of his subsequent training took place on an American aircraft carrier. His letters were screened, but somehow I could read that between the lines.

In London we were now experiencing bombings by what we affectionately called "Doodlebugs." Americans called them 'buzz bombs." These were even more frightening than the air raids we had lived through so far. They would come roaring over the Channel, and when the roar stopped, they would fall and cause so much devastation. We were never given a warning with these bombs, and our guns were unable to shoot them down.

Meanwhile, George had been in India—what later became Pakistan—and Burma, and had arrived in Malaya. He was living in a jungle helping build landing strips in preparation for bombing Japan. Sister Vi's husband was injured at the battle of El Alamein in North Africa under General Montgomery's command. His friend carried him to safety and he was later taken prisoner of war. My sister Rose's husband was a paratrooper in Europe. After the war he was awarded the British Empire Medal by King George for his bravery in saving some German children from a bombed house.

Finally, on May 8, 1945, victory in Europe was declared, and we celebrated VE Day. I was working in the West End of London near Piccadilly Circus and Trafalgar Square. When I walked onto the street from work, people were going crazy with joy.

Nearby there was a U.S. service-men's club called The Rainbow Room. I had Yanks all around me laughing and jumping up and down, singing and dancing. My thoughts were with my husband and the Allied troops from all the countries still fighting in the Far East. It was a huge relief though to know that we could sleep in our beds once again without fear of hearing that awful siren.

All of Britain was so relieved. In London there were street parties organized for the children. We all gave part of our rations to make cakes, sandwiches, and lemonade for them. People carried pianos out into the streets, and there was singing and dancing everywhere. None of the houses had windows anymore, just boards and blackout curtains, but we succeeded in making it festive for these children who had known nothing but war for their entire lives.

George and Doris before their wedding in 1941

The war in the Far East was still being waged, and the news from there was really bad. I wasn't receiving any letters, so it was a terribly worrying time for me. I later learned that George and his squadron were preparing to wade ashore from landing crafts in Kuala Lumpur. The war truly ended for him on his twenty-fifth birthday when they landed, and the Japanese soldiers were lining the beaches with their hands above their heads. It was the day after the first atomic bomb fell on Hiroshima. George forever after was convinced that that bomb saved his life. He was present when the Japanese high command presented the symbolic sword of surrender to Admiral Lord Mountbatten.

Months later George finally arrived home safely to my daughter and me. He had spent six years serving his country in the war—years that should have been the best of our lives.

THE POST WAR YEARS

When the war in Europe and in the Far East finally ended, my husband and his four brothers as well as my three sisters' husbands all returned home to London. When I think back, we were so lucky none of them had been killed, and all of us on the home front had survived too. Life did not just return to the way it had been, though.

When George was finally de-mobilized, it was March, 1946. He had been overseas since 1943 and in the R.A.F since 1940. The Air Force had required him to return his uniforms and issued him a civilian suit and hat. They had allowed him to keep his shirts, underwear, and socks! He owned very little else as his home had been demolished in the Blitz.

I had managed to rent two rooms in a neighbour's house, just down the street from my mum and dad. Rationing was still in effect, and London was terribly damaged from the bombing. The bottom of our road, about a dozen houses away, was now a bombed-out site. Eventually the government erected prefabricated houses there for families who were homeless.

My daughter was four years old in 1946, and she started attending primary school. I was working for a Jewish poke tailor out of his home. Luckily, my parents and sisters all lived on that same street and were able to help out if we were not home. The engineering shop where George had worked before the war welcomed him back. He bought a second hand bicycle in a street market and rode it to work, over an hour each way, six days a week. It was cheaper than the sixpence it would have cost to ride the bus!

Everything was starting to get back to normal when, about a year after he got home, George was involved in an accident at work. This required surgery, and the doctor advised him he should not return to that kind of manual labour. We did not have to pay for any of his medical care, but the paycheck he had earned was sorely missed. He had never worked anywhere else, other than the Air Force, and jobs were hard to find. One reason for this was that many of the women who had taken "men's" jobs stayed working them when the war was over.

In those days, insurance premiums were collected weekly by an agent who called on your home. Our agent, Mr. Smith, who had become quite familiar with our situation, suggested that George apply with his company for a job as an insurance agent.

George was extremely hesitant, as he was very shy and was nervous about the whole prospect. Choices were slim, but he went to the interview and was offered a job collecting premiums in the neighbourhood where he had grown up.

Now his bike was invaluable. Goodness knows how many miles he rode every day. And his work day started when other people had returned home. Premiums were typically a few pence or shillings, and many of his pockets were worn through by all those coins. I was always sewing in replacement pockets in his trousers.

One day, Dad's landlord mentioned that he'd like to sell the house next door where my sister was living. Dad thought it would be great if he could buy it and have George and me rent half of it and share the house with my sister and brother-in law. This was somehow accomplished, and a couple of years later, when my sister had another child, they bought a house of their own. George and I bought the house from my father, and we now had it to ourselves.

The happy couple celebrating fifty years later, 1991

I was working night and day to help pay the mortgage and it was such a welcome relief when George was promoted to Assistant Manager at the office where he worked. The move to insurance was a good one for us. George was eventually promoted to Manager of his branch and then to the position of Agency Manager at the head office at London Bridge.

My daughter married an American and moved to the U.S. in 1963. They lived all over the country, and George and I visited every year for summer vacation. After we were retired we visited twice yearly for extended stays including winter holidays. We enjoyed the United States and its people but never really wanted to leave England. Eventually though, travel became increasingly more difficult.

By the late 1990s, my daughter was living in Texas. George had started to show signs of illness. I decided it was time to live closer to my daughter. It took close to a year to secure a visa and green cards allowing us to become residents of the U.S. Finally, in 2000 we took the big step. By then, George wasn't really aware of what was happening, and my daughter and I had to pretend it was just another vacation. We walked away from our home and all our possessions with just our suitcases. We moved in with my daughter and son-in law until they too retired and decided to live closer to my only grandchild. This is what brought us to Colorado in October, 2001.

By the time we settled in Longmont, George was very ill. He died in 2002 in our home there. We had been married sixty-one years. My daughter and son-in-law live just a mile away.

Longmont and the people here have been good to me. George would be so pleased at all the friends I have, many from the old country. My family is close by, and I love my home and my new life.

Venita's jolly Nana. She's not letting the war get *her* down!

Venita Mann

"Nobody dwelled on the misery of war, we just got on with our daily lives."

―――――●―――――

Venita Mann is another chronicler of the war as it happened in England. Her experience is quite different from Doris Alexander's; Venita's perspective is that of an innocent child. She was only four years old in 1940 when German bombers began their relentless attacks to destroy London and all of England, from September, 1940, until May of 1941—a period remembered as the London Blitz or the Battle of Britain. Also, she and Doris lived in different parts of metropolitan London, which experienced different intensities of bombing.

Even today, Venita personifies the resilience of the English spirit—the unshakable resolve of its citizens, often with characteristic British humor, to survive the hardships and terror of the war in their back yard. You have the impression that little bothers this unflappable lady; she has been well-conditioned. It took careful and sensitive parenting to keep as much fear and anxiety as possible from crippling the psyche of a child growing up in those stressful times. Venita's father was absent, and her mother had additional concerns for his whereabouts and safety. As an adult, Venita observes, "When the men came home, they wanted to forget and to enjoy home and family life again as best they could."

Those of us old enough to remember the regular newsreels that accompanied movies in those days recall the frequent footage of Prime Minister Winston Churchill as he inspected on foot the daily devastation pummeling his city. He was famous for his popular "V for Victory" sign created by holding up his middle and index fingers. The crowds of homeless citizens that accompanied him appeared to be lifted from their despair by the very presence of this inspiring, cigar-chomping figure. (Sir Winston is also remembered for a speech he gave in America early in the Cold War, in which he stood before a large audience eager for a stimulating lecture by this legendary figure from overseas. He said only, "NEVER, NEVER GIVE UP!" *and sat down.)*

Venita writes:

I was born early morning on April 26, 1936, in a maternity home in Catford, southeast London. I had an older sister, Valerie. Since Mum had named her, she suggested Dad name me, and he did, after a character in a book he was reading. Mum liked it. We later learned that in India Venita means "beloved, good and obedient daughter." Everyone laughed at that!

We lived in a semi-detached, two-story brick house in Catford. I suppose it was about 1000 square feet (no basement). I hadn't seen a house with a basement until I came to America. It had three bedrooms upstairs, and my bedroom faced the street. It was just large enough for a single bed and chest of drawers. There was a fenced back garden (what we call a yard in America) and front garden with a low brick wall. Mum and Dad loved to garden; it gave them great joy. This gift was not passed down to me!

Mum made all our clothes on a hand-cranked sewing machine. She bought it second hand and made her wedding dress on it. She designed and made our matching outfits. While she was sewing on it, I used to crank it for her so she could use both hands for her sewing. I still use it.

Wartime 1939-45

"Make do, and Mend"

"Is Your Journey Really Necessary?"

"Dig for Victory"

(Common slogans seen on British wartime posters)

Dad signed up for the Royal Air Force (R.A.F.). He could have been deferred, as he was in his thirties and married with two children. But he chose to serve his country. He worked with radar. He was stationed in the Middle East, including Egypt and Palestine, and also South Africa.

My parents chose not to have Valerie and me evacuated when children were sent to the safety of the country away from London, for which I was grateful. *(British children were also sent to Canada and America.)*

We had an air raid shelter called an Anderson shelter in the back garden, dug out in the lawn and covered with corrugated iron. We always took the cat down with us; his name was Wobbles. My friend across the road had a Morrison shelter, which was

a metal table assembled in the dining room. Thick, sticky paper strips were put on the windows in a diamond pattern so when the windows broke during an air raid, the glass didn't shatter so badly.

We carried our gas masks with us all the time in a box over our shoulder. We also were issued an identity number. We all had identity cards and had to know that number by heart. I still remember mine—1449983.

Our house was close to the railway line that ran from the coast in to London, and the German planes followed that rail line. Our local elementary school was bombed. A neighbor of ours was a policeman, and the first body he pulled from that wreckage was his own daughter.

Venita's father Ewan Mann on duty with the Royal Air Force in Egypt

As I was so young, I just thought this was all normal life and asked Mum what they would talk about on the radio news when the war was over. Nobody dwelled on the misery of war; we just got on with our daily lives.

One sunny day Valerie and I were walking up Further Green Road when we heard a plane and the engine cut, so you knew a bomb would be dropped. They were called "buzz bombs." I was pushing my doll pram, and I remember thinking would it be faster to pull it or push it as I ran home? Apparently I never considered leaving it behind.

After an air raid, I would run round the block and pick up shrapnel (I can still recall the smell) and keep it in a box. There was a rumour that you could take it to the town hall and get money! This wasn't true—maybe a ruse to keep us kids busy and forget the bombs. After the war, an unexploded shell was found in our neighborhood, an exciting discovery but much to the horror of our parents, who nevertheless were relieved it was discovered before someone got hurt.

It must have been hard for Mum on her own with two little ones, so we spent a couple years in Oxford with Auntie Mary and Uncle Wes. Auntie Eileen and my Nana and PomPom (Grandpa) moved in with them too, from Rochester. So there were eight of us in a small, three-bedroom house.

I don't remember where Uncle Wes worked, but Mary and Eileen did "hush-hush" work for the war. They had to sign the Secrets Act and never knew what each other did. It was only in 2001 that I found out Mary was in coding in some way.

Airman Mann at the Mann residence. Windows are reinforced with paper to prevent glass from shattering during bomb blasts.

We wrote to Dad often and he to us. His letters were censored. He never talked much about the war, only what we would do when it was over. One time I asked him to send me a banana from South Africa. He sent a photo of himself by a banana tree. I was *very* disappointed, as I couldn't imagine what a banana was like. In 2001 I had *my* picture taken by a banana tree in Thailand.

Dad came home on leave once as far as I remember, and we spent a few days in Rye, a town on the south English coast. The house we lodged in had a player piano. I spent a lot of time pedaling, my feet just touching the pedals to turn the circular discs that played the piano.

Nana did the cooking, and Mum's job was to go out queuing for food. Everything

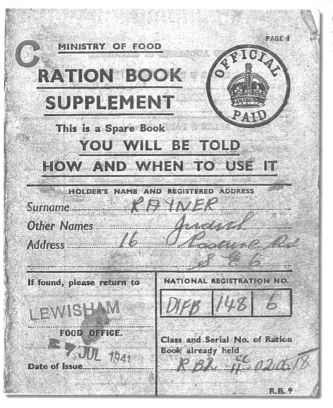

Oficial reminders of tight times in wartime England

was on ration, and food and supplies difficult to come by. If you saw a queue at a shop, you'd automatically join it. People with money could get food on the black market. No such thing as leftovers in those days! For example, a family of five was allotted 4 ounces of cheese, 2 ounces of tea, 4 ounces of meat PER WEEK. We received a Red Cross parcel from America that contained a can of Spam, which we cut wafer-thin to make it last. The old chocolate dispensers at the train station remained in place there, but empty. I thought people were pulling my leg when they said you used to put money in and get chocolate out! After the war, we still had rationing in the 1950s.

When the war ended in 1945, Dad came home to Oxford. I was at Sunday School with my friend, and I asked if she wanted to come home and meet him. I shook hands with him politely, as he had been gone so long. He must have been longing to pick me up and hug me.

So then we moved back to London. There was some damage to the walls of our house. I'll always remember the smell of wet plaster and seeing houses that had been bombed. They looked rather like a doll's house, showing all the rooms open on one side.

Sometimes on a weekend we would catch a train and go to the country for a hike. Mum and Dad loved to walk, and Mum would often bring home branches of autumn leaves. We would pick primroses and bluebells, depending on the season. I often wanted to rest and would run ahead just so I could rest for a while. Also I would go to bed before being told. At night my legs would ache so much. Mum spent hours massaging them.

About 1947, we were coming back on the train from Rochester after visiting Nana and Auntie Eileen. When we got to Hither Green Station, I couldn't get up, and Dad had to carry me home.

In those days the family doctor would come to your house if you couldn't get to the surgery. (*A doctor's office is called a surgery in England.*) I ran a very high temperature and had hallucinations, crying out "Take them away!" at whatever I thought I saw in the corners of the room.

This was the time of polio epidemics, but they figured I had rheumatic fever, and I did have an abnormal heartbeat. I had to stay in bed all the time. Poor Mum was constantly running up and down the stairs. My friend Judy, who lived across the street, would come and play with me, and Valerie played with me too. I was not to exert myself in any way, and if I started laughing, poor Mum would come rushing up, saying "Don't get excited, Venita."

It was discovered I had a hole in my heart, and I was sent to a children's hospital in Surrey. Bed-rest and gradual, limited activity were the prescribed treatment for a few years, so I had plenty of time to read and day-dream of swimming, dancing, and travelling to foreign lands. It was well over ten years for me to do these things, and I am still making up for lost time.

The years after the war were hard and grim. One colourful event to cheer us was the wedding of Princess Elizabeth to Philip of Greece in 1947. Even she needed coupons for her wedding dress, as wartime rationing continued well into the 1950s. As the country started to recover, Prime Minister Harold McMillan made the statement in 1957, "We've never had it so good!"

My mother's younger brother emigrated with his family to Canada, and eventually to the United States. He always wanted someone to visit him, and as I was the adventurous one in the family, I saved up for three years to sail to New York on a student crossing in 1964. The goal was to work my way round the world. I was SO excited to see the Statue of Liberty and to be in America. At Immigration, I was asked where I was headed, and I excitedly said, "on a Greyhound bus to Wichita, Kansas," to which the reply was, "What the hell do you want to go THERE for?"

I traveled the States but ran out of money and ended up in Longmont, Colorado. It was a big adventure, but due to circumstances plus a lack of funds, I didn't get to my longtime childhood dream of seeing the Great Wall of China until 40 years later! Patience is one of my gifts. America seemed a "CAN DO" country. If you have get-up-and–go and creative energy, it is open to opportunity.

But as my daughter Heather says, "You can take the girl out of England, but you can't take England out of the girl, and you've never been boring, Mum!"

Following is the text of one of the letters Venita's father wrote to her. Note the censor-sensitive lack of specificity in the return address and date.

1449983 A.C. Mann
HQ APO S241
RAF Middle East   1943
   My very dearest Venita,

    I have still got the last letter you wrote to me and often take it out to look at and think of you at home. Your description of the tray cloth you are making sounds very nice.

    So you can ride a bike now; perhaps it will not be long before you have one of your own, and I can get one too so that we can go riding together. We shall be able to go to lots of places when I come home, won't we. Perhaps next year

Venita and big sister Valerie posing in front of the family's Anderson bomb shelter

if the war is over, which we hope it will be.

I counted the kisses at the end of your letter—176, not counting the big one. I am well and we live in a tent and cook on a primus stove.

Give my love to Valerie and Mummy and all at home. What are you going to do when I come home? Do you think you will recognize Daddy? Shall I know you now that you are such a big girl? I'm glad you join in all the dancing and plays and Brownies and go camping and have lots of fun. I hope you are getting on well at school and help Mummy at home.

One of these days I shall be sailing home on that big ship and see you all once again, so until then, lots of love and kisses from your very own   Daddy.

X X X X X X X X X X X X X X X X

PS: I am sending you a photo of the "Virgin's Tree." It is called that because a long, long time ago, Mother Mary rested there with the Infant Jesus in her arms. I thought perhaps you would like to show it to your Sunday School teacher so that she can tell you the story.

An Anderson shelter

An eager, bright, young Engberdine

Engberdine Voute

**"For my mother's birthday dinner she was given
tulip bulbs that she fried in vaseline."**

———————————●———————————

*This narrative tells the story of a young girl's perceptions of living under Nazi
occupation in Holland. The family lived at Hilversum, near Amsterdam; Engberdine's
father was an appraiser for an insurance company. Engberdine was barely ten
years old in 1945 when the war ended.*

*Her unusual childhood exposed her to situations adults would find more than
"distressing." As an adult herself now, Engberdine appreciates just how serious
were the difficulties the Dutch population faced during the war and the occupation.
What she remembers and how all that affected her at the time is what makes her
story fascinating as well as informative.*

I was too young to understand the larger picture of the political happenings and
the struggle of the country to fight the occupation, that fear was such an element—fear
of being picked up by the police/Nazis, fear of not having food for the family, fear of
the future, etc. My strongest memory of the years, and especially the last two, is the
fear. I knew more than my parents realized I did, however. For example, we had a
Jewish friend and an *onderduiker* (a person sought by the Germans) who were both
pianists. They would come to our house late at night after curfew to play on our piano.
I knew by their playing who was there, but my mother would deny it to me. I knew
then I was to keep this secret. I had heard that the Germans sometimes picked up a
child to interrogate, because it was assumed a child wouldn't know enough to lie or
to fake ignorance. It was a burden to know too much. It was good to lie during the
war. We were taught that, but it caused confusion about our values.

My parents helped in the underground. They received copies of BBC news taken
from hidden radios, to be distributed to neighbors. Knowing whom to trust was
always an issue.

They depended a lot on the grapevine to keep informed. Some people were totally involved in underground activities. Because of that they didn't have jobs, so they had no income. That meant others had to raise support money for them. They didn't have identity either, so they didn't have ration cards and others had to share with them. *(Remember Miep and the people who supplied Anne Frank's hidden family and companions.)*

Those who outwardly assisted the Germans were counting on being in good positions when the war ended with Germany victorious. Inspectors were usually Dutch collaborators. As the war proceeded badly for the Germans and the outcome was obvious, those people's behavior (and loyalty) changed accordingly.

I'm sure my parents' biggest fear was for the safety of my brothers. The Germans took the male youth back to Germany to work in their factories. At one point they picked up my younger brother and put him on a truck about to take him away. He was not yet sixteen, and my father was able to drag him off. We kept my older brother hidden during all the years of the occupation. My dad "de-registered" him at school so there was no record of his existence—also no ration cards for him. We had a long, narrow triangle storage cupboard in our house with a little door into a bedroom. Father built a fake wall a few feet in and made a dollhouse for me attached to it. Whenever a *razzia* (house search) took place, I had to sit there and play with the little dolls in order to distract the soldiers. It was a successful ploy to keep them from finding my brother hiding inside. They were always looking for hidden people, fugitives, and refugees, and

1945 fashion. Army clothing—the only thing available for the brothers. Cut-off stockings with knitted-on socks to increase length and replace worn feet. Skirt made out of an old coat; sweater re-knitted out of two used sweaters.

articles that were forbidden to be in our possession.

On one occasion, two German soldiers came into our house on a razzia. One was an older man, mean, coarse, barking orders—the other young and well-mannered. The latter asked my mother if he could please take a little nap instead of searching the upper floor, while his superior was doing the job downstairs. He very carefully laid down, leaving his boots dangling in order not to dirty the bed covers. Even at my age it made me realize how insane war is; the far majority of people don't want any part of it.

The occupiers confiscated whatever they considered valuable, subversive, or could be used for their war effort: books, silver, radios, things made of copper, bicycles, etc. There were no tires for bikes anyway; garden hose substituted for tires. We were allowed to keep only two blankets per bed. We were supposed to turn in all forbidden things, but we hid what we could in the chimney. There was nothing to burn in the fireplace anyway.

We lived in one room to keep warm. We picked up our assignments at school to do at home because the school was cold. There was no electricity. My mother cooked on a stove made from a paint can, commonly called a "vagabond stove." We had gas for a while for lamps and also used flashlights. We ran out of candles. We used a stationary bicycle set up to run our tiny generator by pedaling. By 1944, shortages were severe. In addition to

Engberdine's wartime, childhood home. The front of the house shows the steep roof. Draw a line straight up starting at the floor line of the second story; a small triangle will appear—storage space where Engberdine's brother was hidden during the war.

197

fuel, things like shoes were impossible to get. This was a problem for growing kids; one boy was seen wearing his mother's high heeled shoes.

Farmers had quotas, but they would sell what they could to neighbors and keep some grain and vegetables for their own use. They occasionally slaughtered at night. Somebody took a bunch of chickens off to hide on a small strip of meadow that no one knew whom it belonged to, but they found their way back! The farmer had to play dumb about where all those chickens came from. Next time he put them in sacks.

One day a neighbor was cooking a rabbit in a frying pan. Somehow our cat got that rabbit and brought it home. It presented a huge ethical choice for my parents. Not only did our hungry family enjoy the neighbors' dinner (which we shared with the cat), we had to listen to them cry about the loss of theirs.

The south, at Arnhem, was liberated first, in September of 1944; we in the north were liberated later. What followed was called "Hunger Winter." Not all four years of the occupation were bad. It was a process of increasing hardship with the worst situation during the Hunger Winter. When the American GIs came onto the scene, they were mortified at what our people were eating as unfit, and they replaced it with some good soup of their own, which resulted in severe digestive problems, even death.

This happened frequently when well-meaning, liberating GIs shared rations with starving people, whose diminished digestive systems reacted strongly and very seriously in some cases.

I came to the U.S. to Maine as an *au pair* in 1954 and returned to the Netherlands in 1955. I was eager to come back to America again, worked at the Dutch Embassy in Washington, D.C.; then I lived in New York City, Indiana, New Mexico, and Colorado, and I am proud that I have been in all fifty States

Following is a charming account Engberdine wrote previously to describe her experience being sent to the farm of family friends in December of 1944, when she was ten years old.

GOING TO THE FARM

On a cold day the day after Christmas, my father and I walked through the slush of melting snow from my town Hilversum to the next town, about 10 kilometers. There we met Gwen, the daughter of one of our acquaintances. Both of us were to travel to her grandmother's house in Amsterdam and from grandmother's house I would continue to the farm of the Bakkers in the province of Noord-Holland. I knew the Bakker family; I had been there before to "fatten up a bit" during summer vaca-

Farmer Bakker's house and grounds called "De Kreil"

tions. They were always kind enough to take me in without any ration coupons.

Before my father accepted a neighbor's offer to arrange for a ride by car, he made sure (he thought) that no NSB (National Socialist Party) were involved in this deal. Only they and "essential" persons (doctors, for example) were allowed to have cars.

Father, Gwen, and I waited nervously for the car to arrive. My father was concerned that he could not make it home again on his bicycle before curfew time. At last a black car arrived, and off Gwen and I went to Amsterdam. It was difficult to say goodbye to Father; I did not know when I would see him again.

Gwen's grandmother's house was a large mansion on one of the canals. We were led to the dining room by the maid. I'll never forget that room, with its high ceiling and the candles in silver holders on the table, and all that food! It seemed that endless bowls were heaping full of different vegetables, potatoes, even meat and gravy. And the smells, real smells of well-prepared dishes. Grandmother sat at the head of the table, presiding over a dinner party for German officers—well dressed and well fed. She wore several strings of beads that dangled upon her grey silk blouse. With authority she dismissed me. I could not stay and was whisked away to meet a man who took me on his bicycle to an apartment house in a different part of the city. I was dropped off at a flat *vier hoog achter* on the fourth floor in the back—accommodations for lower class people. I had no idea who the woman and her daughters were; maybe she was the cleaning lady of the grandmother?

Having fun at the farm

I expected to continue my trip the next day. That was, however, not the case. How long was I to stay here? And why? I could have stayed at home and be hungry! The two daughters stole my few salted licorice pieces that my aunt had given me. Never have I been so homesick and miserable. The mother, I believe, eager to have me leave, decided to have her older girl walk with me back to Grandmother's house to inquire when I could continue my trip. It was about a half-hour walk over slushy streets against the wind. We rang the bell, were not asked in, but had to wait outside for an answer. The maid conveyed that Grandmother had no answer for us. The door closed and we troddled back again to the "vier hoog achter."

I believe it was two days later, again in the evening, that yet another unknown man came to fetch me with his bicycle. We rode at least half an hour to a cellar under some large house. I knew that one of the tricks of the Germans was to interrogate the youngest member of a family in order to obtain information. They assumed that a child did not know what was important not to tell. I was sure that that was going to happen in that cellar. But no, I was put into another black car and we left. When the car stopped, it was not at the farm, but at the mayor's house of a little town on the way. It was late in the evening, after curfew time of 8 o'clock. There was still some food on the table, even some meat. That fact frightened me. It meant that I was with friends of the Germans, not with friends of mine. And sure enough, the questions came: "How old is your father?" "Do you have brothers?" "How old are your brothers?" etc. As I never talked much and had the habit of putting my tongue in my cheek, it was not unusual for me to just not answer. They gave up and let me go to bed. Another scary experience—I had to sleep with Auntie, something I surely was not used to—sleeping with a stranger in one bed.

In the middle of the night, of course, I had to go to the bathroom. Panic. Where was that place? All was pitch-dark. I remember sliding out of the tall bed and shuffling along the corridor counting doors on the left. I thought the third one was the bathroom. However, it was the master bedroom, and I had awakened the mayor. I am sure I must have left a puddle on the floor, but cannot remember what happened. I cannot remember anything until the next morning, when the questions started again.

In the afternoon I was left alone. I heard loud voices in the office, harsh shouting, and all in German, which frightened me as to what might happen next. But all quieted down and we had a sandwich for supper, made with real bread!

Then suddenly I was told to get my belongings. Yet another black car appeared, after curfew, with all the window shades pulled down. I was told to get in. Now, I was sure bad things would take place. But the driver was a nice man. After a while I peeked around the window shade and recognized the canal close to the farm. We stopped and asked directions at Floris's house. I knew Floris!! Down the driveway we rode to the farm. I jumped out of the car and ran the last stretch. Lief, the farmer's daughter, answered the door, squeezing the *knijpkat*—a hand dynamo flashlight—in the face of the driver. I had no time to wait for their conversation and slipped past Lief into the house.

Why I was taken to the farm safely after all and who all were involved in getting me there, I shall never know. I only know that at last I had arrived. It took about a week to make that hour-and-a-half auto trip!

Renate G. Justin

"My father is arrested, handcuffed, and shoved out the door to the truck waiting on the street."

———————————●———————————

Renate Justin is a retired family physician who has published numerous essays both for the professional and lay press. Her topics include reflections on the practice of medicine and her experiences as a child in Nazi Germany.

COURAGE AND THE UNANSWERED QUESTION

November 10th, 1938, *Kristallnacht,* flames engulf the synagogues in every city in Germany. Late that night Nazis burst into the apartment to which my parents fled after their house and factory were confiscated. The invaders, systematically, throw everything they can lift out the windows to hear it shatter on the pavement below. Things that do not break are quickly appropriated by the citizens that congregate on the sidewalk. My father is arrested, handcuffed, and shoved out the door to the truck waiting on the street. Many Jewish men, in pajamas, are already loaded into the open truck bed. Only the warmth of the tightly squeezed, adjacent bodies, keeps them from freezing in the cold November night. They are on their way to concentration camp.

Moments after the Nazis leave my parents' room, my mother hears loud cries emanating from the apartment below hers. She rushes down the stairs to her neighbors, two elderly sisters, who have for many years taken care of their younger brother, a man who has never developed mentally, but responds to the love and compassion he receives from his sisters. The Nazis have broken into their apartment also, and are shouting at the man: *"Bande hoch!"* (hands over your head). He does not understand their command, and when his sister tries to show him what to do, one of the Nazis strikes her. Then they start to beat the retarded man with their batons. The more he cries out the more furiously the blows reign on him until he lies still on the floor. They leave him there, dead, in front of his horrified sisters. Systematically they continue to empty the apartment of all that is movable.

My mother, looking out the broken window, sees the truck with her husband and men from the small town's congregation, pull off to the next house. In spite of the horror of what has just occurred, she has the presence of mind to call my father's sister, who lives in another town. She tells her, "I have a terrible toothache, my cheek is swollen, and I have a fever. Nothing is helping the pain. If I could, I would just run away." My aunt understands the message.

My mother is not a person who would call her late at night about a toothache! She tells her husband, my uncle, to immediately go into hiding, 'to run away'. When the Nazis come to my uncle's house my aunt tells them that her husband is on a business trip. They ransack her house, but do not find him. He later is spirited into Holland and then England and thus escapes concentration camp.

My mother's sister, whom she also calls, is not at home to receive the warning. The Nazis are waiting for her and her husband when they return. They are both deported to concentration camp and killed in the gas chamber.

My mother stays with her neighbors, the two sisters, and the three women set up housekeeping in their windowless kitchen. It is warmer than the other rooms with the broken window panes. They notice that some blankets fell into a big, muddy puddle below the bedroom window when they were tossed out. No one has claimed these blankets, and so, stealthily, they go outside, retrieve and dry them, then use them to sleep on and to keep warm. The sisters take comfort in the fact that at least their brother does not have to suffer starvation and prolonged torture, although the horror of having to watch him being beaten to death leaves them sleepless and distraught.

The three women try to guess to which camp the men might have been sent; they talk about the unlikely possibility of communicating with them. My mother sends a typed postcard to each of her three young daughters, who attend a school for refugee children in Holland: 'Dad has gone on a long business trip. He is working hard and won't have time to write.' Being one of the recipients of that card I am puzzled by the atypical message. The postcard is not, as usual, written with pen and ink and it is not signed: *'In Liebe und mit Küssen, Mutti'* (with love and kisses, Mommy). Also, if my father is on a business trip to London or Paris, why is he not sending us picture postcards, as is his habit? I take the card to my teacher who gently explains to me what is happening in Germany and that my mother's postcard is giving me the devastating news that my father is incommunicado because he is in Buchenwald concentration camp, not because he is on a business trip. She explains that my mother lied, made up the business trip, for reasons of her own safety and to let us know why we will not hear from our father. At that moment I have to go to class, and the import of the true meaning of the postcard does not penetrate. Later during the day the headmaster of the school calls an assembly and tells the students and faculty about the terrible news from Germany. That evening, when I crawl under my blanket and cry bitterly, my roommates as well as many of the other children at school know why I am crying. Many have received postcards that do not tell the truth.

My parents still own a car, which friends are hiding in an empty barn. Jews are not supposed to drive or possess a car. Disregarding this edict my mother conceives a dare-devil scheme. She takes the car late one afternoon and drives to Hanover. On the way she is stopped by Nazi patrols. "Where are you going? Open your trunk." They search for men who might be hiding. My mother tells them that she is not concealing any men, but that she has an appointment with the *Obergauleiter* (top Nazi of the district), and hopes they will not delay her and make her late. She jokes with them and offers them a ride. She drives on with two Nazi patrols in her car, which protects her from further inspections. She is not stopped again; she arrives at her destination. Her passengers speak briefly with the guards at the office of the *Obergauleiter* and she gains entrance.

My mother, a very beautiful, striking woman, tall, erect, with dark eyes and refined features, leads the guards to suspect that she has private business with their superior. They are afraid to inquire too carefully into the purpose of her visit, in case it would lead to embarrassing revelations.

With great audacity my mother knocks on the door of the district's top Nazi officer. She opens the door, luck is with her, he is alone in his office. He is surprised, looks her up and down, and motions to her to sit down.

"GutenAbend, gnadige Frau." (Good evening, gracious lady). They exchange some pleasantries and then the *Obergauleiter* asks, "What brings you here?"

"I would like my husband released from concentration camp."

"Why was he sent there?"

"Because he is Jewish."

"Surely , you are not Jewish, lovely lady?"

"Yes, I am, but that has nothing to do with my request."

The officer takes down my father's name, address, and birth date, and then stands up, signaling that it is time for my mother to leave. He gives her no indication whether or not he will pursue the matter. On the way out she turns back to him and gives him the name of one friend, whom she recognized in the truck, and requests his release also. She then wishes the officer and his guards a good evening and drives home. Her whole body starts to shake violently as fear and apprehension seize her. Would she and her house-mates be next on the list of deportees? Would her husband be killed rather than released because of her visit?

When she arrives home she again hides the car and quietly enters the apartment to share her story with the two elderly sisters. They shake their heads in disbelief at my mother's brazen bravery.

Nothing happens for many days. One evening late, about three months after the Kristallnacht, the telephone in the entrance hall of the apartment house rings. A quavering voice, which my mother immediately recognizes as that of my father, asks,

"Can you come pick us up?" They quickly decide the safest place for the two men, my father and his friend, to wait for my mother is in the public men's room. Hopefully they will escape notice there with their shaven heads and tattoos which they acquired in concentration camp. My mother again risks taking the car out of hiding to fetch the two men. They are emaciated, dirty, thirsty, louse infested, but alive! She takes them home. They hide, and with the help of members of the Dutch underground, escape into Holland.

A few of the men from the congregation, arrested that fateful night of November 10th were released, many perished. Why were my father and his friend not murdered? My parents never found out, even after the war ended. They speculated that a former neighbor of theirs, who had risen quickly in the ranks of the Nazi party, may have arranged the release, and that it was unrelated to my mother's visit to Hanover. My parents always had questioned this friend's whole-hearted devotion to the Nazi cause. It could have been chance, on the other hand, it could have been my mother's courage and daring which impressed the *Obergauleiter* and caused him to issue the command to spare the lives of the two men.

The motherless Bechtholdt children—Jacob at left, Amelia, Philip, with their father George. The photo was taken in Windsor before the family returned to Russia in 1917.

Jacob & Marie Bechthold

"When I wash dishes, I am reminded that there was food to eat."

————————— ● —————————

When I began this project in 2004, as I searched for subjects, people told me I was ten years too late, which I found to be true in several cases. There was no lack of names to contact but many other relevant folks have left us, and some no longer have clear recollections of those hard times. Their stories could have enlightened and educated us further, but they have been lost, never to be included in the vast literature of wartime.

Jacob and Marie Bechthold lived in Windsor from 1952, Jacob often bantering with other WWII vets at the Windsor Senior Center. By the time I interviewed them, they were in their nineties, still very sharp, and living independently in their own home. Unfortunately, before I finished, they both passed on—Jacob in 2005 and Marie in 2007. They were married for sixty-eight years. The essay that follows is presented in rather sketchy form based on those interviews, augmented a bit and clarified by their children Lore, Bruno, and Edeltraut. "Ethel," as she is known to her family and friends, is a retired Greeley fifth grade teacher. She was too young when the family left Germany to remember the details firsthand, but she recounts from hearing stories around the supper table and at family gatherings.

The drama of Jacob and Marie's story is the stuff of which novels and Oscar-winning movies are made. In reading it, we are reminded how the struggle just to survive was often daily fare for all our forebears. Tragedy pummeled those people; spouses, parents, and children died, children were orphaned and sometimes left to fend for themselves. Illness and crippling diseases that today are just words in the dictionary stalked families of all classes. In the end, those who were able risked everything to bring their skills, their dreams, and optimism to the land of opportunity, half a world away across a vast ocean.

Nineteen fifty-two was not the first time Jacob had been to Windsor. Nor was

Jacob and Marie's wedding party in 1937, full of optimism for the future, unaware of what lay before them in just a few years

Germany technically his native country. He was the descendant of a group of Germans who were persuaded to relocate in Russia during the time of Catherine the Great. She was a German princess married into Russian nobility. Catherine encouraged her countrymen to come to Russia by offering them exemption from military service, religious freedom, and land to farm. The long history of the Germans from Russia or "Volga Deutsch," as they are known locally, is a saga of hard work, disappointment, and ultimate success and prosperity, which has been amply recorded elsewhere.

By the end of the nineteenth century, conditions for their descendants were becoming increasingly intolerable, and many left Russia to seek a better future—in America. The eastern plains of Colorado as well as other High Plains states received many of those immigrants. Great Western Sugar Co. even went to Russia and recruited, before Hispanic workers came to do their work. Those Russian Germans came as stoop laborers in the beet fields, but their typical German diligence and industry were rewarded subsequently by land ownership and prosperity. There are many Germans from Russia in the Windsor area, and as diversified as they are vocationally and socially, they still retain some cohesiveness through a Germans from Russia Society.

Jacob Bechthold was born in Russia in 1912 and brought to Windsor by his par-

ents as an infant. *The family included five other children. Jacob's father worked in the beet fields, fixed shoes and harnesses, and worked in a factory during wintertime. After Jacob's mother died, his father returned to Russia in 1917 with three of the children, including Jacob. (A woman there had invited him to return and marry her!) The other children, who balked at returning to Russia, remained in Windsor with relatives. These included Jacob's older married sister, Katie, and two older brothers, George and William.*

Jacob's father died around 1920, and eight-year-old Jacob was left in the care of an uncle. The following year, the three orphaned siblings decided to return to America. Jacob's sister became ill and died before they left, but Jacob and his brother set off for Minsk, where there were crowds of other refugees. Half of those people died, including Jacob's brother, of cholera, typhus, or starvation.

There were hundreds of orphaned children in Minsk The International Red Cross came to their rescue and took the children to Germany to a camp near the Polish border, where they stayed for six months. It was actually an old prison, set up to provide temporary shelter, food, and basic needs for its young occupants. Jacob went to school for the first time, but the children also worked, herding cows. To stress the anonymity of the children's status, Jacob recalled that birthdays and ages were assigned if they weren't known. Several dozen children could be given the same birthday. Some birthday party!

Through inquiry via the Red Cross, the Windsor relatives were able to locate Jacob at the camp.

Then Jacob was adopted—rather, taken in as an indentured person—by a family in Oberbauershaft. He described how he was pushing a wheelbarrow by the time

Jacob as a driver in the Luftwaffe, with one of his vehicles

Jacob and wartime buddies

he was ten, carrying gravel, mud, and bricks for workers building a house. This unhealthy exposure led to permanent lung damage. By fourteen he was a "hired man." Marie grew up in this same community and knew Jacob's foster family. She describes them as "nasty" people. The exploitation of children in crisis taken in by a seemingly charitable act, is not uncommon in the history of such adoptions. The Orphan Train in America during the Depression and Kindertransport to England in WWII sometimes resulted in such exploitive practices.

We leave Jacob's story now to bring Marie into the picture. Marie's memories of her early years describe hardships unfamiliar to most present-day American readers. After a comfortable life in America, she looks back and marvels at how they survived under such deprivation.

Like Jacob, Marie was born in 1912, in Oberbauerschaft, the tenth of twelve children. Her family was very poor; they were lucky when they had enough to eat. There was little in the way of toys; a ball would be homemade of rags, never a purchased rubber ball. Marie describes how three siblings slept in one bed, four beds in one room. Her father was a field worker on a German farm. Marie's parents were German, not Germans from Russia as Jacob's had been. They attended the local Lutheran church regularly. The Lutheran church in Germany at that time was the official state religion, controlled and regulated by the government. Even the pastor was paid by the government.

Mama worked hard . . . a gross understatement. Mealtime tables were meagerly supplied, and doing laundry for fourteen was yet another labor-intensive chore. Water had to be hauled and heated, clothes wrung by hand.

Her hands would be red for several days before she needed to start again. People didn't throw their clothes into the laundry every day, nor did they bathe regularly. Sometimes a tub of bath water served more than one bather. Bed linen wasn't changed often either. Laundry was hung outdoors and froze in winter.

Marie liked school and was especially good at math. But at fourteen after finishing the eighth grade, it was expected she would quit school and go to work. She worked in a cigar factory and contributed her earnings to the family's modest resources.

The couple married in 1937, and Jacob went off to war in 1940, leaving Marie with two young children—Lore, a toddler, and baby Bruno.

Jacob's role in the German Luftwaffe was as a driver/chauffeur. To receive his license to drive and such an assignment was a special distinction, providing experience and credentials which were to serve him well in later years. His first deploy-

ment was to Russia, and Marie saw him only once or twice during the following four and a half years. On one of his rare home leaves, little Bruno asked his mother, "When is Uncle going to leave?"

Wartime only made things worse. Although Jacob wasn't a combat soldier in the trenches, she worried about him constantly. She knew little of his whereabouts at any given time. Months would pass between letters. Three of Marie's brothers were in the service; only one returned. Many friends, neighbors, and relatives lost loved ones.

Death was all around, *Marie remembers.*

Shortages were acute and widespread. Fortunately, Marie's parents lived with her during Jacob's absence, but they were too feeble to help with many chores or to garden. The children were too young to help so it all fell to Marie. She grew vegetables and raised chickens. However, all the bounty didn't go into the pot. A government agent tallied the chickens and gave her a quota of eggs that had to be turned over. That eliminated the option of cooking a chicken for the family to eat. Instead of meat, she bought bones from the butcher to make soup. Sometimes a meal was not more than home-grown potatoes cooked in water.

When word got around that the baker had bread, a line formed, but by the time an individual shopper got to the counter the bread would be gone. She would have to return to the bakery in the afternoon to go through the process again, perhaps successfully if she were lucky, perhaps not.

We usually weren't hungry; I guess we had enough food but there was not much variety. No bananas or oranges or anything that had to be imported. Wheat was in short supply because it had to come from Russia. Beef was so expensive and then unavailable, because we didn't raise our own.

Jacob recalls, There was no gas for civilians; in the army we burned wood for fuel for trucks and cars. A box was attached to the right side of a truck. The box had a hole in top through which small pieces of wood were fed. Wood had to be from specific deciduous trees, like oak, birch, and apple. Conifers had too much tar. Kindling came from good-sized branches; small twigs burned too fast.

Bombing raids created additional stress. Allied bombers would fly over the village on their way to other targets. On one occasion, a bomb was dropped nearby, perhaps accidentally, terrifying little Bruno, who came screaming to his mother's comforting arms.

It was terrible. Many nights with those two kids . . . one bomb hit close . . . the noise was terrible. The children were so scared, and they cried. I got them dressed; we had to get out of there into the basement. It was dangerous to be there too. We could have been buried down there. They were just bombing houses; in Oberbauerschaft there were no factories until a few miles away. Bruno would grab me around the legs and cry when the bombing started close to our place. "Momma, let's go in the house. Make it stop." Ach, war is a terrible thing. My brother had three kids, and one day he was gone. My sister's husband—one morning they got the notice; he was gone—killed.

Schools continued to operate; the kids had to go to school. They tried to keep things normal. Lore and Bruno were too young to be in the Hitler Youth. While Jacob was gone, we celebrated Christmas the best we could. The kids got one orange and one cookie. There wasn't anything else, no place to buy anything and nothing to buy. We didn't have Christmas stockings like American kids do. We went to church of course; it was close, and we could walk there.

The ultimate question—I always tread lightly when speaking to Germans who lived during that era. "When did you realize that Germany was going to lose the war?"

From the beginning. We could talk to our parents, but not to our neighbors. Nobody talked about it openly.

Despite the supremacy Germany showed over its European neighbors and the late entry of the U.S. into the war, it was a general opinion that the war was going to bring Germany to destruction. Marie was not timid in her condemnation of Adolf Hitler. She spoke the word she had used to describe Jacob's foster family, the one that apparently is as strong as she will express to articulate her contempt for something and remain a lady—"NASTY!!"

At the end of the war there was nothing left: no cities, no food, no housing, no jobs, no railroads, no gas. And we were so afraid of being taken over by the Russians.

Asked how she felt about the war ending, she replied,

Relieved, I can tell you. During the war you had always to be afraid. They announced it over the radio. But now, how would Jacob get home? They walked mostly, the railroads were a mess, no cars because there was no gas, no bikes. One week after, a friend said, "Your husband is alive and he is coming." And we waited. Another week or two—he came, ja.

Now we had to think about how do we get some money? That he gets a job. Ach,

Safely in Windsor---Lore, Bruno, Marie, Ethel, and Jacob

that was a terrible time. But Jacob was lucky; he was a truck driver during the war. When he was home a while, he found a job that was close. He delivered coal. We were in the British zone, lucky not to be in the Russian zone.

Nevertheless, the Bechtholds began looking west to emigrate to America, specifically to Windsor, Colorado. A local pastor, Fred Heidl, was himself a German-speaking immigrant. He did much to help the fifteen to twenty immigrant families who came to Windsor after the war. Local farmers sponsored German families because they needed help in the beet fields. Churches sponsored families too. The commitment by these supporting groups was considerable. For five years the sponsor was responsible for law-abiding behavior as well as financial obligations. If the arrangement didn't work out, the immigrants were shipped back to Germany, and that apparently did happen. Since Jacob's sister was a local citizen, sponsorship was no problem for Jacob and Marie.

The decision to leave Germany was not an easy one. Some of their friends were supportive, perhaps envious; others were not. Marie's parents had died; otherwise the Bechtholds wouldn't have left. Jacob's brother in-law, husband of sister Katie who remained in Windsor in 1917 after the family returned to Russia, arranged for a friend to meet the family at the dock in New York. The crossing had taken nine days, and one can imagine the apprehension as well as fatigue and confusion that accompanied their arrival. The greeter was not entirely sober, but a man who accompanied him was helpful in retrieving baggage and getting the family from the dock to the train station.

None of the arriving Bechtholds spoke English, and their challenges were not over. After missing the train to Denver, they had to stay overnight in the terminal until the next train arrived. Then when the train pulled in at LaSalle, ten miles east of Windsor, Katie's husband wasn't there. Fortunately, a friend of his knew of the family's impending arrival and recognized them, which probably wasn't difficult to do. They likely looked pretty scruffy at that point, bewildered, and unable to communicate because of the language barrier. This man looked after them until they were picked up.

They brought little with them to America. When they arrived in Windsor, they settled into a rented house on Bill Miller's farm near Windsor—a house that formerly housed migrant workers. Jacob had five dollars in his pocket and a debt of $1200 to cover their transportation expenses to Colorado. The children enrolled immediately in local schools. Lore was thirteen, Bruno ten, and Edeltraut three. When Bruno came home from school the first day, he said the teacher had given him a book to read, which of course he couldn't read.

Jacob secured a job at the local grain elevator, although he spoke no English. Marie did house-cleaning. A local pastor tutored them in English, but the children picked it up quickly at school, as children do. The first weeks were difficult emotionally. The girls cried, Marie cried, and they all were homesick. Marie's difficulty was intensified because the children were unhappy.

Every morning little Edeltraut said, "Momma, let's go home in a house with the trees." Then Momma started to cry too. Ja, there were times when we were sorry we made that move. Jake didn't let on how he felt. But today the kids say always "Thank you, we are glad you brought us here."

Once they all settled in, and they did soon after, Marie adjusted to her situation and realized it was the best thing for them to have left Germany. But there was guilt over what they had done to take the children away from "home," where they were so comfortable. They were too young to be much aware of the hardships and insecurity the grownups were experiencing in post-war Germany.

They were just happy the bombing was over.

Jacob, however, never forgot those perilous wartimes and how much better life was for the family in Colorado. When repeatedly urged to install a dishwasher, he would reply,

"When I'm washing dishes, it is a reminder that there was food to eat."

In 1992, when Marie and Jacob were eighty years old, Lore and Ethel took them back "home" to Germany for a visit. It was to be for the last time.

Jacob and Marie in 2004

1948

M and S with son John before leaving the old country for America

M & S

"Back country roads were the chosen route, in order to avoid cities that could be the target of Allied bombing."

———————●———————

M and S illustrate again how there are important things we don't always know about our friends and acquaintances. M and S have been sitting behind me every Sunday for several years at Faith United Church of Christ in Windsor. Each week we "pass the peace," accompanied by a handshake and/or a hug, as we do with all our pew neighbors. Their East European accents are unmistakable, but nary a clue what was behind their presence in our town. Of course it would have been presumptuous to ask. Because of their senior citizen status, I suspected there was a possibility they had been in Europe during the war and would have a story to tell. Initially M was a reluctant chronicler, noting that he lost his three brothers in wartime military service, and it was too painful to talk about such grim times.

We are fortunate M and S consented to share their memories, although anonymously.

As there are no direct quotes, the text appears in normal typeface.

The story begins in Transylvania, a part of the old Austro-Hungarian Empire that later became alternately part of Hungary and/or part of Romania. World War I changed the boundaries and names of several East European countries when the Austro-Hungarian Empire was dissolved as a political entity. Pre-1940 Transylvania was attached to Romania, later divided between Hungary and Romania by a straight line from east to west that bisected Transylvania. Many towns found themselves split between the two countries. After WWII, the area came under Soviet domination as part of the Communist Bloc, and all of Transylvania is Romanian since 1945.

For several centuries, until after WWII, a large population of ethnic Germans inhabited the area, hence its very Lutheran orientation, and children were educated in parochial schools. Presently the area has lost its German character, as few ethnic Germans remain. There were few Jews in pre-war Transylvania. They lived mostly in urban areas, earning their living as merchants. S remembers a kindly, elderly Jewish gentleman who had a candy store in her village and was very kind to and generous with the neighborhood children.

Most of us don't know much about Transylvania except as the homeland of Count Dracula and for its natural beauty stemming from its setting in the Carpathian Mountains. Centuries-old churches of stunning style and architectural distinction can be seen throughout the area. Given the numbers of armed conflicts that have criss-crossed the area throughout the ages, it is remarkable that so much remains intact.

It is an area that has managed to retain much of its traditional East European flavor. Vintage photos of S show elaborate costuming with intricate hand embroidered decoration. Family heirlooms possess the same exquisite treatment of ordinary household items, a characteristic common to traditional folk cultures. At the same time, on a recent trip back to Romania, M and S were surprised and even shocked to see horse-drawn wagons still in common use. Lack of the postwar modernization other countries of Western Europe experienced can be attributed to being under Russian control for so many years.

Fortunately the area was not besieged during WWII, although German troops marched through on their retreat from Russia. The Ploesti oilfields were a more stra-tegic target for Allied bombing raids, but they were a safe hundred-plus miles to the south.

Born in 1922, S was the only child of a couple who lived in Treppen, a small town in the north, near the Russian border. Her father was a farmer. People who worked the land commonly lived in a nearby village. Unmarried during the war, S lived with her parents and worked on her father's farm. The family was German by heritage, speaking a German dialect and also high German. (High German was spoken in church; a lower form spoken by villagers at home.) Romanische, a Romance language deriving from Latin, was the official language of the area.

In September, 1944, it became apparent that to avoid approaching Russian troops, S's family and other members of the community and surrounding areas needed to evacuate to safety somewhere farther west. They had the luxury of a week's prepara-tion, unlike many other refugees elsewhere across Europe. A wagon pulled by two horses was loaded with what necessities the family could carry—food for the horses, their own nourishment, a few extra clothes, and bedding. No one knew how long they would be in flight. Neighbors and other members of the community joined the exodus caravan. Back country roads were the chosen route, in order to avoid cities that could be the target of Allied bombing. The men of the group slept under their wagons; women and children slept in the wagon bed with a tarp-like covering to protect them from the weather. Many of their days on the road were cold and rainy.

The journey was naturally stressful, and fear that the Russians were closing in on them added to their anxiety. Crowds of refugees were on the roads, all headed south and west to an undetermined destination that would assure their security until the end of the war. Initially S's family headed in the direction of Budapest, although that city was not intended to be their final refuge. The journey through Hungary was made easier by S's father's knowledge of the Hungarian language. He had served in the Hungarian army during WWI.

Their meager supplies were occasionally supplemented by food provided by villagers and farmers along the way, and water was sometimes available from local wells. Otherwise, they had to depend on rain to supply them with fresh water. They picked the countryside clean of any wood they could burn. There was intermittent Allied bombing, but it was restricted to more strategic targets, in the cities. German soldiers were prevalent, but as they were not adversaries, they were not hostile or threatening to the refugees.

Although Romanians disliked these German intruders, Romania was not subjugated as an "occupied" country as were for example, Poland, Holland, France, Norway, etc. Unless, of course, you were Jewish. Hungary and Romania actually fought side by side with the Germans against the Russians. East Europe traditionally feared, disliked, and distrusted Russia and understood clearly the consequences of a Russian victory. It didn't take long for their fears to become reality. Every account of Russian occupation of the Eastern populations beginning in 1944 is one of depravity, pillage, and brutality.

Thus the refugees were able to plod along, making twenty to thirty kilometers a day. After traveling for two months, from September 20 to the end of November, they finally were able to stop in the area of upper Austria called Karnten in a small town between Linz and Salzburg (Hitler's birthplace at Braunau is nearby). There Austrian authorities were able to billet the refugees in private homes, mostly with farmers who exchanged their lodging for work on the premises. Food was provided by vouchers, like ration coupons. S's family didn't have to work for their hosts. They stayed with a family consisting of a brother and two sisters who had a small plot and didn't need additional help.

When American forces moved in in 1945, a camp for the refugees was developed nearby at Voklabruk, which provided shelter, food, and security. Four thousand refugees occupied that camp. S. describes it as a former tire factory. (In other locations, some Displaced Persons refuges were located in cleaned-up former concentration camps.) While the Americans were in charge of Voklabruk, conditions were satisfactory, but after they left and Austrian authorities took over, the environment worsened. Notable deficiencies were the result of authorities stealing supplies intended for the refugees. Truckloads disappeared, likely for resale on the black market. S's family lived there for the next eight years. She found employment at a plant nursery nearby.

In December, 1944, S's father was hospitalized in a nearby town, with pneumonia and pleurisy. While he was there, the hospital was bombed and patients were evacuated to another site. Conditions were critical that winter as the war was drawing to a close and Germany was falling to its knees. Among the shortages, there was no medicine. S's father died the following August in the hospital. He was buried close by, but the grave has since been removed and destroyed.

During the stay in Austria, S enrolled in a nurse's aid training program and worked in the camp hospital, a former Catholic school operated by nuns.

In the meantime, M was serving in the Romanian army. His family came from Rode, in the Romanian sector of Transylvania. After the end of the war and M had returned, they too evacuated, fearing Russian troops threatening to occupy the area. Some of the townspeople stayed, while others fled. The family at that time consisted of M's parents and one daughter who had four children. The four sons served in the military, but M, the second youngest, was the only one to survive. M became separated from the family during this evacuation.

After walking thirty kilometers, the group of assembled refugees were put onto a train going to Austria, which also stopped in Karnten. M didn't know where his family was at this point. He worked for a farmer and began to look for his family. He found them living in ground bunkers in the American zone. Later the family moved to the Voklabruk camp, where M met S on Christmas Eve, 1945. They were married four weeks later, on January 24, 1946. Son John arrived the following year.

The World Council of Churches was hard at work across postwar Europe assisting in the enormous challenge of resettling thousands of displaced persons. Volunteers from America assisted as liaisons between local governments, the military occupation forces, refugees, and the sponsoring agencies in the U.S. In 1952 the opportunity came for M, S, and five-year-old John to emigrate to America. S's mother returned to Treppen.

The conditions that enabled this move to America involved a contract for one year which provided housing and wages, but no food allowance. Steamship passage was paid for by the church, and each adult traveler was given $29 cash.

When M and S arrived in New York in April of 1952, they had no idea where their final destination would be. The World Council of Churches was active in the U.S. as well, finding sponsors for the thousands of Europeans who came to America. Colorado wasn't selected by M and S; they were assigned to it. When they arrived at LaSalle, near Greeley, the same station that received Marie and Jacob Bechthold a few months earlier, they were greeted by a rotund, smiling man wearing a big hat and holding up a sign listing a number of immigrant families whose arrival was expected on that trip.

That gentleman was Hugo Becker, pastor of what was then the German Congregational Church in Windsor. He would become a guardian angel for the immigrants. He spoke German and tutored the German arrivals, as well as M and S, who knew no English. This was very important assistance to all the immigrants during their adjustment to productive life in the US.

S's mother immigrated to America in 1965. Visas were not issued automatically, and the Colorado senator at the time, Peter Dominick, had to intervene, similar to Elsie Streeb's situation in 1952.

ALLIED FORCE HEADQUARTERS
Office of the Commander-in-Chief

27 December, 1943.

Dear Pastor Becker:

I deeply appreciate your message to the
armed forces. I earnestly believe in the
power of prayer and it is most encouraging
to receive a message such as yours.

Sincerely,

Dwight D. Eisenhower

Pastor H. Becker
N. E. 7th and Stanton St.
Portland 12
Oregon

**Thank you note from General
Dwight Eisenhower, a prized
family momento and tribute
to Pastor Becker**

Office of the Commander-in-Chief

Pastor H. Becker
N. E. 7th and Stanton St.
Portland 12
Oregon

Pastor Hugo Becker

"He must have felt a calling to help alleviate the chaos of postwar displacement by using his skill with the German language as well as his natural compassion as a man of the cloth."

There is an additional dimension to the experiences of civilians affected by the war. We must not overlook the unsung individuals and agencies that impacted the people who were directly impacted, like those we have been describing. Pastor Hugo Becker of Windsor is one of those who contributed to the postwar care and well-being of what were known as "DPs" or Displaced Persons. His work began in Europe before he came to Windsor.

The Becker family lived in Portland, Oregon, where Pastor Becker led his own church. He was German-born, from Frankfurt. He must have felt a calling to help alleviate the chaos of postwar displacement by using his skill with the German language as well as his natural compassion as a man of the cloth. After Christmas in 1945, he was granted a two-year leave of absence from his Portland church to go to Europe under the auspices of the World Council of Churches to work in various DP camps. These were scattered all over Europe, largely in the Eastern countries. The International Refugee Organization worked under the broader authority of the WCC, and it was with the IRO that he operated. The YMCA/YWCA was also significantly involved in addressing the needs of millions of these homeless people from all over the war-ravaged continent. Becker's family doesn't know exactly where he was assigned, but his charges included groups from the Baltic States—Estonians, Latvians, and Lithuanians, plus Poles and other nationalities. He came home to Portland for six months, then was re-assigned to Europe for two more years.

After that last European stint, he felt it wasn't fair to his home congregation to be a part-time, on-again-off-again pastor and he resigned. Windsor, Colorado, was his next calling, and he accepted a position in 1951 as pastor of the German Congregational Church. (That congregation later merged with Zion Evangelical Lutheran to form

Faith United Church of Christ, which exists today.) At that time, he became involved in helping Windsor immigrants like M and S and Marie and Jacob Bechthold. Because of a significant German population around Windsor and the wartime existence of the POW camp between Windsor and Greeley, numbers of immigrant families, including ex-POWs, were welcomed to the area.

Pastor Becker passed away in 1977. He has descendants presently living in Windsor, and his daughter Gerta Rutz provided this information about him.

A copy of this touching letter appears among Pastor Becker's records of his time with the World Council of Churches. He adds, "Here is one of the many letters DP boys and girls have written to the boys and girls in the USA."

"To day I am sending a letter over the Large Ocean to get me an American Friend. I am an Estonian boy, 15 years of age and I am living in North Germany at Oldenburg. We have here several DP camps. These camps are built out of wood, so that we have here only huts and not many stony buildings. In the camps we have a Boy Scout troop in the YMCA. I am a member of the YMCA and a scout. I am attending the third grade of the local Camp High School, and

Sunday School – Latvians
D.P. Camp Dobbenteich Oldenburg.

we are very grateful to the Allied Forces that we may live here.

I was sent with my mother in 1944 to Germany, my father was deported to Siberia. The life in Germany was not easy for us til the Allies occupied Germany. We became again free and may live now again our own life in camps. I hope to go to England, but I do not know when. The life in the camp is dull and not pleasant, but we have no other choise (sic) as long as we are in Germany.

Please be so kind and write soon, because I am very interested to know about your life in America.

Please remember me to your friends and parents, so I remain,

Yours sincerely,

J.J."

Camp life could have indeed been dull for an adolescent boy, but the YMCA report from which Pastor Becker's remarks were taken shows that at least at some locations there were movies, a library, church services and religious education, athletic activi-

Pastor Becker in the center

Divine Service arranged by Estonian and Latvian YMCA in Lübeck, Germany D.P. Camp Artillery Barracks on March 11ᵗʰ 1947

ties including competitions, musical and dramatic presentations, card games, and classes of all kinds—from language courses to sewing and carpentry. There are long itemized lists of leisure time supplies requisitioned for various camps served by the YMCA. Pastor Becker conducted lectures and discussions on American life. The report adds, ". . .Interest is great and the discussions vivid."

A bit of Pastor Becker's personal reminiscing in the report tell us, "In the DP Camp Wehnen, a little room behind the washroom has a YMCA sign on the door. I entered; it was a little workshop where beautiful handiwork is made—cups, chests, toys. I looked over the few tools, nicely placed, chisels, hammers, saws—many of them made by the DPs themselves. But their pride is a lathe just completed. The driving wheel and the stand all made by hand out of wood, but the knife, chisel, and other parts are from a German tank shot down by the Allies. The handle is from a German anti-aircraft gun, the belt from an electricity cable."

Not all camps leave a picture of such ingenuity and vitality. One Yugoslavian worker complained of insufficient food rations and ". . . for recreation we have no

Pastor Becker

books, newspapers, games, playing cards, sport material . . . Our situation is difficult. I may tell that we had not met the right man who has understood us. Your YMCA Unit is our last hope."After all these many years have passed, one wonders whatever may have happened to JJ and to other inmates of camps like his. International and U.S. relief aid made gigantic contributions to the welfare of millions of those disrupted lives. As part of the final victory team in both theaters of war, Americans are remembered for the humane style in which their military occupation of Europe and Japan was carried out.

Stateside

Home Front

by Jean Messinger

———————————— ● ————————————

As a teenager in a small town in southern Wisconsin during World War II, I was barely aware of the horrors the Nazis brought to Germany and to the rest of Europe. Japan and the world it represented could have been on another planet. My small world was entirely WASP—more like WASC, because the area was largely Roman Catholic. If it hadn't been for the war and its accompanying Holocaust, I wouldn't have noted in any way that there were a few Jewish families in our town. Beaver Dam was a pretty church-y community, and more distinction was made between the three Catholic congregations: one for Germans, one for Irish, and one for the Polish. "Intermarriage" was defined in a unique way in our community, but the concept was just as problematic.

My older brother, his contemporaries, and brothers of my friends were gone, half a world away in places with names none of us had ever heard of and depended on radio commentators to pronounce. These young servicemen were symbolized by blue stars, one for each on small white flags that hung in front-room windows in house after house on my route to school. For those who would not be returning, a gold star replaced the blue to represent that tragedy. Yes, a gold star, to subtly indicate the anguish and turmoil going on inside that house. There were two on our block—boys I knew.

The war touched us all by human absence and loss, but otherwise citizens in my town were not affected much. The local stove manufacturing factory where my dad worked re-tooled and made shells for the U.S. Army, and there was plenty of employment. A few items were rationed, like butter, sugar, coffee, meat, and gas, with no real resulting hardship. Automobile tires were not available, and of course auto production was terminated for the duration.

233

Beaver Dam was a prosperous manufacturing and farm community with a large population of German and East European immigrants. It served as market center for the rich agriculture industry of Dodge County. Thus, in day-to-day living, the impact of the war was seen mostly as inconvenience. Adults likely experienced anxiety and insecurity, but I was not aware of it, nor personally affected by it. It was only later as an adult and parent that I realized what an emotional challenge it must have been to get through those years, which closely followed the difficulties of the Great Depression of the 1930s.

Labor shortages were acute in the Midwest farm belt, as they were in other areas of the production economy. In Dodge County, crops needed to be harvested and processed, and the efforts of women, students, and under-draft-age males were stretched to meet the demand. In 1944, German POWs arrived to help with the harvest as well as to work in many canning factories around Wisconsin. Beaver Dam had a Green Giant pea-canning plant, and nearby Fox Lake processed corn. I worked at both sites, as most high school and college students of the area did during the summer packing season. We had a good time—the first paying job for many of us, at 65 cents an hour, twelve to fourteen-hour days, seven days a week.

I went to work on the night shift on my sixteenth birthday, forking cans in a box car. A German POW was assigned to do the heavy work for a classmate of mine, her mother, and myself, as we laid rows of empty cans onto a conveyor belt which took them into the factory to be filled. I was terrified of this "enemy" stranger. I never could have described him because I never looked at his face. The other two workers were of German extraction and they used to bring him baked goodies from home. I was horrified at the time but admit I would do that myself today, without hesitation.

There were signs throughout the factory forbidding fraternizing, which I found odd—who would want to fraternize with these "monsters"? I was mystified by the cordial and casual relationship between prisoners and the rest of the workers, particularly the males. I avoided any contact whenever I had occasion to move through the factory, as I lived in mortal fear of being mugged and disposed of in a dark corner, in some barbaric fashion. Guards were not visible, and talk around the factory was that after they delivered their charges to work assignments, the guards would spend the day in a nearby tavern.

At least some other citizens did not share my personal apprehensions. The local fairgrounds in the center of town served as camp for the prisoners. On Sunday evenings, a crowd would gather around the fence to watch them play a vigorous game of soccer, followed by some spontaneous, exuberant German choral singing and a joint rendition of "Deutschland Uber Alles." (Prisoners at camps around the country were noted for their skillful and enthusiastic singing.) Although my family was partially of German heritage, we didn't join in this bit of international socializing, which to me was shocking as well as seemingly unpatriotic at the time.

A recent published account of the POW canning factory experience in Wisconsin tells similar warm, human stories about the relationship between prisoners and their keepers. There were such incidents as Uncle Herman occasionally coming out from Milwaukee to visit his nephew interned at a camp, and no doubt Aunt Maria sent along her special strudel to share with his buddies. They showed up in local taverns and churches with relatives and local townspeople. Such stories make me proud about the way we treated an enemy's sons, fathers, and brothers— that Americans can be the kind of people we are—generous, compassionate, keeping a sense of humor. It says something that many of those prisoners found America palatable enough to immigrate here after the war, that we could hold our heads high and welcome them back to carve out a new life for themselves and their families in America.

Camp markers on Business Route 34 near Greeley, Colorado

The Wehrmacht in Colorado

Not much is generally known about the POW camps in the U.S. Over 300,000 Germans were brought to the States, and many farmers and canning factories around the country benefitted from their labor. There were several camps in Colorado. Working prisoners were paid, and at $24/month their compensation exceeded what Japanese American physicians earned while working in the hospital at Camp Amache during internment—$19/month. Most prisoners did not leave until late 1946, as the American military didn't have available transportation facilities to carry them. There was nothing for them to return to, and their labor was still needed until American troops returned home en masse. Some spent additional time in England before they actually returned to Germany.

Between 1-25 and Greeley on Business Route 34, on the north side of the road just east of the light at the entrance to Promontory, are two low, blocky, masonry structures which are actually markers to record the former existence of a POW camp. Few people outside the area are aware of the camp, although some of the buildings used there have found adaptive re-use in Greeley, Windsor, and Denver. Ample files exist in the archives at the Greeley Museum and the Greeley Tribune, and they make fascinating reading as memoirs and analyses by scholars. Prisoners did return to the Greeley/Windsor area after the war, but none are living here at the present time.

Not all prisoners in American hands were converted by the humane treatment they received at the hands of their American captors. In some camps there was intimidation by loyal, hard-core Nazi types. Escapes were generally not successful in that escapees were most often picked up and returned to camp; percentage-wise they were not very frequent. Security varied from camp to camp, and it was recognized by the prisoners themselves that "it was a long swim back to Germany and farther still to the Russian front."

A story is told in Greeley about a few prisoners being reported missing. By the time the alarm turned to diligent search, the men returned. They had just gone into Greeley to watch the rodeo. Another incident describes how a guard left his gun behind and sent a prisoner to retrieve it for him. Occasionally prisoners would load onto a camp bus and be taken to a local baseball game.

Not a bad place to be during a shooting war.

POW camp 202 near Greeley   *Photo courtesy of City of Greeley Museums archives*

Letter from a Former POW

"A giant war camp awaited us in Greeley."

———— ● ————

The Greeley Museum received a copy of this letter which was written to a Colorado friend of Erich Geissler. In it, Mr. Geissler of Fichtelberg, Germany, described his recollections of life as a Prisoner of War in Camp 202 near Greeley, Colorado. In the spring of 2004, Jennifer Eidswick, a student in Professor Peter Kastner's German 413 class at the University of Northern Colorado, translated Mr. Geissler's letter as a class project. Her translation of Mr. Geissler's October 13, 2003, letter follows, reprinted as received, by permission from the Greeley Museum archives.

It bends the rules a bit to include a military veteran's story, but it is a noncombatant narrative, and it contributes in a significant way to what is known about the camp. Mr.Geissler not only describes camp life from an inmate's perspective but gives insights into the psychological issues accompanying that imprisonment. What he shares about his feelings nearly sixty years after the experience is an instructive exercise and a unique contribution to the mass of recorded memoirs of the war.

"RECOLLECTIONS OF THE POW CAMP, GREELEY, COLORADO, USA

During the last World War, from October of 1941 to the 29th of January 1947, I too had to serve as a civil service worker, a soldier, and a war prisoner. The greatest portion as a prisoner. I would like to compose what is still left over in my mind from the time of January 1944 to May of 1945, into writing.

On the 3rd of March 1943, (during the African War), while in the vicinity of El Bathan, I was seriously wounded. On the 5th of March, I arrived at the military hospital 650 Carthage that was set up in a section of a monastery. The 8th of May 1943, brought a premature end to the war for those of us who were injured. It was then that

English troops took hold of Carthage, and thereby also the military hospital. This day was also simultaneously the end of the entire African field train.

After more months, we wounded were separated into smaller groups of about 25-40 men and sent westward into different military hospital camps. It was during this process that I came upon others near the Algerian border. There we were handed over to American soldiers and taken to a small military hospital tent near Oran (no house, no bushes, only naked hills and sand). At the end of the year 1943, we were transported from Oran to the harbor, where we boarded a "Liberty Ship" and were kept in the lowest storage hold. This freighter was a single-walled ship, built in a short time, barely sea worthy and only meant to transport materials overseas. After about four weeks at sea, with only one hour daily of fresh air above deck, we finally landed in Norfolk, Virginia. This world travel continued with an approximately two-day train ride that ended in Greeley, Colorado.

A giant war camp awaited us in Greeley. Beyond the enclosed barracks—administration buildings, team rooms, garages, etc. for the Americans—the prisoner portion was separated into three compounds with four companies per compound. Every company decreed over five housing barracks: a kitchen, a barrack for materials, a laundry facility, a bathroom, a shower, etc. Fifty prisoners were placed in each of the housing barracks.

The fifty beds were provided with white-coated mattresses, allotted a quilt and white sheets. Our barrack had a shield hanging on the wall with handmade wood letters that said, *"Goetz von Berlichingen."* This was the name given to our barrack thereafter. We ourselves were at this point newly dressed and provided with adequate laundry. Every article of clothing that was to be worn on the outside was labeled with crackly white letters that said PW (Prisoner of War) on the back.

Every Company was designated as the charge and responsibility of a U.S. officer. The director of the entire camp was a Colonel by the name of Griffin. Oddly enough, an extremely fair and humanly officer. In case of illness there was a sickbay, run by a staff doctor and his nurses.

Hobbyists could access a workroom with many tools displayed, basically for cabinetmakers. I myself also supervised this room for many months.

For "our safety" and that of the Americans, a mesh-wire fence (about three meters high, and above that, about one meter of barbed-wire) was erected parallel in distance from a second similar fence. Between them (the fences) were guards with dogs posted in trestles. At approximately every 100 meters, there was a watchtower equipped with two spotlights, so that everything could be well supervised by day and night.

Almost all of the prisoners were constantly on labor assignment at the different farms in the surrounding areas. The main crops were sugar beets, potatoes, and onions. The earnings per month were about twenty-four (dollars) in warehouse charges. This money could be spent in the camp (at the cantina).

A very small group, including myself as well (as a result of the war), did not want to work for the enemy. I, myself, had, as a result of my injury, total stiffness in my ankle. I used that to my advantage. The non-workers were given only three dollars. That didn't bother me, personally. I organized myself at the oven with an iron, free-lancing and ironing clothing for the fellow prisoners (pants, ten cents; shirt, ten cents; jacket, thirty cents, etc.).

The food, until the end of the war, was unimaginably good and rich. Those in our company who were competent in the kitchen were managed by a young cook, who back home in Germany had done his apprenticeship in a first class hotel, and was allowed to practice his culinary arts for us. Lunch and dinner were always plausible, but adequate and very tasty. Occasionally, if accurately timed, the head chef would gladly fulfill special requests. One example was breakfast. Daily assortments included: coffee, hot cocoa, milk, white bread, marmalade, sugar, and cake. On Sundays we could have an additional large piece of cake. Who out of us could have afforded this at home? Overall, the kitchen staff was composed of German prisoners. I myself worked for a part of the time in the kitchen peeling potatoes.

Sports were also very popular. In the early part of the year 1944, a group of athletes persuaded the camp management to build a sports field. A short time later, American pioneers came with motorized crawlers, excavators, and other miscellaneous vehicles. They leveled an adjacent area, built a new fence, and in a few weeks we had a soccer field with a 400-meter track and a 100-meter track.

Every one of the twelve companies organized from among themselves a team of eleven. The jerseys were made from undershirts that the kitchen staff had dyed with the help of their products or leftovers from the sink (red beets, onions, green vegetables, etc.). For the game action we used game plans, similar to back home. So it was that the games were carried out, the head of the compound and lastly the respective head of the camp calculated. For the three thousand prisoners, as well as interested Americans, this was always suspenseful entertainment.

At about the same time a Christian organization (the name of which I don't know anymore, but they were similar to the CVJM) donated numerous forms of musical instruments to us. In no time, 20-25 highly talented hobby musicians from the camp formed a brilliant orchestra, that for us, and also the Americans, arranged concerts for our entertainment. It should be noted that the musicians were not allowed to take their instruments home.

Among the three thousand prisoners there were also many teachers. One of them founded, together with the camp management, a night school. They wanted to keep themselves and those interested prisoners mentally up to date. The subjects taught were math, German, and English.

The 8th of May, 1945, ended the war for everyone in the world—except Japan. What I found out later from my former fellow prisoners was that the German prisoners in Greeley were in good hands up until their discharge. At the end of May, I, myself, was placed with a group of about one hundred men in a camp in the vicinity of the U.S. Camp Carson—an army city. The city of Colorado Springs was not far away. Afterwards we came to a branch-camp. What awaited us there was something completely different. Hard work in the farming industry from early (e.g.in the morning) until into the night, with extremely less food. Though it was nearby, Greeley had nothing to do with this.

Briefly now, a picture of the trip back home. At the end of 1945, a large group of prisoners were shipped off together, myself included. The railroad took us through New Mexico and Arizona to Los Angeles, where we boarded on the 12000 BRT US-Troop transporter *"General R. House."* Upon this ship we were allowed to move freely. The almost three-week-long boat trip went through the Pacific, the Panama Canal, and the Atlantic towards Liverpool to a one-year holdover in England. Finally, on the 29th of January, 1947, we arrived back at home.

In retrospect, the time in Greeley seems akin to a dream-like experience, and I thank God frequently that I was able to spend a portion of that dreadful war, that played itself out in Europe and Africa, unintentionally away from home, in Colorado, 2000 meters above sea level and in the foothills of 4000 meter high mountains, in the wonderful countryside. The winters with their powdery snow, the summers with their beautiful, sunny days, blue skies, and their agreeable climates.

So it was for me, all in all, even as a prisoner, a part of my life that will always continue to be a good memory for me. Thank You, Greeley."

The Hazel E. Johnson Research Center at the Municipal Archives, City of Greeley Museums, 714 8th St., has documentary and photo files, plus numerous other reference materials about Camp 202, including Erich Geissler's original letter (in German). For more information contact the Greeley Museums at (970) 350-9220.

Erich Geißler
Bayreutherstr. 21   13. Oktober 2003
95686 Fichtelberg
Germany.

Erinnerungen an das POW-Camp Greeley/Colorado/USA.

Den letzten Weltkrieg musste auch ich vom Oktober 1941 bis
29. Januar 1947 als Arbeitsdienstler, Soldat oder Kriegs-
gefangener miterleben. Den größten Teil als Gefangener.
Über die Zeit vom Januar 1944 bis Ende Mai 1945 in Greeley
möchte ich das, was meine Gehirnzellen übrig gelassen haben,
kurz niederschreiben.

Im Afrikakrieg wurde ich am 3.5.43 in Tunesien in de Nähe
von El Bathan schwer verwundet. Am 5.3.43 kam ich in das
Kriegslazarett 650 Karthago, das in einem Teil eines Klosters
eingerichtet war. Mit dem 8. Mai 1943 war für uns Verwundete
der Krieg vorzeitig beendet, weil englische Truppen Karthago
und somit auch das Kloster samt Lazarett eingenommen haben.
Dieser Tag war gleichzeitig das Ende des gesamten Afrika-
feldzuges.

Nach mehrere Monaten verlegte man uns Verwundete in kleineren
Gruppen von ca. 25 - 40 Mann westwärts in verschiedene Laza-
rettzeltlager. Ich kam dabei unter anderem in die Nähe von
Thibar und schließlich an die Grenze von Tunesien/Algerien.
Dort wurden wir von amerikanischen Soldaten übernommen und in ein
kleines Zeltlazarett nahe bei Oran gebracht (kein Haus, kein
Strauch, nur nackte Hügel und Sand). Zum Jahresschluss 1943
transportierte man uns zum Hafen von Oran und wir kamen an
Bord eines "Libertyschiffes" in den untersten Laderaum. Diese
Frachter waren einwandige Schiffe, in kürzester Zeit gebaut,
kaum seetüchtig und nur für den Materialtransport nach Über-
see bestimmt. Nach ca. 4 Wochen Seereise, mit nur täglich einer
Stunde Luft holen an Deck, landeten wir schließlich in Nor-
folk/Virginia. Die Weiterreise erfolgte per Bahn, dauerte ca.
2 Tage und endete in Greeley/Colorado.

Martha and Paul

Martha Matula

Love at the POW camp

Martha's story reminds us that even during wartime, humor is part of the human scene.

I was born in 1925. I grew up in Windsor and attended church in Windsor but high school in Johnstown. I lived closer to Windsor, but the Johnstown school bus came closer. I still had to walk a mile to catch that bus. After I graduated from high school in 1943, I went to work on my dad's farm as his hired hand for a year. My brother had to go to war. He joined the Air Force, and my dad needed me. I drove the tractors and did all kinds of work.

At the POW camp near Greeley I started at the Post Exchange. There was an ad in the paper, and it sounded like good money. I asked my dad, "Can I go over there and apply for a job?" He probably thought I'd never get one. I don't recall how much they paid, but the money was far better than I could get anywhere else at any other job in Windsor or Johnstown. The government was good to have around, because they paid so well.

So I applied and got the job. I started in the fall; it was close to Thanksgiving time. That was an advantage because there was no work on the farm. I was making good money, and so my father said, "OK, you can go ahead and keep working over there." I think we were paid once a month. With my first paycheck I went to Denver to the American Furniture Store. I bought two pretty 9 X 12 rugs for my mom and dad for their living room and their dining room. I was so proud to be able to buy my parents new carpets, and that was for their Christmas. Of course, I was living at home, and I felt I should do something to help out.

I worked at the Post Exchange for about four months. One day a Captain Thomas came up to me and said, "Have you ever considered another job here?"

I said, " No. Are there any other jobs for women?"

He said, "Yes, down at the motor pool. They need drivers. I recommend if you are a good driver, you go down to the motor pool and apply. I want you to tell the motor sergeant that I said you're to have a job."

I didn't really know Captain Thomas, but he would come into the PX and buy things from me. I suppose he thought here's a young, single farm girl who needs money, and he was going to help me out financially.

I said, "But you don't even know about my driving record. Do you trust me that much?"

He said, "Well, it's a lot better pay than you're getting here, my dear; you'll make more money."

I was eighteen years old, and I told him, "I'm a good driver, and I like to drive fast. I've been driving since I was ten years old on the farm. I drove trucks and tractors."

He said, "Well, we have to have a fast driver. I have to go to the branch camps up in Gould and Walden." They had prisoners up in the mountains. They were doing construction jobs, roads, and so forth. They had them working on all kinds of things; the Germans were good workers.

The prisoners around here worked in the beet fields, and they came out and worked in the fields on my dad's farm. My mother was a good Christian woman, and she always fed everybody; she didn't care who they were. She wanted to go out and feed those workers, but the guard wouldn't let her do it. She felt so bad because she had baked a chocolate cake for them. I think there were about eighteen of them

It must have been up to the guard's discretion (or perhaps how hungry he was), because this is contrary to reports from some other farms.

At the camp, we weren't supposed to fraternize or even communicate with them. But I got acquainted with some of them; they knew I was German. We could communicate; I could understand them, although I wasn't good at talking German. Sometimes I would speak in English. There were times I could talk a little with them like when I would be waiting for my car to be serviced. I'd be sitting outside the motor pool and they were working on the grounds. They would be gardening; they had built little flower boxes on their barracks and put flowers in them. They would take any little scrap of lumber they could find and build something. They were very creative.

I got acquainted with one of the boys who worked in the dentist's office, because I would have to take the captain over to get his teeth taken care of. While I was waiting for him, the prisoner that was working with the dentist would come out and we would visit a little. One day he came over and put something in my hand. It was a little pendant he had made from stuff from the dentist's office. He had made this flower for me.

Then there was another one—I had gotten acquainted with him when I worked at the Post Exchange. He was one of the boys that came in and cleaned. I would see him sitting down during a break. He was always drawing, painting, or making something. It was a good year later, because I was still driving, when I ran across him one day at the Post Exchange, and he had a package. He handed it over and said simply, "Here." When I got to the car, I opened it and it was a scarf, like a table runner. It was made of blue material; it had a fringed edge, and he had painted a bouquet of roses in the middle.

The prisoners weren't sent home right away after the war ended. There was nothing for them to go home to, and there weren't ships available to transport them. They were treated nicely out there, and some of them didn't want to leave. Most of them that I met were kind; they weren't arrogant. They were happy to have food and happy

Martha showing a table runner hand-painted and given to her by the POW

they weren't in Russia. Many of them came back to the Windsor/Greeley area.

Let me tell you what happened when I went to apply for the job at the motor pool. This master sergeant was sitting at the desk. I went in and said to him, "I'm supposed to come down here and work at your motor pool."

He said, "Who says!?"

I said, "Captain Thomas said you're supposed to hire me, that you need more drivers, and you're to hire me."

He said, "Well, I appreciate that a lot. That's all I need down here is another woman! That's the last thing I need!" There were two other women working there already. The camp hired civilian women to drive their cars.

The sergeant was pounding his hands like this . . . I noticed he had such pretty, clean hands and was wearing a beautiful red ring. Here's a motor pool sergeant; how come he has such nice clean hands? Because on the farm when you worked on machinery, your hands got greasy. My brother's hands and my father's hands—they didn't look that nice. I'm thinking, this guy doesn't work.

I said, "The captain told me I have a job here."

He snarled, "Well, I'm gonna look into this! I'll investigate further and we'll let you know."

I said, "I'll be seeing you, because I'm going to be working here."

He said, "We'll see about that."

He was real arrogant about it, real snotty, and I thought—you jerk, you! It was the captain who gave me the job and you're only a master sergeant. You can't stop me.

A few days later Captain Thomas came to me at the post exchange and said, "I've got everything cleared and you're to start work on Monday morning." I told him what happened with the sergeant when I went down there before. But I went on Monday morning like he said to, and the sergeant was not a happy camper.

He assigned me a car; it was a Chevrolet of that ugly green with a big star on the front, and he said, "This is going to be your automobile to drive, and you better take good care of it! I don't want to see a smashed up car in here. You women drivers don't take very good care of our cars." He was real belligerent.

I thought, OH BROTHER, and I told him, "I've never had a wreck in my life, and I've been driving cars since I was ten years old"—back and forth like that.

Sometimes the officers would tell us we had to get to the airport in thirty-five minutes! When we went on long trips, like to Gould or Walden, there were always two drivers—two women. Captain Thomas needed to go up there to supervise the jobs the prisoners were doing, to oversee it all to see that everything was going the way it was supposed to, that the camp was running right. And he would usually stay overnight. We were put up in motels or hotels, and our meals were all paid for. The girl I worked with was from Greeley and a little older than I was. We would change off; we were allowed to drive just so many hours and then we had to change drivers. But if it was just to the airport, I would take Captain Thomas down to Stapleton or to Buckley. Sometimes they would go on commercial planes. Sometimes he went home to visit his wife, who was living in another state.

I also drove for Major Meyers, an older man and very much of a gentleman, very kind. He always complimented me about my driving.

About a month after I was hired, Captain Thomas called me and said, "I need to be in Denver real quick! Get up here as fast as you can. We've got to go right away; we have a deadline to meet."

I said, "I'll be right there!" I took off and was driving pretty fast down the main street, and over to the right I saw a whole bunch of naked German prisoners lying on the grass out in the sun taking a sun bath. They were STARK NAKED! And they were all just lying there, some on their backs, some on their fronts. I had never seen so many naked people in my life! I never saw ANYthing like that in my life. My mouth dropped open, and I kept looking over there, and I ran into a fire plug. I was really booking it because I was in a hurry, and I tore that fire plug off from the ground, and the radiator went back into the motor. Cold water from the fire plug spurted all over everywhere, and these guys got up and started running—all these naked guys! They were screaming and sopping wet. I got out of the car and I'm sopping wet too.

I walked into the officers' club, where I was supposed to pick up the guys that were in a hurry. No, I didn't go to the motor pool!

"What is wrong with YOU?" Captain Thomas said. "Where's the car? You're late!"

So I told him what happened, and I said, "What am I going to do!? The car is wrecked!! Am I going to have to pay for that car?"

He said, "Just calm down; I'll cover for you. We'll take care of this. I'll get someone else to take my job today, and I'll go down to the motor pool with you."

I'm dripping wet; my hair is hanging down. He kept covering his mouth with his hand because he couldn't keep from laughing. It was unbelievable, and I was SO embarrassed.

So we got into Captain Thomas's car and drove down to see the wreck. He looked it over and said, "Hmmm. Kind of messed up, isn't it. OK, let's go down to the motor pool."

We walked in and that same sergeant, Paul Goss, said, "Just what I figured. Another accident from a woman!"

The Captain said, "Well, it really wasn't her fault."

"Whadya mean, it wasn't her fault? Who forced her to run into the fire plug?"

The captain explained everything to him and the sergeant started laughing. Then he said, "Right now we're short of cars. What are we going to do about that?"

The Captain answered, " I'll let her drive my personal car for a few days or weeks. You put in an order for another car right away. Fill out this form."

Goss said, "Who's taking care of the cost of it? How do I write this up?"

The piece of jewelry given to Martha by the POW

The captain said, "You do this paper work, and I'll take care of the rest."

Then we left, and the captain said to me, "It's not going to cost you a dime. We have ways to cover this stuff. The car will be replaced at no cost to you."

I kept saying over and over, "Thank you, thank you, thank you . . ." I found out later all this was covered by insurance; every driver was covered by government insurance. It didn't cost the government anything; it cost the insurance company.

A few months later, there was an officers' club dance. Major Meyers was actually head of the whole camp. I was driving for him one day and he said, "I'd like to extend an invitation to you and your boyfriend to a dance at the Officers Club. You can bring a civilian and enjoy the evening. There'll be good music and fabulous food." At that time I was dating a farm boy from Johnstown and he'd given me his fraternity pin. We'd been dating since my senior year in high school. He was going to college in Fort Collins. But I had told my mother, "I'm not marrying a farmer, and I'm not marrying a German." Because the German farmers made their wives work so hard.

To the contrary, I had always told my daughter she could do very well by marrying a farmer, and if he were German, so much the better. But I'm from Wisconsin.

So we went to the dance. My date was wearing his cowboy hat and his cowboy boots and his western clothes. All the rest of them were dressed in their uniforms, all nicely pressed and looking so sharp. We danced the first dance. Then Paul Goss, the motor pool sergeant, came over and asked me to dance. I asked my date if it was all right if I danced with my boss. He said, "Sure, go right ahead." So we danced. They were playing "Let Me Call You Sweetheart, I'm in Love with You." He had a beautiful singing voice, and he sang this song in my ear. And I'll tell you what—sparks started flying. We danced the next dance, and the next dance. Then I went back to my boyfriend, and he was not happy. I danced a couple dances with him, and pretty soon Paul came back over and asked me to dance again. By the time the evening was over, my boyfriend was very much not happy and took me home real quick.

That was the end of that relationship, and then Paul and I started dating. We dated until he was out of the camp in '45. I worked as a driver until the camp closed in 1945.

After the war he went back to Indiana. He had a garage back there. He wrapped up the business, came back to Colorado, and we were married in June, 1946. Of course that was the end of my plans to go to college. I was twenty-one when we got married; Paul was eight years older.

Paul was a very good husband, and he was an excellent cook. We ran a Spudnut shop in Greeley for a while. He managed a garage and eventually went into the insurance business. He was a very handy guy, he could fix anything, he could clean house, he was a gardener; there wasn't anything he couldn't do. His father was a minister in Indiana, and Paul was one of nine children. He started earning money when he was real young in order to help the family. His younger brother told me that there were times if Paul hadn't brought in money, they would have gone hungry. Paul would go to high school during the daytime and work in the garage at night. He knew hard work.

He had this beautiful singing voice, and he used to sing in a quartette at church. He knew all the old hymns. When our daughter was two or so, she asked him to sing her favorite song, "I'll go out in the yard by myself" ("I Come to the Garden Alone").

We had four boys; then we had this little girl born at home. Paul delivered her because we couldn't get to the hospital on time. He was out in the kitchen making a pumpkin pie and getting dinner ready because I was lying down; I didn't feel too good. I kept calling him, but he didn't hear me because the mixer was going and a kitchen fan. I was yelling, "Help! Help! The baby's coming!" and by the time he got there the baby was almost there. The cord was around her neck, and she was black. He got that off, whopped her on the butt and she turned pink. He cleaned her up, called the doctor, and the doctor said there was no need to my going to the hospital; everything was under control and Paul had done a fine job. Then he went back out in the kitchen, finished making his pie, and fixed supper. By eight o'clock that evening, the house was full of people come to see the baby. The Gosses finally had a girl! I was forty; Paul was forty-eight.

The next day he brought a bouquet of red roses and a bouquet of pink roses—one for Momma, one for the baby.

In 1976, Paul suffered a massive stroke and was in a coma for seventy-five days. He was fifty-nine when he died. He was my protector, he looked after me, and I didn't have to worry about anything. I wasn't in the business end of it; I stayed home and took care of raising the children. I was so dependent on him, it was really hard to be left alone. Then I had to get out and make a living. I still had a ten year-old and an eleven-year-old at home and two boys in college. The oldest boy had just returned from Vietnam. I think a lot of what happened to Paul came from his concern for that boy in Vietnam; he was shot down twice. Paul couldn't sleep, he prayed and grieved for him, and it took its toll.

We've been through a lot together, this family, but God has been good to us and faithful. I was alone for sixteen years before I remarried. My first priority after Paul died was to get those kids raised and through school."

    Martha's story doesn't end there, but she has told what is relevant to our collection of wartime memoirs. She has made her life without Paul meaningful. Through lay ministry at her church, she has brought comfort and meaning to many others by what she has learned from her own trials. Illness and tragedy have accompanied her on her life journey, and through it all, she has survived and triumphed. Now happily married to another jewel of a husband, Don Matula, Martha is an inspiration as well as a good storyteller, who can reminisce with humor as well as purpose.

Dashing, handsome, young Gernot

Ava Molnar Heinrichsdorff

"Go back where you came from, you dirty little alien!"

———————●———————

*Ava and husband Gernot deserve a volume of their own; they are a highly tal-
ented and accomplished pair. They have called Colorado Springs home for many
years, and each has earned the highest esteem of people in that community as well
as acclaim from their respective professional circles throughout the nation.*

*Ava's parents, Ferenc (world-famous violist) and Maria Molnar, and Gernot's
mother Irma can also be described in no less terms. Ava briefly describes below their
respective wartime experiences. Perhaps one day Ava will write "the rest of the
story."*

THE MOLNARS

I remember my parents' horror on Pearl Harbor Day. We three had emigrated
from Hungary to a nation that they thought was "Shangri-La." (James Hilton's *Lost
Horizon* with its portrait of the "Shangri-La" social paradise had recently become a
best-seller.) And now "we" (since we already felt like Americans) were suddenly at
war.

I was ten that year. My father, violist Ferenc Molnar, was teaching music at
Stanford University, and since he had been trained as an engineer before choosing
the concert artist career instead, he soon volunteered to teach mechanical engineering
at Stanford as well. My mother, Maria, trained and then volunteered as an X-ray
technician. These were their wholehearted contributions to the war effort.

But all three of us were just learning the English language, and I still had a strong
accent.

On the first day of my very first paying job, which was helping Mrs. Pintler with
housework for 25 cents an hour (she had just taught me to wrap a knife in a cloth to

dust the slats of her Venetian blinds), I was walking home from her house. As I approached our little neighborhood grocery store, Mr. Lippincott's, I realized that I could now buy myself an ice cream cone with some of my new earnings.

I chose my favorite flavor, black walnut, and Mr. Lippincott dipped it in his tub of chocolate coating. The cold ice cream hardened the chocolate right away. It was perfect.

I had just said something like, "Ssank you, Meestair Leepeencote!" and walked out the door when I felt it—warm on the right side of my forehead, then cooling as it went down my cheek to the corner of my mouth.

Then I heard the angry, "Go back where you came from, you dirty little alien!" from a woman who had spat into my face. My ice cream cone was on the hot sidewalk, melting.

I ran home crying, and when I told Mami what had happened, she screamed, hugged me, and burst into tears. When Papi came home it became "a scene," with

Mami demanding in Hungarian, "How could you bring us to such a dreadful place?" and Papi striding to his desk, putting his head down and beginning to weep.

During the 1930s, the string quartet with which Ferenc Molnar was violist had repeatedly toured Europe and America. The U.S. Congress honored the quartet by inviting them to become United States citizens. My father was thrilled, so my parents took out First Papers and started studying for the citizenship exam even though the citizenship process would take five years.

But now, since Hungary was allied with Germany and therefore part of the German-Italian-

Ava and her mother Maria Molnar

Japanese Axis, we were no longer respected aliens; we had become Enemy Aliens. Respect for my parents quickly changed to suspicion. On our party-line telephone, people who heard our accents would sometimes shout invectives and curses. Some of the operators (since in those days when you lifted the receiver an operator said, "Number, please?" and you told her what number you wanted to reach) could make even "Just a minute!" sound hostile.

So when my father took his engineering students on field trips to factories, he was not allowed to enter; he had to wait outside while they were toured. "Listen well, take notes, and write your own exam based on what you think is worth remembering," he would tell them.

Papi, who for a number of reasons was disgusted with the Hungarian government, was enthusiastic about having found the citizenship he wanted, but Mami had merely acquiesced. When pregnant with me she had stayed home in Hungary while he was on tour, since she wasn't at all sure that one could properly have a baby in a foreign country.

But after that woman spat on me, Papi had to try to persuade her. "Give America a chance," he pleaded. "We still have a couple of years to change our minds if we need to."

"When this nation makes Ava suffer so?" she retorted. It wasn't only about that spitting woman. Since I was the smallest and youngest in my class, as well as being "that foreign one," I was often the victim of the "normal" cruelty of my eleven-year-old classmates.

But Mami handled her homesickness for Hungary admirably. She not only learned to speak and write English but started writing newspaper features, then historical cartoons, and then novels in her new language. The settings of her novels, though, were Hungarian. Through this artistic melding of cultures she became not only an accomplished, successful author but also an ardent American.

THE HEINRICHSDORFFS

Irma Franzen was from childhood a rebel. Her family, who were renowned architects in the Witten area of Germany, were chagrinned when this errant girl insisted on continuing her education in botany and horticulture far too long, to the point where she became the first female landscape architect on the European continent. Not only that, she consorted with freethinkers who entertained radical ideas in religion, politics, and philosophy. She had two children out of wedlock, she sometimes lived in a nudist park, and she wanted to work for a salary. In the 1920s, all this was outrageous for "a girl of good family."

Gernot's mother Irma, a very modern, compassionate, and talented lady

So, around 1930, her embarrassed older brothers found her a decrepit house in a tiny fishing village on the North Sea, far from their home city. "Here," they said, " here is a home for you. And consider this to be your share of the inheritance."

To legitimize her daughter and son, Irma married a fellow landscape architect whose name was Heinrichsdorff—for just one day.

Since a small fishing village is not a place where a landscape architect can find professional work, Irma Heinrichsdorff opened a vegetarian restaurant. As war approached and then broke out, she could no longer get enough foods for a balanced vegetarian diet, so she expanded the fare to include meats. Then she expanded the restaurant to a guest house and then a summer vacation home for children—what we call a summer camp. Her brothers were glad to send their children to her for vacation.

But when some summer sessions ended, certain children could not be sent home, because they suddenly had no home to be sent to. Their parents had disappeared. For example, the mother of two boys was a Jew. These boys' parents had sometimes visited Irma as her guests for weeks (without ration cards, since Jews didn't get those), but then they vanished and afterward died in a concentration camp.

Irma kept these children as her own and raised them to adulthood. The entire village protected them, including one of their teachers, a man who was in the Gestapo-SS. Irma often had to entertain and placate high-ranking Nazi party members; for years she risked her life for these foster children. When the postwar trials ensued, Irma testified on behalf of the teacher who had protected these boys. He was then acquitted.

Irma's son Gernot was in the Hitler Youth, like nearly all German children at that time. In their little fishing village, this group was similar to many Boy Scout groups; it emphasized sports, crafts, outdoor life, community, and friendship, not national-ism.

During the war, Gernot was trained as a pilot. But Germany ran out of gasoline before he flew in combat; pilots were shifted to the Infantry and sent into battle with-out Infantry training. Gernot was wounded and became a prisoner of the Americans. For more than a year his mother had no idea where he was or whether he was even alive, since the one postcard prisoners were allowed to send did not reach her.

The war ended in 1945, but it wasn't until July of 1947 that he was released from being a prisoner of war. Finally, he automatically became a civilian again. What an ecstatic welcome he received from his surprised mother!

But he had only one day and night at home. That part of Germany was under Canadian occupation, and the day after his return from prison, a group of Canadian officers appeared at their door to arrest Gernot. Two people, perhaps to ingratiate themselves with the Occupation, had accused him of being a Nazi Party member and of having been in the *Freicorps Adolf Hitler Verdaechtig,* an underground move-ment.

"But I never even joined the Party!" he exclaimed.

"You have a membership number," they told him. Gernot saw no evidence and was given no opportunity for any defense. He was immediately confined in one of the concentration camps where hundreds, maybe thousands of Jews and others had been killed. There he was starved to about 95 pounds before he was released about seven months later. Since starvation often causes heart problems Gernot also had those to recover from.

For a young man who had Jewish foster brothers whom his family had risked their lives for years to protect, it was an ironic experience.

Ava Molnar Heinrichsdorff was born in Hungary but has made English her professional language. For twenty-five years she chaired the English Department of the Colorado Springs School where she taught writing, literature, philosophy, history, ecology, anthropology, and dance. She is also a published writer and an editor, has had a career in international folk dance and belly dance and has worked professionally in horse and livestock photography. She continues in several of these endeavors.

Gernot was born in Germany and came to the U.S. in 1952. In Colorado Springs he made indigenous, environmentally-sound landscape design his mission long before the word "xeriscape" existed. His gardens exist in several states and foreign countries and have received numerous, prestigious awards. He writes, lectures, teaches, and has served in various capacities for relevant professional associations. He is also a talented sculptor, working in several media.

Irma studied in England to achieve her credentials, then designed gardens in Germany. In 1953 Gernot brought her to America, and she resumed professional work through his Colorado Springs firm.

Gernot, still handsome as ever

Boat in the bottle and hand-painted plate made for and given to the Ostermillers by one of their POW workers

Gene Ostermiller

"If you're going to work for us, you're going to eat right."

———————————●———————————

During the war, Gene's dad Pete farmed acreage on Weld CR 56 between what is now I-25 and Berthoud. Like many farmers in the area, he was grateful to be able to use the labor of the nearby POW camp. Time spent away from the camp was considered a privilege by some prisoners (and perhaps guards), and so the arrangement was to all parties' mutual benefit. There were strict rules governing the management of these workers, but among friendly German farmers in the area, the atmosphere was congenial and casual. Lucky were those assigned to Pete Ostermiller's farm.

Gene's parents were of the Germans from Russia heritage so common in Weld County and the northeastern part of the state. Both parents spoke German, although the differing geographic origins of the POWs and the senior Ostermillers brought differing dialects to the table (no pun intended), making easy communication a challenge. The Ostermiller children were not taught German, as there was a time during the great immigration waves of a previous century when immigrants wanted to assimilate as quickly and as obviously as possible in order to show their American loyalty. Consequently, their offspring missed the opportunity to become naturally fluent in another language. Besides, Pete remembered how difficult it was when he arrived in America as a boy not knowing English. He wanted to ensure that his children wouldn't experience that same discomfort and confusion about their language, even though they were native-born Americans.

One of the heartwarming stories (and there are many) that comes out of the POW experience is the report of how some farmers for whom the prisoners worked often provided a substantial noon meal for their workers. No farmer's wife can bear the thought of anyone going hungry. As homemakers and mothers, they were naturally appalled by the meager sack lunch provided by the camp kitchen—a meal that usually consisted of a lard or margarine sandwich and a bottle of water, plus an

265

occasional apple or orange. Tea bags and the makings for coffee were also provided by the camp, but the quantities were so meager, according to Gene, " The result barely colored the water." So Mother Ostermiller supplemented, sharing those tightly rationed commodities from her own pantry. She regularly fed her ten children three meals a day plus seventeen extra, POW appetites. It must have been a challenge to this busy lady, who was coping with wartime shortages despite the bounty of the home farm.

That bounty included pheasants Gene's older brothers hunted on the property. The pheasants sometimes found their way to the prisoners' dining table.

Margaret and Pete Ostermiller

Appreciating the energy needed to spend a hot day working in the beet fields or whatever task was required of their workers, some wives set up a table or two under the front yard shade trees and served up fried chicken and apple pie. Home-made grebble was a special Ostermiller treat and reminder of home. (Grebble is a deep-fried delicacy, rather like a raised donut but lighter in texture.) Some guards objected to such hospitality, no doubt regarded as pampering, and certainly against the rules. But all personnel on the premises participated freely and enjoyed the luxury (and no one complained to the head office!). However, one day a U.S. Army captain from the camp arrived at the farm on inspection duty. He objected to the levity with which the prisoners were managed. Unintimidated, Pete sent him on his way. (He may have been offered a compensatory sack of grebble to make his rejection more "palatable"?)

Some guards were more congenial than others but naturally needed to keep their professional distance from the prisoners.

Some were downright mean. They tended to follow the workers, calling out something that sounded like Hubba! Hubba! Hubba! to make them hurry.

When the Ostermiller truck arrived at the camp each morning to collect a crew of workers, small wonder that a loyal group was there waiting to jump into the back end of the truck. Gene reports that the same workers came every day.

We never had a bit of trouble with any of them. They got along fine with each other and with us. They helped each other and were good workers. Most of them were no more than kids. They worked in the beet fields all through the area. Beets were a more common crop then than they are now.

They also helped with the cultivation and harvest of corn, potatoes, alfalfa, and grain. Potatoes were picked up from the field and put into burlap gunnysacks that were laid out in rows, then loaded onto trucks that took the harvest into nearby Johnstown. There the sacks were sorted, bagged, and shipped.

We had one worker we got to know pretty well. His name was Carl Lempkl. My brother Ray used to take Carl into Johnstown to help; then he'd buy Carl a malt. The prisoners weren't supposed to leave the field, of course.

The Ostermiller children helped too. Like many farm children, they milked cows before school and had regular chores to do. At ages nine and ten during the summers the prisoners were on hand, Gene drove tractors and other vehicles. An occasional prisoner did too, although they were officially banned from operating machinery. Some prisoners were outwardly more amiable with the children than others were; probably some had children of their own. Gene's little three-year-old sister Carol was a particular favorite. She used to enjoy a ride now and then on the shoulders of a burly worker. The element of mutual trust in all this interaction is noteworthy.

One worker made a white canvas cap for Gene, a model of the type of caps the prisoners wore, except Gene's had designs of a Great Dane on the front, a baseball on one side and a bat on the other. We wondered if the prisoner was from Denmark!

On the other hand, a time or two we got a crew that were apparently Nazis. They were a nasty bunch, hostile, uncooperative. The regular fellows that worked for us said they didn't want to go to war, didn't want to fight. And they were darned happy

Gene on the farm 2008 holding the ship-in-a-bottle made by a prisoner

to live out the war where they were.

From other sources, reports indicate that hard-core Nazi prisoners sometimes intimidated their fellow inmates, although they all had served in the same military forces for the same cause.

Prisoners weren't supposed to venture out of the fields in which they were working, not onto the private premises, and certainly not into the house. But the Ostermiller family accordion and piano often provided the occasion for an impromptu musicale performed by prisoner musicians—not Mozart but lively polkas, nostalgic for all within hearing distance.

At Christmastime, Pete bought cigarettes for his workers, and his wife baked holiday goodies. In order to pass these off at the camp, Pete had to arrange to get the men assigned to outdoor tasks so he could have access to them.

At the end of 1945, internment came to an end for the prisoners at Camp 202, but return home to Germany took more than another year. Emotions were mixed on both sides at the parting. Pete showed his appreciation, not without affection, by providing some of his "boys" with an ample supply of spirits to celebrate.

The Ostermillers continued to have contact with Carl Lempkl, who not only corresponded with the family but visited two or three times, as Gene recalls. On another occasion, the son of an ex-prisoner, an exchange student in Iowa, came out to the farm to visit. Another ex-prisoner requested that Pete help sponsor his son to come to the States. This young fellow lived with the Ostermillers for about six months on his path to permanent resettlement.

There were other Camp 202 prisoners who later immigrated to the area around Greeley, but all have passed on.

Gene presently farms land on WCR46, not far from the farmstead described above. Pete celebrated life to age ninety-six, a citizen who could be proud of his humane treatment of other fathers' sons. Perhaps he thought of how he would want his own sons treated if the circumstances were reversed.

POSTSCRIPT

In 1985, my husband and I were traveling in Norway. We reached the Russian border at Kirkenes and booked passage on a small coastal steamer to ride down the Norwegian coast back to Bergen. The trip took six days, one that stopped at every village along the way, taking on chickens, fish for market, school kids, and occasional travelers. There were only a few cabin passengers, and during the course of the trip, we made the acquaintance of a middle-aged German couple. From introductory conversations, we learned that the man had spent time in a POW camp near Greeley, Colorado, and worked for a Berthoud farmer. They had kept in touch for a while, but contact had faded in recent years. He wrote his name and the name of his "employer" on a piece of paper—Carl Lempkl and Pete Ostermiller. I put the paper into my billfold where it remained for TEN years. We lived in Colorado Springs at the time, and I couldn't have found Berthoud on a map. In 1995 we attended a church picnic at Highland Lake, near Berthoud, and were seated across the table from a man who identified himself as a farmer from Berthoud. I showed him the names on the paper and asked him if he know Pete Ostermiller. He replied that Pete had passed on, but he had gone to school with Ostermiller boys and he would give the paper to his friend Gene. Ten more years went by and I heard nothing. Then one day a friend took my husband and me out to a farm in the area to watch the pickle harvest (yes, farmers call them "pickles," not cucumbers), and we were introduced to the farm's operator, Gene Ostermiller. After another few years, we connected again for the above interview.

Harold, center, purchasing the prize-winning lamb at the Weld County Fair

Harold Long

"The Nazi sympathizers were not cooperative and not good workers."

———————————— ● ————————————

Harold Long is another farmer who depended upon POW labor during the war. Harold was leasing a farm at the time, five miles north of Windsor on Highway 257.

Regular help was furnished housing, equipment, and certain foodstuffs like milk, eggs, and potatoes. But all the regular farm laborers were off in the service, and I employed twelve women who came out from town to work in the beet fields. They were hard workers.

The farmers were happy to get the prisoners, and there was work all season for them, weeding, thinning, harvesting beets, and other crops. If it hadn't been for the prisoners, I don't know what we would have done. The farmers would have been hurtin' bad. They came too late in the year, probably 1944, to thin the beets, but they helped with the harvest. We had them for a year and a half. They left in 1946. We had a contract with the government, paid the government, and the government paid the prisoners less than what we paid the government—probably 50 cents a day—and they were lucky to get that.

I would call the camp and request a certain number of workers. A guard used to bring them out in their bus, about twenty of them. If you needed more than they could put on the bus, you had to go get the extras with your truck. My brother and I worked together, and we could always use a big crew, a busload.

We raised potatoes, sugar beets, corn, barley, and alfalfa, also pintos but we didn't need prisoners for that. We'd have to have a row of potatoes dug for each person. One time we did about twenty rows, and I got a call from the prison camp. "Don't dig any more potatoes; they're on strike." When the guards did something the prisoners didn't like, they would refuse to work. It would freeze every night by that time of year, so we went around the neighborhood to get help to get those potatoes dug. The strike only lasted an hour or so, or we could have lost probably five acres of potatoes. I think at the camp they told them, "If you don't work, you don't eat." They said, "We'll eat."

A machine went down the row and dug the potatoes. The prisoners picked them up and threw them into a sack. Then a truck would go along and pick up the sacks. The American guard told us we were lucky; the majority liked us and wanted to help us get our potatoes harvested. A funny thing about potatoes. We had to pay so much for each sack, so the real small potatoes we wanted to leave lying on the ground. But they just couldn't do that. They couldn't figure out how Americans could be so wasteful.

Prisoners weren't allowed to operate machinery; they did all hand work. For beets, they picked them up, laid them in a row, and someone came along with a knife and cut the tops off.

There weren't many Nazis, but the ones that were Nazis really hated it here. Once in a while when they got off the bus, a guard or one of the prisoners would come up to me and say, "Be careful. Watch that one; he's a Nazi." The Nazi sympathizers weren't cooperative and not good workers. I had one bunch of workers and the GUARD was a Nazi. He and I would argue about the war. One time when the American Air Force blew the German Air Force out, I told him, "I guess you guys are done."

He said, "Don't worry. Hitler's got a secret weapon," and that was the atomic bomb.

I told him how foolish that war was, how many people got killed. That guard said, "Ach, what's a life? Look how much fun it is to make 'em." You could tell the way he acted, he was the only real Nazi I had in the bunch; the rest were real nice guys. If you tried to talk about Hitler, you found out they really hated him.

At the camp, American soldiers were the guards, but out in the field, sometimes there would be a German guard who would sit aside with a gun and watch the others work. I expressed shock that this man was given a gun to watch over the other prisoners. I was told later that the gun didn't have real ammunition in it.

If they did something wrong, they knew they would be severely punished. They also knew they were being well-treated.

After the war ended, they worked here for a while, and we were allowed to treat them, to give them cigarettes. But we always did give them cigarettes, sandwiches, etc. There were guards that wouldn't want you to do that. They still needed to be guarded and under surveillance after the war ended, because otherwise they would have gone off and found a way to stay here, illegally. At the camp they counted them regularly, onto the truck, off the truck.

Harold eventually bought his own farm, which his son is working now. Harold didn't remain in contact with any of his prisoner workers, and he doesn't know of any of his that returned to the area after the war. However, he did have experience with a German DP who came here sponsored by a farmer friend. The arrangement of sponsorship required the sponsor to be responsible for a year, then the immigrant was free to work for whomever he pleased. This particular DP did not work out well with his sponsor, so Harold's friend asked Harold to hire him. Harold quickly ascertained the fellow was not a good worker and severed their relationship quickly. It turned out this DP was a lawyer; he had never worked with his hands and was totally unsuited for farm work. Harold's friend later admitted that he regrettably "dumped" the man onto Harold. The DP had other skills, however, and was reported to become a successful entrepreneur in the U.S., owning a string of hotels. Now in his ninetieth year, Harold keeps an eye on things from his house in the country near Lucerne.

● ● ●

Bertha and Art Streeb also farmed in the Windsor area and used POW labor. They didn't experience any of the hostile, uncooperative attitude of Nazi sympathizers that some other farmers did. Art could speak German and had a good time with "his boys" (a term used by other farmers interviewed). The Streebs later sent CARE packages to individuals they knew who had returned to Germany, but otherwise didn't keep in contact for long. None of the workers they knew returned to this area.

Several accounts relate to the prisoners' connection to the children of their employers. The Streeb children were young, at an age when prisoners loved to pick them up and hold them—surely against the rules. Clara Rutz, also of Windsor, remembers, "I was out in the yard with Ron, born May 12, 1945, and one of these prisoners saw that I had a young baby. He said, 'I've got a baby at home that same age.' He wanted to touch him."

It would be many months before that soldier daddy was able to hold his own baby.

All in all, the prisoner labor force seemed to work out well for workers and their employers, and many positive memories were taken back to Germany as well as retained in Weld County.

Ida May and her daughter Betty Tangbakken display Ida May's personal history book. It was featured in an article by Sarah Sangosti in Longmont's Daily Times-Call/Bonus Special Section March 2005.
Photo by Paul Litman, reprinted by permission from "Daily Times-Call"

Ida May Brunemeier

"It was so very wonderful to have him back home safely."

———————————— ● ————————————

We can only regret the passing of the kind of lady Ida May Brunemeier represents. Living much of her long life on eastern Colorado farms during times of
Dustbowl drought and Depression of the 1930s, plus wartime, the challenges met
by Ida May and her contemporaries are fortunately behind us, we hope. Novelists,
playwrights, and filmmakers often create larger-than-life characters from such
"ordinary" people, and their fictional challenges seem beyond us. They seem stronger and more tested than ordinary people, surely more than anyone WE know, and
we are inspired as much as saddened by their travails. But they triumph, just as they
do in reality. Actually, we do know real-life models for such heroic personalities.

Today, the Ida Mays of the world are stereotypical grandmother figures,
although not many attend exercise classes at age eighty-eight, like Ida May does.
Their image is quite different from the young grandmothers of today who run their
own businesses, are lawyers, CEOs and public media personalities, who don't mend
socks or make strawberry jam (and probably don't know how). Making the family's
clothes, canning, raising and processing vegetables, beef, chicken, and pork for
home consumption, nursing children with diphtheria, scarlet fever, and spinal men-
ingitis, doing laundry in a wringer washer or on a washboard (with no running
water), baking bread daily—are tasks unknown to most of today's housewives and
mothers. When a rattlesnake bit the baby, or Grandpa fell down the cellar stairs, no
cell phone 911 call could summon help. For certain, "soccer mom" is a term several
decades removed from mothers who watched that the pickup baseball game being
played in the street or back yard didn't break a neighbor's window.

With modesty and an unconscious sense of private dignity, Ida May has written
her life story, from which the wartime segment printed here has been extracted.
There isn't a trace of self-pity, self-applause or recognition of what an extraordinary
role model she provides for her progeny. From her life story, readers also learn how

Farmer Art back on the farm

to butcher a hog, make soap, and numerous other skills familiar to and required of farm women of an earlier era. Ida May's memoirs are intended to inform her family of its roots while identifying relationships, and giving historical background for who they are and where they came from. By implication, they testify how they contributed to their communities by honest labor, hard work, and good citizenship. These are characteristics that can no longer be taken for granted in the general population. And these are the kinds of folks we would need to fight and win a war several years later.

Ida May's Danish predecessors came across the prairie to Kansas in an ox-drawn wagon, made a "soddy," where they lived until they could build a house. Grandmother washed clothes in the creek.

She was very lonely and afraid; the wind blew, coyotes howled at night, and there were probably Indians in the area. She spoke no English, and even if she could speak English, there was no one to talk to. The cow, hungry for salt, ate the last of her soap. Grandma wept; washing would be difficult without soap.

Ida May's mother and her husband Art's mother both died when Ida May and Art were seven years old. Ida May and Art were married when she was eighteen in what Ida May laughingly calls a "shotgun" wedding.

Art sold his shotgun for sixteen dollars so we could get married.

At the same time, Ida May is no anonymous matriarch living a quiet retirement; she has her own claim to celebrity. Anyone driving north on I-25, just before the Loveland exit, sees Johnson's Corner on the east side of the highway. It is a well-known truck stop that features very special cinnamon rolls in its restaurant. They used to be advertised as Ida May's World Famous Cinnamon Rolls. Ida May proudly recalls that Johnson's Corner was once mentioned in "Travel and Leisure Magazine"— the only U.S. restaurant to be mentioned for its good breakfasts and (her) deluxe cinnamon rolls.

My first job at Johnson's was washing dishes and helping the cook. Baking was going so well, we started making dinner rolls. One day I had more dough than I needed for rolls, so I made several pans of cinnamon rolls. The manager, Clayton Bearly, said, "That's a wonderful idea! The graveyard cook can bake them in the morning for the breakfast and coffee crowd." From then on I made cinnamon rolls daily. The demand grew greater. I did this for over two years. Another baker and helper were hired, and the cinnamon rolls kept rolling out. They have become a great source of income.

When the attack on Pearl Harbor occurred half a world away, Art and Ida May were minding their own business, farming near Burlington and raising two young boys (to be joined a year later by a baby daughter). Soon after their lives would be touched by the conflict in several ways.

Art was in the field picking corn when the news came on that the Japanese had bombed Pearl Harbor. When he came in for dinner I told him the terrible news the radio was broadcasting over and over. Our minds fled to thoughts of our brothers

Those World Famous Cinnamon Rolls were Ida May's creation.

already in the service. My brother Cecil was in Company I from Burlington. The 157th Infantry Regiment was one of the first to go. Art's brother Ralph was in the tank corps, later with General Patton in the Battle of the Bulge. He was injured there and sent to England to recover. His brother Dave was in the Air Force, later stationed in North Africa. We listened to the news a lot and prayed they would all be safe.

I think Art felt that he too should be out there helping to keep our country free. He and a neighbor tried to enlist, but they were rejected because they were needed on the farm.

By spring we held an auction and moved to a 20-acre farm near Loveland. Art's brother Kenneth, still a teenager, was allowed by their dad to bring their truck to move us to our new home. It was a beautiful place, and we settled right in. The children were happy there too. We farmed, plus Art worked at the Kuner-Empson pea-canning factory while our crops were growing. I took care of 300 Leghorn chicks and the canning of our wonderful garden crops. In the fall after harvest, Art went to Cheyenne to work at the Union Pacific roundhouse and came home weekends. He paid for his board in Cheyenne with eggs from our hens, sometimes milk and butter as well.

Spring rolled around, and Art received a letter telling him he was drafted out of the Burlington draft board. He passed his physical and enlisted in the Navy. We sold our farm, machinery, and livestock at auction and bought a small house in Loveland.

March found him bound for Farragut, Idaho, for boot camp. This was a difficult time for me and for other wives whose husbands were in the military. The federal government provided $90 for the wife and $20 for each child each month. I was expecting our fourth baby in July. I had my hands full with my three precious children—cooking, washing, and caring for the house, yard, and garden.

The mail came twice a day; it seemed like a week from

Photos of Ida May and the children.
Art carried these while in the service.

morning mail to afternoon mail. Art wrote every day that he could. He had a difficult time getting through boot training. He had to have surgery, and after his recovery he was transferred to a different company. When it was time for him to go on furlough he got scarlet fever, which held him back again.

At last he came home on leave for ten days in late June. I was in the back yard finishing hanging up the laundry, when he came into the yard. I really made fast tracks, and I was in his arms. The children were so happy their daddy was home. We kept busy visiting and having visitors. Ten days is just too short to make up for three months being apart. It was crying time for both me and the children.

He was re-assigned to San Diego for gunnery school and then to the *Cape Grieg,* a Merchant Marine ship, as Navy armed guard. Art's brother Bill had also been drafted and gone to boot camp in Farragut. Both Art and Bill became armed guards on merchant ships. They were not on the same ships, however, and did not see each other until after peace was declared.

After Art left, it was back to waiting daily for the mail. He sent his address at gunnery school just in time for me to send him a telegram that we had our third son, John Philip Brunemeier, born July 10, 1944, in the Loveland hospital. Relatives came to stay with the children while I was in the hospital. We all enjoyed John, who was nicknamed "Jackie." We took pictures to send to Daddy when we wrote to him.

When Art returned to port at San Pedro, California, his sister Margaret and I took John, then four months old, on the Greyhound bus to meet Art there. There were several military men on the bus. They were eager to hold John; it made me think they probably had babies at home.

Art's second trip was to India. They had a terrible storm on the Tasmanian Sea. Art was on deck and was nearly washed overboard. They returned safely four months later, and the *Cape Grieg* was sent to dry dock for repairs. Relatives took care of the children again, and John and I rode the train to California. We stayed for a week. We went to Long Beach, rode the trolley, and enjoyed the amusement park there. We played a lot with John and loved just being together.

Art was sent to the base in San Francisco and was there for a while. When Japan surrendered, he was dismissed with an honorable discharge. It was so very wonderful to have him home safely.

After the war ended, the Brunemeiers settled back into a busy and productive life farming. Ida May's brother Cecil didn't fare so well.

Art, Ida May, Jim, Jerry, and Betty

They were in five major invasions and were nearly wiped out at Anzio Beach.*
When they were in the south France invasion, a beautiful police dog adopted Cecil.
He couldn't bring him home and had to leave him there. They were among the first
troops to come home. Cecil came to my house and stayed for a while. My boys played
war every day. One day they were "dirty Japs," the next day "dirty Germans." They
had toy guns. Cecil was so touchy from the war that he asked me to take their guns
away. I did. Then he worked at the Pueblo Ordinance. He survived many battles of
the war but was killed when he climbed a telephone pole, and the pole broke and fell
on him.

*The 157ᵗʰ Infantry Regiment, composed of mostly Colorado servicemen, was
commanded by Colorado's own hero, Lt. Colonel Felix Sparks. This highly-deco-
rated unit liberated the concentration camp at Dachau. Felix Sparks retired to
Denver as a brigadier-general and passed away at 92 in 2007.*

The Brunemeier children and grandchildren have continued to serve their country in the military.

Ida May's story is not the most dramatic of these memoirs, but it verifies what defines the American Spirit and the quality of people those words describe. It also paints a picture of how the home front coped. Fortunately, America escaped bombing destruction, invading forces, and the postwar disruption experienced by European and Far Eastern populations. But there were hardships, sacrifices, and losses on a personal level, and ordinary American citizens demonstrated well that they were up to the challenge.

Art & Ida May's Golden Annversary

Proud dad, proud son—Martin and Paul

Annie Hall

"Don't be surprised if you don't hear from me for three months."

Annie's story, like Ida May's, describes the issues young women with children faced when their husbands went off to war in the 1940s. During every wartime, each spouse, child, and parent faces the same anguish from uncertainty and separation. But WWII had its own set of challenges that came from the entire nation being mobilized. For example, dependent housing was in short supply, as some wives followed their husbands from one stateside assignment to another. Train travel was an ordeal. As Annie describes, just boarding the train was a physical challenge. There was waiting and waiting in the station, schedules were unreliable, and a serviceman on leave might spend too much of his precious furlough just getting home and back to the post on time. Many resorted to hitchhiking. No motorist could pass a serviceman thumbing a ride from the side of the road, in all kinds of weather.

Millions of American wives could tell a story similar to Annie's, and no doubt it will bring back memories to some readers. It was a time when families had to pull together to provide living space, share child care, give the troops something to fight for and return to, and to support each other when the dreaded telegram arrived.

My husband Martin and I were both born and raised in Iowa, went to different schools, met and married at Mount Ayr; that's 100 miles south of Des Moines. Work was very scarce during the Great Depression. We went to Aurora, Illinois, in the late '30s. Martin had a brother there who thought we could get jobs; work was more plentiful there.

We both got jobs in two days. Then the war started. Martin wrote back to the draft board at Mount Ayr to see how close he was, if he was going to be inducted into the army soon. He did that because he didn't want us to move into a new place (if he was going to be promoted to another store) if he was going to leave. There was just our ten-year-old son Paul and me. They sent his "Greetings" back, and he was in right away, in early 1943. Martin was thirty years old by then; he was older than the major-

Martin and Annie

ity of them. Maybe they forgot about him; he had left Iowa. They tended to keep their own boys and sent the ones that lived out of state, was what we figured out.

He took his basic training in Texas, then he was transferred to Fort Smith, Arkansas. I stayed in Aurora. I got a job in a defense plant as a timekeeper at All Steel Equipment. About 400 people worked there. The plant is still there; it makes big road equipment. They made things to fasten the holder of shells together for packing and shipping. They didn't make the shells, but they worked with metal and did a lot of things—anything that had to do with the war. I was paid thirty-five cents an hour. We also did piece work. I was interested in that; we had to make a quota, and above that we got a little extra.

At Christmastime Martin got a few days off, and he said it sure would be nice if I could come down to Arkansas. So I called the school to see if Paul could get off for a few days.

I got a leave of absence from my job. We rode the "third rail" into Chicago. When we got to the depot, the iron gate was up, and I got as close to it as I could because huge crowds were wanting to get on the train. First ones there got seats. They opened the gates, and my son and I ran. It was something to have silk stockings during the war. I was so proud of them, going to see my husband. They were torn to pieces by the time we got onto the train, from suitcases and everything and everybody scraping my legs. We did get on and got a seat.

They had a prisoner in the car; he had a guard with him. He was actually a POW; we thought perhaps he had gone AWOL.

While we were at Fort Smith we stayed in a hotel, and the three of us slept in one bed. We were lucky to get anything. It had been six months since we had seen Martin. The funny thing was, his buddies that were in camp with him came to the hotel room just to visit. They came to see ordinary people besides servicemen. I thought it was nice that they did that. They knew we had a son, and it was like visiting family for them. It must have reminded them of their own family.

I found this small apartment during the time we were in Fort Smith at Christmas so we would have a better place. It had cooking facilities and a big room with a bed and cot, makeshift just to get by. The lady who owned this house had a helper. She was so sweet and kind to us. We didn't have any cooking equipment, and she brought me enough to get by. And she brought us a little Christmas tree and decorations. I'll never forget her. She lived in the attic.

We went out to the base to have Christmas dinner, but they had quit serving by the time we got there. They had run out of food or something. We milled around for a while, then came back to town. All the places were closed up for Christmas. So we went home and I fixed bacon and eggs.

We had bought a Monopoly game for Paul, and we spent a lot of time playing Monopoly. When Martin had time off, he played too. Some of his buddies would come, and we'd all play Monopoly together.

We knew Martin was going to be shipped out soon, but we didn't know when. When I left Fort Smith I went first to my mother's in Iowa. I asked her if she would take Paul back to Illinois so he could get back into school, and I would return to Fort Smith and stay with Martin as long as I could. I got an extension of leave from my job, about four weeks.

So I went back to Fort Smith. Couldn't get the same apartment, but she had a room. That dear sweet lady used to bring me cookies, fruit, and stuff of her own. There was only one bathroom, and you were lucky to have one in those days. There wasn't anything said about when it was OK to take a bath. I took a bath later in the day to be nice and fresh when my husband came in from work. The nice lady came down and told me nobody was supposed to take a bath after two o'clock, because her boyfriend was coming, and he wanted to use the bathroom!

Well, the day came when Martin had to leave, and that was a heartbreaking day. I had no idea where he was going, and he didn't either. He said, "Don't be surprised if you don't hear from me for three months." We said goodbye, and I got on the train. I sat with a young lady, and she made a selfish remark, which I guess was just "young" thinking, "Well, you've lived your life; we've just been married, and it would be worse for my husband to go than it would be for yours."

I went back to Aurora; my mother was there with Paul. I put her on the train, and I went back to work. I had overstayed my leave by just a few hours. The supervisor used that as an excuse to replace me. She had a friend she wanted to put into my job, because I wouldn't tattle to her about what was going on in the department. The new job they never really showed me how to do. There was a big conveyor that would come around and dip in things to paint these bracket things. They didn't tell me how to shut off the machine. They were stacked so high, and I couldn't reach anything because I'm short. When it got full, those things just kept coming off! Finally a foreman came around and helped me. I quit that job after two weeks. I was so upset; the supervisor's husband wasn't in the service, and to think they treated me that way. It hurt. I went to work for another company that made shells there in Aurora, until the end of the war.

Meantime, there is a memory I would like to share about a grocery store where we traded during the war There weren't big supermarkets then, just neighborhood, family-run stores; the one where we traded was only two blocks away. We didn't have electric refrigeration in those days, and we shopped at least every two days. The dear grocery man where I traded whispered to me, "If your grocery bill is a little higher than you thought it should be, don't say anything." When we got home with closed brown paper bags, we might find bananas or some other goodies, meat especially, hard-to-get items that he kept in the back room for us who worked, especially in defense jobs.

Next time, I thanked him. He said the social ladies would come during the day and buy up all of scarce items, and that was not fair to the rest of us. How grateful we were, so nice of him to do that, and we let him know.

Also, Paul had heard over the radio that people were even cooking potato peelings and eating them. He wanted to know if we should be doing that. I told him not yet, but we will if we have to. What a sweet gesture of gratitude from him.

We didn't have meat every day, and mainly the cut was round steak, kept in a back room cooler hanging up. The butcher would carry it to the meat-chopping block, slice off enough for our size family. It was so sweet of him.

The first Thanksgiving Martin was gone, Paul and I went downtown for Thanksgiving dinner. That was a real treat in those days, to go out to eat. After we ate, we walked outside. Paul walked over to the curb and threw up his dinner. He was upset because his dad wasn't there. And it just broke my heart.

I had to do "Daddy" things with Paul; we often took his friend along, and we went fishing, to the zoo, and had a lot of fun. Paul wouldn't talk about his dad during the war when he was gone. He wouldn't bring up the subject. But when the war was over, he couldn't talk enough. It was quite a strain on him that his dad was away.

Martin was stationed in Germany. As a foot soldier, he walked clear across to the edge of Czechoslovakia. He worked himself up to sergeant in the 4th Armoured Division. There were times I wouldn't hear from him for six weeks. We didn't know where he was. One day I heard on the radio that the 4th Armored Division was at such-and-such place. I was ecstatic to get word. When he could, he wrote every day, and I think I got most of that mail.

Martin described being in the trenches with German troops also in nearby trenches. When the war ended, each side got out and shook hands with their former enemies. They were both glad to have it over and be able to go home. They kept Martin over there to train the other troops coming over as replacements. He said it was a pathetic situation.

These were just young kids. They were taking them awfully young then. You would hear them crying at night in their bunks. They wanted Martin to come back to the States and get his family and go back to Germany to stay. Paul was so against it.

So, Martin was discharged, and in 1947 Annie received word that her sister in Boulder had cancer. She and Martin came out to Colorado to assume parental duties for her sister's motherless children, and once again the family was able to depend on each other to meet and survive a crisis.

Lorna as Lorna Hoagland in 1940-41

Lorna Hoagland Knowlton

"I saw the giant B-29 dwarfing the B-17. It left me breathless."

Lorna's recollections describe how the war brought new freedoms and adventure to a Midwest college girl. Her exploits and independence may not seem so revolutionary to the liberated young woman (and her parents) of 2008, but it was a big step sixty-seven years ago. It's been a long journey from Kansas to Colorado via Wisconsin. A writer herself, Lorna tells her own story.

December 7, 1941: Sitting with friends at my university, supposedly studying, we were shocked to have our radio music shut off and the voice of President Roosevelt come on with the astounding news of the bombing of Pearl Harbor and the announcement of our entrance into the war. We were speechless for the first time in our young lives.

Several weeks later at the end of our semester, all the boys we knew left school bag and baggage and enlisted in one branch of the service or another. Since I was more interested in the boys than in anything else on campus and was gung ho to get into the war, I finished the second semester and immediately tried to join the WAVES (the Navy's women's corps). I did not pass the physical and was always convinced that my parents had influenced the doctor to find something wrong with my body. They were horrified at the thought of my joining the service.

After that failure, I sought a job at Boeing Aircraft in Wichita, Kansas, where most anyone could get a job at one of the many airplane factories there. My brother-in-law was working at Beech Aircraft in Wichita, and my parents thought he and my sister could keep an eye on me, so they finally approved of my action.

I was hired as a clerk/typist on the second shift (3:00 P.M. to 11:00 P.M.) at Boeing, but overtime became a norm. If you showed up every day for work at that time and worked while you were there, you were advanced. I quickly moved into typist and then into secretary to the department head on that shift, at a higher salary with each advancement, of course.

Finding a room to rent in Wichita at the time was nearly impossible. Some people I knew lived in a cleaned-out chicken coop out back near the alley of the owner's home. My sister and brother-in-law lived in a tiny apartment made from the storage area of a home.

Getting to and from work without a car was difficult. All buses didn't run during the night, and that was when I needed to return home. I finally found a tiny room to rent (formerly a large closet in a nice home) on the east side, which my parents approved. Nearly everyone with a house in Wichita rented out some part of their home. I had to make two bus changes to get to the place where a large bus made the run out to Boeing at the proper hours.

Getting home at night was another matter. I shudder to think now how I rode home partway at one or two o'clock in the morning with a shift leader of our floor and several others—no women. Someone was watching over me.

The B-29 bomber was being built in the Wichita plant, because secrecy was of the utmost importance and also because at that time people thought the Japanese were going to attack via the Washington/Oregon area. The construction of B-17 bombers continued while the larger B-29 was being created.

As a green, inexperienced young girl from a small, central Kansas town, I was still investigated from every angle by the F.B.I. These men journeyed up to Osborne and interviewed all of the professional men in town—teachers, churches, anyone who might have known me. Of course in a little town like that everyone knew everyone else, so that was a little foolish, I thought. I didn't know about this until I left Boeing and they gave me the file they had on me. Needless to say, I was amazed. And most interested in what all those hometown authorities had to say about me.

As secretary to one of the big boys (and they were really just boys and felt their importance so that they tried to hide their ages), it was often my job to go into the head office to take dictation. I had to walk a long distance from the door on deep, elegant oriental rugs to the far end of the room in deep silence, where sat the U.S. President, Vice-president, Secretaries of Army and Air Corps, plus the V.P. of Boeing, watching me enter. Needless to say, my shorthand must have been a bit shaky. I know I was!

I was moved up to the first shift after working at Boeing for a few months, and this made my travel problems less defeating. An eight-hour day was unknown, and even a ten or twelve-hour day became rare. We worked through weekends and holidays, and my first Christmas away from home is memorable.

I seldom had reason to deliver anything to the huge work area where the planes were constructed. Finally, one day when the Washington, D C. Army Air Corps officers came to anoint us with that special award they gave to war plants that met their quota, I saw the giant B-29 dwarfing the B-17 bomber. It left me breathless! I could not imagine a plane that large, and I believe my co-workers felt the same. Considering the role the B-29 played in ending the war and later its status in every aspect of air travel, the B-29 certainly created and kept the role of Master of all.

Dee Cole and Kay (right) going native on a trip to the Netherlands

Kay Egger O'Keefe

"I don't want to go there; I want to go to PARIS!"

———————— ● ————————

Kay O'Keefe is a vital 87-year-old with a quick wit and remarkable memory. Her war years and postwar life as a military wife were a total change from what she was prepared for growing up on a South Dakota ranch and probably a far cry from anything she expected! A glamorous, exciting, and romantic experience to be envied by any young girl from the American Midwest.

Deadwood, South Dakota, is not only an HBO series, it is also my birthplace. But I grew up on a ranch near Sturgis, South Dakota, with five brothers and two sisters. We were a happy, somewhat rowdy crew. Life on the ranch was mostly work for everyone, as we had several hundred head of cattle, lots of chickens, turkeys, pigs, some goats, guinea hens, and about 100 horses—work horses, riding horses, two race horses, and several polo ponies. We all spent a lot of time on a horse, attending to the animals.

I remember standing with my mother on the gravel road that ran past the ranch, and she told me, "They say if you stay on this road, it goes all the way to Chicago."

I thought to myself, I don't want to go there; I want to go to PARIS!

In May 1938, I graduated from St. Martin's Academy High School in Sturgis with a scholarship to Duchene University in Omaha (an all-girls school that later merged with Creighton University and became co-ed). However, the country was still recovering from the Great Depression. There wasn't a lot of money around except for necessities, so I was unable to go.

I was just seventeen but managed to find a job in Deadwood as a bookkeeper. I knew how to take shorthand, type, and keep books, thanks to the nuns at St. Martin's. Later I found a better-paying job in Rapid City as bookkeeper at a Dodge-Plymouth Agency. This was a lively, fun place to work, but when World War II broke out in December, 1941, it put the skids on the automobile business, as the car factories started building tanks instead of automobiles. However, we somehow managed to stay afloat through it all. I always had a car to drive—a plus even though gasoline was strictly rationed, along with everything else.

Early in 1945, I decided if I was ever going to get to Paris I'd have to first leave Rapid City. Reluctantly, I quit my job, which I really liked, and went to Washington, D.C. It was a madhouse, swarming with wartime activity and people, no place to live. I had some friends who were stationed at the Naval Air Station at Patuxent River, Maryland. They convinced me to come there to work while I kept an eye open for overseas opportunities. I did this, had a good job, and a good time there. After the war in Europe ended in May and then the war with Japan ended in August, I saw an article in the *Washington Post* that said that the U.S. Department of State was recruiting people to staff the Consular offices in Germany, which had been closed since the beginning of World War II. I applied and was accepted! Oh Happy Day! We were given a choice of Bremen, Berlin, Hamburg, Frankfurt, Stuttgart, or Munich. I wisely chose Munich, the old capital of Bavaria, land of Bierhalls, Gemutlichkeit, and wonderful music.

First, we all took an intensive training course at the Foreign Service Institute where we supposedly learned how to be diplomats. Mrs. McNair, wife of a general who had been killed in the Normandy Invasion, gave us a course on Foreign Service etiquette. We called it Mrs. McNair's Charm School. We sat for hours listening to German language records in an effort to cram some German into our skulls. I'm not sure how much any of this rubbed off or sank in, but toward the end of February we were ready for our assignments.

Some of the girls flew to London and then on to Munich, but Kay Toomey, Olga Lucashewich and I flew to Paris (I made it!) on the second flight that TWA made there after World War II. It was terribly exciting; the first sight of the Eiffel Tower sent me off into the stratosphere. The State Department put us up in the grand old Crillon Hotel. We stayed three days and crammed every minute enjoying all Paris had to offer, which was a lot, even then. We took a train to Frankfurt and then to Munich.

The American Third Army had conquered Munich, and they had all the places to live that had not been bombed out. They were supposed to have arranged apartments for us, but when twenty-five American girls arrived, they weren't sure where to put us. There were also about twenty Vice Consuls in our group and they billeted them with Third Army officers who were living in comparative luxury. They finally put the girls in an abandoned, former German enlisted men's quarters—very spartan, no hot water, and an open elevator shaft which one jumped on as it went past, to get to the third floor.

296

After a couple weeks of this, the State Department requisitioned two large apartment buildings near the downtown area that had miraculously escaped the bombings. The apartments at 21 Prinzregentenstrasse were large and very comfortable, and each apartment was assigned a maid. We had a small bar built for our apartment and christened it the "Chez When." Our maid was a wonderful lady, Brita von Panwitz, who before the war had had a lovely home and servants of her own.

The Consulate General was located in the heart of downtown Munich on Ludwigstrasse, in a building once again left standing but with destruction all around it. All the cities of Germany were pretty much destroyed from American and British bombings and were still in shambles and piles of rubble when we arrived.

As the Allied troops advanced into Germany toward victory at the end of World War II and Germany was falling apart, the Nazis did not know what to do with the Jews and other victims from the concentration camps that they had not killed. The end was coming too fast to kill them all and cover up the camps, though they tried. Some they just simply left in the camps; others they abandoned in sealed trains. Still others they set free with no food, water or destination. Hence, hundreds of thousands of refugees who had been torn from their homelands roamed the face of war-torn Europe.

Many relief agencies followed the troops into Germany as the camps were liberated: the International Red Cross, United Nations Relief and Rescue Agency, the American Joint Distribution Commission, and others. They opened and staffed Displaced Persons camps and helped relatives in the U.S. and other countries contact displaced persons. They also furnished documents necessary for immigration.

The American Consular offices were in charge of processing and issuing immigration visas. There were several Displaced Persons camps near Munich and for the first several months we were there, we all worked on interrogating these poor souls from the camps and issuing visas to the U.S.

For us girls, life was very good. Besides a maid, we were also assigned a Consular vehicle and a chauffeur who picked us up and took us to work and home each day, and any other place we wanted to go, day or night. We had a very active social life—parties, parties, parties. We traveled. Europe was very safe and we went everywhere. We could easily drive to Zurich, Venice, or Innsbruck after work on Friday for the weekend, and we did. We lived across the street from the opera house and attended performances several times a month. When we traveled, we always made it a point to attend the opera in whatever city we were: Prague, Milan, Rome, Paris, Vienna, and I learned to love opera. Pretty heavy stuff for the girl from a ranch in South Dakota! When there was nothing else to do, there was always a lively bridge game going on in one of the apartments.

Then there was The Haus der Kunst, a former art museum that had been converted to the downtown Officers Club. We ate our meals there, accompanied by strolling violinists. At night it was a fun night club with a couple of bars and a good band that played Big Band music. It was a beautiful building located on the edge of the English Gardens. I've been back there since, and it is once again a wonderful art museum.

In July 1946, Kay Toomey and I traveled to Rome to attend the canonization of the American saint, Mother Cabrini. Kay's father, a professor at Catholic University in Washington, D.C., had obtained tickets for us to the canonization from his friend, Monsignor Carboni, who was Secretary of State at the Vatican. But how to get to Rome? There were no train schedules—too soon after the war—but we went to the Munich train station (the *Bahnhof*) anyway, hoping for the best and got on a train to Italy. We got as far as Brenner Pass on the Italian border and the tracks ended there—end of the train trip.

We found an Italian man who with his wife and child was taking a load of chickens to Bolzano in his rickety pickup truck. Kay and I rode in back with the chickens, considering ourselves lucky to get a ride, for a fee, of course. I think we gave the driver some cigarettes, which was better than currency, as they were in short supply in

Kay searching for souvenirs through the ruins of Hitler's Eagle's Nest

Kay Toomey on the left and Kay O'Keefe in Rome at the Colosseum

Europe. In Bolzano, two little Italian boys took us to the Americanos (more cigarettes). Sure enough, there were two GIs stationed there at some outpost. They had a jeep, and they gave us a ride to Venice (they had their own cigarettes and seemed quite happy for the company of two American girls). From Venice we were able to catch a train to Rome.

We stayed at the Excelsior Hotel on the Via Venetto, had a gorgeous room for $1.00 a day as the hotel was still operated by the U.S. Army. We attended the canonization, which was a magnificent ceremony in St. Peter's Basilica. Monsignor Carboni also arranged a private audience for us with Pope Pius XII, who had been Pope during the war. He later came under great criticism for not doing more for the Jews who were sent to concentration camps by the Nazis.

However, it was a great privilege to have this ten minute audience with him; he was very gracious though rather austere, and was most interested in the Displaced Persons programs in Germany. The next day our names were in *L'Osservatore Romano*, the Vatican newspaper, on page two. I suppose there were other more important things to report on the front page.

The return trip wasn't nearly as exciting as the trip down. We were able to get a train from Rome to Geneva, Switzerland, and from there to Munich.

In early 1941, a new Consul General, Sam E. Woods, was assigned to Munich. He was well known among diplomatic circles as the man who tipped off Washington about Hitler's plan to invade the Soviet Union. At the time, he was serving as Commercial Attaché in the Embassy in Berlin. This, of course, wasn't revealed until World War II was over, and it was included in Cordell Hull's memoirs. He was interned for six months in Bad Neuheim with the other American diplomats serving in Germany at the outbreak of the war. After being exchanged for German diplomats interned in the U.S., he was assigned to Zurich, Switzerland, as Consul General and spent the war years there. When he came to Munich, I was assigned as his Administrative Assistant, which was a great move for me.

While in Zurich, Woods became acquainted with Welhelmina "Minnie" Busch, the youngest daughter of Adolphus Busch, co-founder of Anheuser-Busch, and worth about a $50 million fortune. Minnie had left her home in Bavaria, an opulent castle outside Munich on Starnbergsee, to spend the war years in Zurich. She had been married twice— both times to Germans—one she divorced, and the other died. She really was more German than American and because of her close German ties was placed on an American "black list." Woods, with his considerable connections in Washington, was successful in getting her removed from this list. In the midst of all this, Minnie became enamored with Woods and he with her. After twenty-four years of marriage, his wife flew to the U.S. and divorced him, agreeing to this for the sum of a million dollars.

Shortly after Woods arrived in Munich, Minnie returned to her castle Hohenried

Minnie's castle near Munich

Fourth of July celebration at Sam and Minnie's castle (Quite a crowd there!) American diplomats and foreign service personnel always celebrated the Fourth when on assignment abroad.

(100 rooms with full furnished basement!) and in February 1948, she and Sam were married in an elaborate ceremony in the castle chapel. I did not attend the ceremony; however, I wrote the invitations to the many prominent personages who did attend. The bride wore a dazzling diamond tiara, a 50-karat diamond ring and was arrayed in white. She was sixty. He was fifty-two.

Both Minnie and Sam were very good to me. They included me in many fabulous parties at the castle; their Rolls Royce would arrive to pick me up. There were always lots of visiting Congressmen and Senators as well as local former royalty at these soirées. They would also have me down to spend Christmas Day, which included a lavish dinner and a ride in a horse-drawn sleigh around the estate, and of course, gifts. What a kick in the head this fairytale-type occasion was!

Mr. Woods was a wonderful man to work for, and I was very devoted to him. Minnie died of a heart attack in November of 1952, and Sam died of a cerebral hemorrhage in May, 1953. (Alas, I was not named in the will.) They are both buried on the grounds of the castle. When Minnie died, she left her fortune to Sam, and when he died, he left it all to his family in Mississippi and to his former wife.

On Easter Sunday 1948, two of the other girls and I decided to go to Garmisch to have dinner. Garmisch was nearby—a beautiful alpine village, and we went there a lot. The U.S. Army had two great hotels there, the Riessersee and the Eibsee, and we knew the guys in charge real well, Al Maid and Lou Montfort. On the way to Garmisch the car got a flat tire. The chauffeur got the spare out of the trunk and lo! it was flat, too. So there we were, three damsels in distress and more than a little annoyed at our "dummkoph" chauffeur. As we were pondering our fate, along came a carload of dashing American Air Force officers. They fixed the flat, sent the chauffeur back to Munich and took us with them to the Yacht Club of Starnbergsee, where they'd been golfing.

One of the guys was a handsome, auburn-haired fellow, Bill O'Keefe. I took to him right away (he was a good dancer) and he to me. This was the beginning of one of the great romances of the twentieth century. He was stationed at Furstenfeldbruck Air Base outside Munich along with a group of fun-loving fellow officers. Among them was his roommate Norm Magee and another funlover, Al Crull. Bill and I saw as much of each other every day and night as work schedules and his flying allowed. We introduced Magee to Barbara Swain and Al to Zola Lackhove, two of my good friends who worked in the Consulate General. The six of us had great times together.

At the end of May 1948, I went back to the States on home leave, sailing first-class on the *SS America*, which was the premier U.S. ocean liner at the time. Three of the gals and I went together. It was a fun trip, and when we sailed into New York Harbor and saw the Statue of Liberty greeting us, we got all choked up; we didn't realize we were so nationalistic.

We spent some time in New York and in the Department in Washington, D.C. and then I flew home to South Dakota. In August I flew to New York and went back to

Captain Bill O'Keefe, one-half of the Great Twentieth Century Romance

Europe, once again on the *America*.

My friend Dee Cole (later Byrnes) went back at the same time, and we had a good time on board ship. We took the boat train from LeHavre to Paris and lo and behold, there were Bill O'Keefe, Barbara Swain and Norm Magee to meet me. We spent a few hilarious days in Paris and the four of us drove back to Munich together. Barb and Norm later married, and Bill was the best man.

The Great Twentieth-Century Romance continued until November, when Bill got orders to the

Minnie Busch and Sam Woods

U.S. He wanted to get married, and I told him I'd think on it. I thought and thought, but I really wasn't ready to quit my wonderful job and return to the U.S. I tearfully let him get away.

Life continued on pretty much the same—work, parties, travel. Zola and I went on a Mediterranean cruise, sailing from Genoa to Elbe, Barcelona, Algiers, Malta, Sicily, Naples, and back to Genoa. Shortly after this, Zola went home to Pennsylvania and married Al Crull.

There were always a lot of VIPs coming into the office to see Mr. Woods. The most famous one that I met there was Colonel Charles Lindberg—a soft-spoken, unassuming person in spite of his fame, some of it unwelcome.

In 1949, Katie Guidrey (Hedrick) and I went on a German pilgrimage to Lourdes, requiring thirty-six hours sitting up on the train with eight pilgrims in our compartment. We were the only Americans. In Lourdes we stayed in a dormitory-type accommodation (cold water and cots). We did all the things one does in Lourdes. We made the candlelight procession to the grotto, attended mass there, bought rosaries, and holy water. There were many crippled and ill people praying for a miraculous recovery, which was a touching sight. Finally, we got tired of being pilgrims and took a train to Biarritz, checked into a luxury hotel for a couple of days, indulged in good food and wine, then went back to Lourdes and caught the pilgrimage train back to Munich.

Katie had purchased a little Ford, and she and another gal and I drove to Rome for the Jubilee Year of 1950 celebration. We did a lot of other travel together, including a trip to Britain. Katie had been my apartment mate the years I spent in Munich, and we have remained friends ever since.

In December 1950, I received orders transferring me to Sydney, Australia, with a subsequent transfer to Canberra as secretary to the American Ambassador. There were farewell parties every night and a grand send-off at the Bahnhof with champagne, caviar, flowers—the works. I had spent almost five wonderful years in Munich and leaving was a happy/sad occasion. I left many memories and many good friends there, German and American.

Katie had orders transferring her to Rio and we left Munich together for Paris, spent a few days there, then on to LeHavre to board the *America* for the trip to the U.S. The North Atlantic in December can be rough and was. Lots of people were seasick but it didn't faze us. We just enjoyed.

I hadn't kept in particular touch with Bill O'Keefe. It had been two years since I'd seen him when I arrived in New York. Our old friend, Al Mold, who used to manage the Riessersee Hotel in Garmisch, met the ship and convinced me to send Bill a postcard telling him when I'd arrive in Rapid City, which I did. Bill was then stationed at the Rapid City Air Force Base. Coincidence? After spending some time in New York and Washington, D.C. in the State Department, I flew home to Rapid City. And there to meet me was William! As soon as I saw him, I got that old familiar feeling, and the Great Twentieth-Century Romance heated up again, causing a dilemma for me—to marry or go to Sydney. I was coming up on my thirtieth birthday.

I somewhat reluctantly resigned from my wonderful job, and we were married in Rapid City in January, 1951. I became an Air Force wife!

We were in Rapid City a year when Bill received orders to Korea, where the war there was still going strong. We spent Christmas with my family in Sturgis, then took off for Washington, D.C., as I had decided to go there and work while Bill was gone.

I assumed I'd go to work for the State Department, but I had a friend in the C.I.A.

that I'd known in Munich, and he offered me a better job than State offered, so I took it. We weren't allowed to say we worked for the C.I.A., so when anyone asked where I worked, I had to say "for a government agency." Then they knew right away I worked for the C.I.A. It was a good and interesting job.

Bill flew back from Korea on New Year's Day, 1953. I quit my job, and we reported to Shaw Air Force Base in South Carolina. Once again, I was an Air Force wife, doing what military wives do—a lot of volunteer work, luncheons, coffees, bridge parties, an active social life plus eventually raising a family.

We enjoyed our Air Force years, moving often to different bases in the U.S. and an assignment in Europe. It was fun, and a rewarding, exciting, and educational time in our lives. We made friendships that have endured to this day.

Lieutenant David A. Smith, Tuskegee Airman

Epilogue

"...this is a white man's school."

────────────●────────────

BY VIVIAN ROBINSON SMITH

African Americans participated in various aspects of wartime activities and were amply represented numerically. However, for this collection of wartime memoirs, I was unable to make contact with more than one. African Americans are not Jewish, nor of Japanese heritage, nor were they victimized by what Nazi Germany was doing on the European continent. My efforts to locate a USO entertainer, Rosie the Riveter, or some sort of government employee were unsuccessful. They are out there, and hopefully will be included in another recording. There were, however, many wives and dependents of African American servicemen.

Vivian Robinson Smith has filled that slot as the wife of a Tuskegee Airman. Vivian's account is far too brief, however, and readers will wish to hear more of this disturbing account. Her story was received after publication deadline, thanks to her daughter, Sharon Smith Daniels. We had no time to pursue in depth the many issues and situations described, nor have I had the privilege of meeting either of these ladies. But ninety-year-old Vivian's recollections are vivid as well as disturbing and perhaps more powerful because of their brevity. One short episode gets the point across.

Most of Vivian's abbreviated account relates to her husband David, but as a family, as she describes, they all experienced the same humiliating and unfair treatment, wartime or not. Although it seems out of place with the rest of the civilian narratives, my justification for including her memoir is that a prewar civilian code, Jim Crow, carried over into the military during wartime. In other words, there is irony in the reverse application of what is impacting what. Jim Crow's demise would have come eventually, but wartime social changes may have hastened the onset and intensified the rationale for the Civil Rights movement of the 1960s. Like the irrationality of sending Japanese Americans off to fight while their loved ones were treated as dangerous aliens, it is likewise difficult to justify refusing African American offi-cers access to their service clubs. Stories have circulated that German POW officers were welcome in clubs that refused admission to our own, like David Smith.

I was born in Keystone, West Virginia in 1918. I graduated from West Virginia State College, in Institute, WV, in 1939 with a B.A. degree in business education. My first job was teaching at Gary High School in Gary, WV. I met my husband, David A. Smith, in college. We married in June 1941, and now live in Denver, Colorado.

When I was a child, my parents, siblings, and I often traveled to Virginia to visit relatives. My father had a Model T Ford. We were able to purchase fuel at gas stations; however, we were not allowed to use the restrooms. As a result, my father would pull off the road at wooded areas so we could use the "bathroom." If traveling by train, we had to sit in the Jim Crow cars, certainly the worst accommodations of the carrier. We could only attend theaters if we sat in balconies. We were unable to try on clothes or shoes in department stores. At Richies Department Store in Atlanta, there was a separate section for Coloreds to sit to try on shoes.

To briefly identify who Tuskegee Airmen were, they comprised an all African American pursuit squadron based in Tuskegee, Alabama. The group included pilots, navigators, bombardiers, maintenance and support staff, instructors—all personnel concerned with flying their planes. They were involved in an Army Air Corps exper-imental program to train African Americans to fly and maintain aircraft. Prior to 1940, African Americans were barred from flying for the U.S. military. The achieve-ments of this unit paved the way for full integration of the U.S. military. (For more information, see "The Tuskegee Airmen" and much more, on the Internet.)

David was drafted into the Army Air Corps in 1943 and was sent to Jefferson Barracks for three months' basic training. *(My brother also received his basic train-ing at Jefferson Barracks, Missouri, in 1943. JB is a very old military post in the U.S. system. A green, eighteen-year-old Northerner, my brother was puzzled and trou-bled to see that African American inductees were quartered in a separate part of the camp in a swampy, mosquito-infested, undesirable and unhealthy environment.)*

David applied to and was accepted for Officer Candidate School in Miami Beach, Florida. When he reported to the Admission officer, he was told, "Here's one thing I want you to know: this is a white man's school. If you keep your nose clean and do what you are told, you'll get those bars on your shoulder; otherwise, we'll get you out of here quick like a minute."

After successfully completing Officer Candidate School, David was sent to Tuskegee and became an Intelligence officer of the 477th Bomber Group.

Although in uniform, discrimination continued to follow African American servicemen. The War Department received complaints that base commanders and nearby communities did not want them stationed at their locations. Some would accept limited numbers or only Southerners.

David and his fellow officers were sent to Freeman Field, Indiana. There were living quarters there, one-bedroom apartments, so my daughter and I joined David.

After a short time, these officers decided to go to the Officers Club, where they were refused admittance and told the club was for whites only. The Black officers decided to go in anyway. Later, the Black officers were told to report to the Commanding Officer in Headquarters and were again told there were certain buildings on the base where they could not go, and the Officers Club was one of them. This was a direct order.

David was the first officer called into the Commander's office and was given the written order, which in essence stated, "I will not try to go to the White Officers Club." David, together with 101 Black officers, refused to sign the order. Those 101 officers

were then sent to Fort Knox where they were placed under arrest. Subsequently, the Black officers were released and sent to Tuskegee for further training.

David was honorably discharged from the military in 1946. We returned to Denver where David opened Dave Smith Realty Company, which continues to operate.

The rest is history for the Tuskegee Airmen. David is now ninety-two years old.

**David and Vivian (above),
the Smith family (below)**